Amherstburg, Ontario,
Dec 25, 1989.

With my best wishes
and
Regards.

Hon Eugene F. Whelan P.C.

WHELAN

WHELAN

*The Man
in the Green Stetson*

by
EUGENE WHELAN
with
Rick Archbold

Irwin Publishing
Toronto Canada

CANADIAN CATALOGUING IN PUBLICATION DATA

Whelan, Eugene F., 1924-
Whelan : the man in the green stetson

I S B N 0-7725-1621-9

1. Whelan, Eugene F., 1924-   . 2. Cabinet
ministers — Canada — Biography.* 3. Politicians —
Canada — Biography. 4. Liberal Party of Canada —
Biography. 5. Canada — Politics and government —
1963-   * I. Archbold, Rick, 1950-
II. Title.

FC626.W48A3 1986   354.7104'092'4   C86-094176-0
F1034.3.W48A3 1986

Designed by The Dragon's Eye Press
Typeset by Fleet Typographers
Printed and bound in Canada by T.H. Best Company Limited

1 2 3 4 5 6 7 8   93 92 91 90 89 88 87 86
Published by Irwin Publishing Inc.

To Liz, Terry, Sue, Cathy
and my extended family — with special thanks to
my friends, staff and supporters
over the years — whose encouragement and friendship
helped make all things possible.

CONTENTS

Prologue: November 27, 1972

I'd wanted the job of Minister of Agriculture so long that, once I had it, it took me a good while to get used to the idea. And even after all those years in caucus as a backbencher, I found I was feeling a bit the way I did when I first arrived on Parliament Hill – scared and humble. Now that I had what I'd wanted, could I really handle the job? I was still thinking this way when I went to the swearing-in ceremony of the new Cabinet at Rideau Hall. It was a very solemn occasion, made more gloomy by the fact that we Liberals had almost lost the election and many old friends and colleagues were missing. The atmosphere was a bit like a funeral. When it finally came time for me to go up and sign the book – to put my name down in the Oath Book along with the names of Macdonald and Cartier and Laurier and King – I just stood there like a statue with the pen in my hand; I didn't do anything for the longest time. I was standing there asking myself whether I had the right to sign, whether I would be able to fulfil the obligations of the office and keep the oath of secrecy. I'd never had to worry about these things before. People must have been getting fidgety in the dead silence because out of the blue sky Don Jamieson – who was the new Minister of External Affairs – piped up and said, "You spell it W-H-E-L-A-N." That broke the mood for all of us and I turned to the Governor General, Roland Michener, and said, "Is it okay, your excellency, if I just put my X down there?" That finished us – it completely broke the ice and everyone started to laugh. Before this we were all so formal, you'd have sworn we were signing a death warrant.

1

When I Was a Kid...

I've never had much use for banks – or bankers, for that matter. It's an attitude I formed when I was still quite young, the year my father died.

My father's name was Charles Bernard Whelan. He was fifty-seven when he died of cancer and I was only six. He'd been sick for quite a while and for the last year or so he'd had to stop working the farm. He would sit in his chair or lie in bed during the day and we kids were supposed to keep quiet. Imagine trying to keep nine kids from making noise! I was just too young to understand and I know I used to get on my dad's nerves. I can remember one time he took after me with a lilac switch because I was making too much noise. I hid under the table.

When I was very small I remember watching him ploughing and milking the cows; he looked so strong and confident. I can still see him in the barn in the morning eating a raw egg with a shot of White Horse Whiskey; that was his appetizer before breakfast. He was never one to drink much, but he always had his shot of whiskey in the morning – it was quite a common thing to do in those days. The raw egg was supposed to give you vitality and make you virile.

Once he got sick, my four older brothers Bernard, Edward, Martin, and Tom couldn't keep up the farm and that's what led to our problem with the bank. Bernard, who was the oldest, was only fourteen in 1931, and my mother insisted that he stay in school and finish his education. Dad was a strong believer in the importance of schooling, although he hadn't made it through high school himself; very few farm kids did in those days. (Perhaps if he'd lived, there would have been enough money for me to go to college.) So the day came when he had to sell our dairy herd of pure-bred Holsteins. I was only five years old at the time but I can still remember the auction sale as one of the most exciting events of my young life. There were lots of people because my father had a fine herd.

It was at the beginning of the Depression but I was too young to realize how serious things were—what the sale meant to our family. The cows sold for as high as five hundred dollars a head but, being farmers, those who bought them didn't have that kind of money so they gave my father promissory notes. Which was fine, but pieces of paper don't buy food and clothes and medicine. So my dad took these notes to the bank and used them as collateral to borrow some money to pay his doctor's bills and support the family. Then the Depression hit and my father died and the farmers couldn't honour the notes. My mother was left with practically no income. She was almost forced to have all nine of us adopted by relatives—I was supposed to go to a family named Rose in Cleveland, Ohio. Mrs. Rose was my mother's half cousin. It was a near thing.

We were saved by the Mother's Allowance—forty-five dollars a month or five dollars for each child under sixteen. That's not the federal Family Allowance that Mulroney's Tories were talking about taking away, but the old provincial allowance for needy widows. My mother certainly fit the bill with nine hungry mouths to feed. As soon as the bank found out she had this pittance coming in, they took after her to start covering the interest on my father's debt. They made her pay five dollars every month. So that left forty bucks for the family. Every

month she'd send one or two of us down to the bank in Amherstburg – the Canadian Imperial Bank – with the five dollars. It was
a three-and-a-half-mile bike ride each way. We were years and
years and years paying off that debt but eventually – sometime
in the early 1940s – we did. That was how I first learned to love
banks and bankers.

Years later, after the Depression, some of the farmers who'd
bought cattle from my father at that auction were still coming
around to repay my mother. When the Depression first hit, a
couple of farmers brought back the cows when they couldn't
pay for them, but by then the poor critters had starved to the
point where they weren't much good. I remember one fellow
who'd moved away and gotten a job in Sarnia. My mother
hadn't seen him for years and he drove into the yard one day
and said he'd come to pay for the cow. That must have been
after the war – fifteen years or more after the auction took place.

I was the middle child. As I grew up I fought with my four
older brothers and I helped to look after my two younger brothers Henry and Bryce and my two younger sisters Gertrude and
Helen. Because of my age, I suppose, I also helped my mother
around the house more than the others. I even got to be a pretty
good cook. In a funny way being the middle child in a big family
with only one parent was a good education for politics. I learned
to look after myself and not depend on others; I learned to be
tough and to stand up for my rights; and I learned to care for
others less fortunate than myself. As far as mothering goes,
I didn't get too much. My mother didn't have time. She was too
busy trying to make ends meet.

Even though my father died when I was so young, he was a
strong influence on me. My older brothers would tell me stories
about him – about his political accomplishments, for instance.
He was a staunch Conservative, who'd served as reeve of Anderdon Township and warden of Essex County, and he believed
strongly in the importance of taking an active part in public
life. Not long before he died, he called in my older brothers and
gave them quite a lecture about their duty to serve. He told
them to choose whatever party made sense to them, not necessarily the Conservatives; the important thing was to partici-

pate. When I got older, my brothers told me about this lecture. They must have really impressed it on me because, apart from my older brother Ed, I was the only one in the family to go into politics. Ed ended up moving to Saskatchewan in 1946 where he eventually became an MLA for the CCF and then a Cabinet minister for the New Democrats. At one point my mother had two sons who were Cabinet ministers, one provincial and one federal.

My mother also was a big influence, of course, even though she didn't have much time for love and affection. I think several of my brothers and sisters were afraid to get married because they saw how hard her life was. She was pretty young when suddenly she was on her own and looking after all of us. In those days women weren't expected to manage anything outside of their houses and their children, so she had to learn fast and it must have been difficult for her. But she certainly survived. When she died early in 1986 she was ninety-three and she'd been a widow for fifty-five years. People used to tease her about different men but she'd always laugh and say, "Who wants a woman with nine kids?"

It wasn't because she was homely. My mother was a good-looking woman with jet black hair. She was about five foot, eight-and-a-half inches tall which was a lot for a woman in those days. My theory is that she simply didn't have time to consider remarrying. She was always working.

One of the things mother did was to raise wyandotte chickens both for the eggs and for meat. Big, pure-snow-white chickens. A hen would weigh six pounds and a rooster seven or eight. A lot of people bought her eggs and chickens. It brought in a little money and sometimes she would pay for things with chickens instead of cash. For instance, she paid our family doctor with eggs and sometimes she'd barter chicken for coal to keep us warm. And we ate a lot of chicken ourselves – chicken and eggs and oatmeal, which was cheap. We ate eggs sometimes as often as three times a day. Sometimes when mother served us fried eggs one of us would say, "Ma, I'm seeing spots before my eyes so there's either something wrong with my eyes or we got eggs again." You can imagine how many fried eggs would be on that platter to serve ten hungry people.

She would often cook chicken and dumplings, boiling them in a big pot and then saving the broth to make soup. We didn't waste anything. In Essex County then no one worried about garbage collection because there wasn't any garbage. People didn't have anything to throw away; they couldn't afford to. Now people throw away nearly one-fifth of all the food that farmers produce. When I was a kid there weren't any mountains in Essex County, but we've got three of them now. They're called sanitary landfill sites.

Another way my mother made a little money was by sewing and by cutting hair. That's how she was able to afford the telephone, which was considered quite a luxury. It was her lifeline to the outside world, so even though it cost $1.55 a month, the expense was worth it. She'd cut hair for most of the kids in the neighbourhood and they would leave her ten cents or fifteen cents or twenty-five cents for doing three of them—that sort of thing. And a lot of kids couldn't pay, but she used to cut their hair anyway. The odd time some of the older children and even adults who couldn't afford a barber would come. She would never refuse anybody.

I don't know how my mother did it. She kept us in food and clothes and pretty well left us to look after each other. But she ran us with a pretty stern hand if we got out of line. I'll never forget the time I went to get some cookies she'd baked that were in the pantry. She'd put them out of reach on the top of this big old cupboard that had all the dishes in it from her wedding—things she really loved. I climbed up onto the cupboard shelf so I could get at the cookies and the whole thing came crashing down and just about everything broke. I knew I was really going to catch hell so I ran straight into the orchard just south of the house. It had a mixture of apple trees but the tallest ones were northern spies and I picked one of those and I climbed to the top and hid until dark. Then I started to get hungry and frightened to be alone, so eventually I went back into the house where I got whipped really good, I can tell you. When my mother whipped us she often used a lilac switch. (We had lilac brushes growing right near the house.)

My mother was stern but fair and she certainly impressed on us one philosophy – that all people are equal. I remember coming home from school once and we were talking about these two pretty little blonde Czechoslovakian girls in my class in grade school. I referred to them as "honkies." Well, my mother was having none of that and she gave us such a speech, I'll never forget it. She told us, "Those girls are no different from you, they're just from another country. They're just as good as you, and they're equal in every way. And I don't want to ever hear that kind of talk from you again." That was only one of many occasions when she hammered her belief home. She had a natural, deep respect for people, and I like to think it rubbed off on me.

My mother's maiden name was Frances Kelly. (That's how I got my middle name of Francis.) Before she got married, my mother had been a telephone operator for the Bell Company. First she'd worked as a housekeeper, keeping rich people's houses clean, so the operator job was quite a step up. She made almost twelve dollars a week working six twelve-hour days.

She worked at one of those old-fashioned switchboards where you were pulling and plugging all day. It was in Amherstburg and it served the whole of Anderdon Township and Malden Township. In those days everybody who wanted to make a call had to talk to the operator, so people got quite friendly with her. Most of them would call her Frankie, the doctors and merchants and so on. If someone was on night duty at the chemical plant they'd tell her to call them at home and give them a wake-up call. She was very conscientious and she helped a lot of people.

For example, she'd always do what she could to make sure that the doctor got there when someone was sick, or that the priest got there before a person died. She'd call the station agent and tell him where the local passenger train (it ran three or four times a day between Amherstburg, Essex and Windsor) should stop to pick up the doctor or the priest, whomever. In those days the roads where all dirt roads, which often meant mud, so the train was often the only way to get close to someone in need.

On the job she treated everyone the same and she didn't take any nonsense. A favourite joke was to call her up and say, "Frankie, would you get me Heaven." And she'd always come back without a pause: "If you don't get off that line, I'll give you hell." And of course in those days everyone had party lines. There was one old guy, whenever he called on the party line and he wanted the line private, he'd pick up the phone and say "Now all you women get off of this line, 'cause we're going to discuss castrating horses." Nowadays we'd think of party lines as an invasion of privacy, but then it just increased the sense of community. People liked to eavesdrop on each other. Everybody used to listen on the party line, but no one seemed to mind.

When I was first starting out in politics my mother's old job turned out to be a tremendous benefit, just as it had been for my father. Everyone knew Frankie Kelly and knew that it was Frankie's kid running for reeve or running for warden. For many years afterward people would send her gifts and Christmas cards and many of her old customers became friends of the family. People didn't forget what she'd done for them. One such family was the Pettypieces, hard-working Irish people. When I started farming on my own they loaned me money at very low interest. And they didn't ask me to pay it back for a long time.

As I said, my mother was working as a telephone operator when she married my father. He was nearly twenty years older and had known her since she was a little girl. There's a funny twist to the story – not of how they met, but of how they finished up something their grandparents had started. You see, my grandfather Bernard Whelan came from Ireland at the time of the potato famines and went first to New York City. He stayed for five years and then he came to our area to marry a girl named Murphy whom he'd met back in Ireland. Perhaps he'd saved up enough money working in New York that he figured he could now afford to marry his childhood sweetheart. Well, when he arrived, it turned out she'd been married to a man named Kelly for about five years.

At that time the local Irish settlers would have get-togethers once a week, each week in a different house. Everybody brought food and there'd be eating, talking, dancing and drinking. After discovering he'd been jilted, Grandpa Bernard went to every one of these parties. I guess he was lonely. When people asked him what he was doing he'd reply, "I came here to marry the Murphy girl and she's already married." At one of these parties there was a girl just standing nearby who overheard this remark. And she said, "Well, why don't you marry me?" Just like that. Her name was Bailey and her mother was a Mayville, which is a French name. She was not a Catholic. Her mother was the local mixture, part Irish, part French, and part Indian. They got married six months later and she became my grandmother Whelan. When she married, she became a Catholic.

Meanwhile my grandfather's former sweetheart named Murphy—the one who'd married a Kelly—was giving birth to baby Kellys. And one of them was a son named Timothy, who later married Mary Richard. Their oldest daughter was named Frances; she became my mother. And she married a certain Charles Whelan, son of Bernard. And that was my father. So my father finished off what his father Bernard had tried and failed to do. He married a Murphy girl—even though her name was Kelly.

My grandfather Bernard Whelan was an educated man, but he wasn't much of a farmer. According to the story that's been handed down he went to Trinity College in Dublin, but this would be surprising since not very many Catholics went there then. After he got married he rented a farm from Squire Cunningham, a rich man from Ireland from whom many Irish people rented. My parents' families—both the Whelans and the Kellys—rented from him and his descendents for about a hundred years.

My grandfather's farm was on fifty acres of land right in the middle of the bush. My grandmother ran the farm and he helped her. He mainly used his education to help the local people, most of whom couldn't read or write. He would write letters for them and help them draw up their wills. That sort of thing. He wasn't cut out for farming, but in our area there wasn't much of anything else for him to do. His children and grandchildren became farmers and none of us until my generation went to university. The only one of us who made it was my youngest brother Bryce. Sadly he never finished. While he was there he had a nervous breakdown and he was never the same after. He was married and divorced with two kids and went from job to job until he finally ended up in a psychiatric hospital. And he was the brightest one of us all – he was handsome as could be and he could learn anything. I think his problems had a lot to do with the fact that our father died when he was so young – he was only six months old at the time.

My father Charles was a farmer – and a politician. After he married my mother, he bought a small farm from the heirs of the McQuaid estate. It was fifty-six acres. Most farms then were fifty acres, but the railroad from Fort Erie to Chicago – it was known as the straightest railroad in North America – went right by the side of our farm and then crossed the river at Amherstburg. So the crown land on our side of the railroad track was ours to farm, which gave us the extra six acres.

All nine of us were born and raised in the log cabin – I often joke that Abe Lincoln and I had that in common. The log cabin had originally belonged to Pat McQuaid who'd lived there in the 1860s. McQuaid was the grandfather of the Biddle Brothers, the famous Canadian gangsters. There was a good movie made about them not long ago – *Mrs. Soffel* – but the movie didn't reveal the fact that they got their start in Anderdon Township in the very house where I grew up. The Biddles were dirt poor and the Biddle boys used to steal pies off of window sills. Later on they robbed banks and were put in jail.

Our house was a pretty big place – it was a storey and a half with three bedrooms upstairs and two more on the ground floor. The logs went right up to the eaves – and the sheeting was big wide boards you couldn't even drive a nail into. They must have been walnut or something, they were so hard. But it was cold in the winter. The windows were so rotted that the air came in all around them and we had to wear toques, socks and mitts to bed in the winter. The house was on a migratory bird path and in spring and fall we used to joke that the birds didn't fly around our house, they just flew through it. Later my brothers and I helped my mother fix up the place and she continued to live there until eight months before she died.

My mother always got up first and on winter mornings we

could hear her rattling the Quebec heater in the living room to get it going. When we heard that rattling it was like our alarm clock and we'd all rush downstairs to dress in front of the heater. I can remember my brother Henry stooping over one time to put on his pants and he backed right into the stove – he had a brand on one cheek for years. Otherwise we didn't use the living room much. When we were in the house we spent most of our time in the kitchen which was a big room, twenty-four by twenty-four, that had been built by my father.

I grew up in a community that was mostly French and Irish, but there were many other elements. The south half of Anderdon Township was mostly Irish and the northern half was French, but there were German families that date back to the American revolution, descendants of Hessian soldiers who fought for the British and were given land grants in Canada. Some of the English, Irish and Scotch families are descended from the soldiers who fought in the War of 1812, members of General Brock's ragtag army. They used to say that the British would never have had an empire if it wasn't for the Irish soldiers who did all the fighting and dying for them. Most of the French settlers came in the early 1720s but there were about two hundred of them, mostly *coureurs de bois*, who'd been in Brock's army. Most of the Irish settlers came later, in the mid-1800s when things were so bad in Ireland. Later in the nineteenth century Italian people came to work in the local quarry, stonecutters and masons. During the Civil War escaped slaves came to Anderdon on the Underground Railroad and there were always black kids in school with me and black people were respected members of the community. When I was growing up there was almost always a black member of the Amherstburg town council. And for quite some time there's been a black policeman. There's a young black man, Wayne Hurst, now on town council who's from one of the oldest families in the town.

In the late 1800s and early in this century came Hungarians, and Slovaks, and more Germans and Italians. By the time I was growing up there were no Indians, just an Indian burying ground on the Detroit River. The Indians who were there when the explorers first came were Wyandots. Then later came the

Iroquois. Quite a few of the older families – like mine – had Indian blood.

From the late 1800s until the early 1920s the road by our house was used as the springtime route for the stage coach between Sandwich and Windsor because at that time of year the road along the river was often flooded. My older brothers could still remember the last stage coaches, but I never saw one. Back in the days before Prohibition there was a tavern at the corner of Texas Road and the Third Concession, less than a mile from our house. It was known as Hell's Corners because the place was pretty wild then – lots of drunken brawls and sometimes worse. There were two saloons, a wagon works and a lime-burning kiln. The drivers knew if they ever stopped at Hell's Corners there'd likely be trouble, so they'd just gallop right through. And often the people in the tavern would take shots at the coach. My mother told stories about some of the fights and some of the killings at Hell's Corners.

I knew a man whose father had been the hotelkeeper in those wild days. He remembered one incident from when he was a little kid, only about seven years old. A fierce-looking Indian who was in the tavern picked him up off the floor and set him on the bar. Then he pointed this big gun at him and said, "Little boy, I'm gonna kill you." He held the gun right to his head. When my friend told me this story he said that at the time he'd thought this was the funniest thing in the world and so he started to laugh and the Indian laughed too because this little pipsqueak wasn't scared of him. Then he picked my friend up off the bar and just set him down gently on the floor. I first heard this story when my friend was in his seventies.

The world I grew up in was a lot more peaceful than that, but it wasn't your typical Ontario farm community. Not only was there this rare mixture of people, there was the combination of farming and industry and the closeness of the growing city of Windsor. At one time Amherstburg had been bigger and more important than Windsor, but by the time I was a kid Windsor was getting to be a big place. Nevertheless I didn't actually go into the city until I was thirteen years old. More and more local people were working in the plants in Windsor (and even Detroit), but the main local industry was the Bruner Mond Chemical Plant, a British firm which made soda ash and calcium chloride; it was bought by Allied Chemical after the war and is still going strong. A lot of the people who lived in Amherstburg worked there and some farmers worked at the plant to supplement their income from the farm. So when I grew up there was always this big chemical plant right around the corner.

The elementary school we kids went to was founded in the 1800s by my Grandmother Bailey on my father's side (the same Bailey Grandpa Bernard Whelan married instead of Miss Murphy). It was a frame building that had replaced the original one which burnt down after about twenty-five years. It was used until about thirty years ago when it closed down and people started going to the Central School in Amherstburg.

We had grades one through eight in the one large room that had a big old potbellied stove in the corner and no electricity, so on dark winter days we worked by the light of kerosene lamps. I don't think the school had electricity until the time I was elected to the school board (when I was just twenty-one). There was no running water – no bathroom – just two outhouses, one for girls and one for boys, in two corners of the schoolyard. Around behind the outhouses was one of the places where we kids fought because the teacher couldn't see us.

In the winter you never spent time reading a magazine in those outhouses because it was too damn cold. They had no heat so you just ran and went and then ran back into the school. Sometimes we left newspaper over the seat. That way you could just flip the snow off and sit down. Generally newspaper was what you used as toilet paper, too. People talk about using the *Eaton's Catalogue* but that was never a best seller with us – it was too smooth. Until we got running water at home, pretty much the only toilet I ever saw was in an outhouse.

The older kids went to school only about six months a year because they were needed on the land the rest of the time. We each had a set of overalls that my mother made for us. During summer holidays we wore our overalls with no shirt and in warm weather we went to school barefoot. We just padded along in that nice soft clay dust in our bare feet. It felt good. But by the time I'd graduated into high school they'd put gravel on the road – crushed limestone that had sharp edges. It really hurt our feet and it was hell on our shoes. We kids thought it was the meanest thing anyone could've done.

My mother didn't have much formal education but she'd taught herself quite a few things through reading and just by observing the world and she believed very strongly in seeing that we got the best education we could. When we were starting school she helped us learn to read. And she watched how we were doing all down the line.

My teachers were Irish – Miss Curran was the first one I had. She came from Corunna, Ontario, which is near Sarnia. She was a good teacher and not too strict. She had a novel way of dealing with kids who wanted to fight. Instead of trying to stop it, she'd referee it right there in the schoolyard. Then she'd give them both the strap and give us all a lecture about the difference between civilized people and barbarians. As a result, even the oldest and most unruly kids liked her and respected her. When she left to go to Sarnia to get married we all cried.

I guess we were a pretty rough bunch. The next teacher, Miss Macpherson, lasted only about three months. We were always getting into fights and making fun of Miss Macpherson when she wasn't looking. I wasn't one of the worst but I learned to raise hell early in life. It stood me in good stead when I became a politician.

Miss Macpherson's replacement was Miss Donnelly from Lanark County near Ottawa. She knew our tough reputation and the first day she came in like a dragon breathing fire. I'll never forget what she said: "This is a tough school and it has a bad name and I'm going to straighten it out." I just sat there grinning in the front row. We all thought, "Best of luck, old gal." Miss Donnelly wouldn't stand for swearing or fighting or smart remarks. I used to get strapped by her about three times a day, but I never paid much attention to her. She had much more of an effect on my younger brother, Henry. She used to lift him out his seat by his hair. As a result, he hated school and he hated her. Today, a teacher would be put in jail for that sort of thing.

Miss Donnelly didn't understand us. We weren't such bad kids, really. I think it's natural for rural children to be a bit rougher and more unruly. But we didn't mean any harm. We wouldn't steal or do anything like that.

I didn't say much in the classroom because in those days I had a habit of stuttering. When I first started out in politics I still would stutter and often I'd get the order of words mixed up. It still happens to me sometimes and it's part of what the press used to make fun of – my "unique" way of speaking. But eventually the stutter disappeared. I think it just naturally went away as I became more self-confident.

At school we grew up to be close friends with some of the kids we used to fight with every day. There was a certain amount of division along ethnic lines, but mostly our rivalries were territorial. The kids at our school were mostly "bushwackers," but some were "quarrysuckers." The bushwackers came from the east side of the school and were mostly farm kids. The quarry-suckers came from the other direction and many of them lived near the limestone quarry for the chemical plant where many of their fathers worked. Bruner Mond provided the school with cinders from their boiler house to keep the schoolyard from getting muddy. After fighting in that stuff we'd be an incredible mess, especially after a rain or snow. I may sound like we were always at war, but actually we didn't fight that much of the time.

Two of my best friends from elementary school were Danny Rosati and Sammy Di Nunzio. Danny was a little bit older than me and Sammy was about my age. They should have gone to the quarry school but because the quarry school was a public school the priest got them to come to ours. As quarry kids they had a little bit of a rough reception when they arrived. It didn't help that both their parents came from Italy when they were little kids and so could barely speak English. The bigger kids would start us all fighting and we gave them quite a hard time. Since Sammy was older than me but not as big I used to take him on, and Danny would stand up for him, so I'd end up fighting with Danny. That was something new for our school. They were quarrysuckers and Italians but they stood up for their rights. It took me a while to learn that their rights were just as much theirs as ours were ours.

We also played baseball and hockey together and occasionally we'd have a power struggle over a hockey stick or a bat. I remember one time Danny and I got into a tussle over a baseball bat and he hit me in the nose with a stick. When I went home I was bleeding like a stuck hog and my mother put cold rags on it and asked me who I was fighting with. I told her who it was and she said, "Well, you probably deserved it." That's all she said and that's all there was to it. One side of my nose is flat where it was hit so I guess it was broken. Danny Rosati and I are still good friends and we laugh about those times now.

Edmond Matte was someone I used to stand up for in the schoolyard – he was small so bigger kids used to pick on him – and he never forgot the winter day when he got into a fight with several older and bigger kids. They were beating the hell out of him, so I went and stopped them. With the snow and the cinders you can imagine the mess. At the time I had a little home-made sleigh and, since little Edmond was bawling away, I gave him a ride on it around the schoolyard. He was only about seven years old at the time. Edmond never learned to read or write much in either English or French, but he became a damn good farmer. When he was starting out, he worked for me as my hired man and when I first went to Ottawa to cultivate all those Cabinet ministers he was back home cultivating my vegetables and my grain.

Because this was a separate school, part of what they taught us was religion. My mother was not what you'd call a strict Catholic but in a way she was more strict than most people. She would certainly never eat meat on Friday because you were going to Hell if you ate meat on Friday. For Lent she used to send to Manitoba to get whitefish. She ordered it out of a farm magazine and the train brought them in big boxes packed in ice. Since we didn't have a refrigerator we ate all the fish before Lent was over.

She didn't make us go to church every Sunday but we went quite often. When she couldn't go she'd send us with neighbours. In the early days we used to go in a buggy drawn by our old work horse Belle – she was a cross between a Belgian and Percheron and she had more sense than any of us kids. Belle was the only horse left from the team of four my father had and she knew the way to church and the way home, when to run and when to walk. She was a very gentle horse, too.

We didn't go to Sunday School because we learned our catechism at elementary school, and the priest came to school about once a month to teach us and test us on our prayers. If you didn't know your prayers the priest would sometimes punish you. I remember we had a young Father Kelly and an old Father Kelly in our parish – both of them at the same time – and one day the two of them came to the school and told us the next time we didn't know our prayers we would have to kneel in the corner of the room for an hour with a kernel of corn under each knee. I went home and told this to my mother and she said, "Who was it told you that?" And I said, "Father Kelly." (Remember, my mother was born a Kelly.) "Well," she said, "that's so much Irish blarney. You tell him the next time when you see him that that's no way to teach a kid his religion."

Actually the priests in our parish were generally quite liberal and advanced. Most of them were Basilians, which is a teaching order, and they used to permit open and free discussions. They didn't teach us that you'd go to Hell if you ever went into a Protestant church – and this was long before Vatican II. We learned to have minds of our own and not do just what the church told us.

Danny Rosati tells the story of the time just after he was married when a priest came to his house and saw a book there that was banned by the church. The good father told him to get rid of that book and Danny replied, "You give me no credit for having brains or for having any intelligence whatsoever? You don't think I know what is right or wrong? Just because they've been banned by the church doesn't mean I shouldn't read them and make my own judgement." Danny is very religious to this day but he'd still argue with a priest or anybody. We both learned that from the Basilians.

No way you should take everything the church or anyone feeds you as being the gospel. After I grew up and learned something about marketing I realized that the Catholic Church was involved in a clever marketing scheme for fishermen. That was the idea behind setting aside one day a week to eat fish. I found this out many years later and I remembered this one time when I met with Cedric Ritchie, who is still head of the Bank of Nova Scotia. After I became agriculture minister I met him once at a dinner in Ottawa, but before then we'd corresponded back and forth. I don't usually like bankers, but I liked him—he always answered his letters himself and a lot of them didn't. Anyway, at this dinner party someone mentioned that I was going on a trip to Rome and he said, "What are you going to Rome for?" I said, "I'm going to try to get the Pope to make Friday a fish-eating day again." And Ritchie said, "Gee, that's a good idea." At this time his bank had a lot of loans out to fishermen and fish plants and the industry was in a slump. So I said, "What will you do if I get the Pope to set aside two days for fish eating?" And I remember very clear what he said: "If you do that, I'll turn Catholic." I always liked him because he was easy to talk to, unlike a lot of bankers.

My mother was strong on one thing and that was family prayers every night before we went to bed. We'd gather in the kitchen around the big table and she would lead us through our prayers. It didn't take long, usually only about five minutes—but it was important to her. Religion wasn't just what went on in church, although in later years she went to church nearly every Sunday until she broke her hip a few years before she died.

The September I started high school was the first time I'd ever worn shoes to school so early in the year. They wouldn't have allowed bare feet at General Amherst Secondary School in Amherstburg. Those first days were pretty exciting since it was traditional for all the first form (grade nine) students to be initiated. But I was determined to escape this torture, which could be pretty severe, so every day at noon I'd hop on my bike and ride uptown to hide. One day a bunch of older kids chased me all over town and I managed to cut one of them off so that the rider was thrown right off his bike. I can still see him somersaulting through the air. His bike was damaged, too.

That afternoon after school they were waiting for me. They had let the air out of my tires and I had to push my bike over to the garage. On the way they ambushed me and started to beat the hell out of me. I was quite a mess – all blood and dirt. Luckily, two senior girls happened to come along and saved me. They were pretty girls, too, so I was saved by two fair damsels instead of the other way around. They washed my shirt in the gas station tank where you put the tire inner tube to test for air leaks, and then I went home. One of their mothers called the principal and that was the end of initiation for that year. Up till then the teachers at General Amherst hadn't known it was going on. Or they'd turned a blind eye.

Even though we were Catholics, we went to the public high school because it was free. The separate school had no funding from the government and charged five dollars a month. With three of us in high school at the same time that would have just about taken care of most of our remaining Mother's Allowance and we'd have had practically nothing left to live on.

My two oldest brothers, Bernard and Ed, had by this time quit school to go to work. Once you hit sixteen the Mother's Allowance stopped whether you were in school or not, so that was actually an incentive for poor kids to stop their education. Eventually Bernard and Ed both got jobs at Church & Dwight in Amherstburg making Cow Brand Baking Soda. This was just before the war. Because they were earning good money, my mother wrote the government that she didn't need the money for the rest of us any more because her two oldest sons were wage earners and paying their board. They started at thirty-three cents an hour, which we thought was tremendous pay. When they got up to thirty-eight cents that seemed like a huge boost. They used to work ten hours a day and sometimes six days a week.

People used to worry about who was going to take care of my mother after we'd grown up but we couldn't understand anybody else having to take care of our mom. At first the two oldest ones were looked on as supporters of the family. Later Martin and Tom and then I would do our bit. I can remember working on local farms for a dollar a day when I was sixteen years old – and that included two big meals. I lived at home until I was married and my two bachelor brothers Martin and Tom lived at home until my mother went into the nursing home.

While we were on "welfare" we had to get a card signed once a month—to prove we were still in school and still "needed" the money. The man who signed the card was a Scottish Presbyterian named Walter K. Sidey who'd come to Amherstburg from Belleville, Ontario, sometime in the 1920s; he taught all nine Whelan kids and he had quite an influence on me. Whenever he signed the cards or gave us our report cards, he'd have each of us in and he'd talk to us for a while. He knew we didn't have a father so he took a special interest in us, asked us questions and gave us advice, that sort of thing. He and his wife had no children, so I guess in a way he adopted us a bit as his own.

My marks were never that high and he would always give me a friendly little lecture. He'd say, "Eugene, you could do better if you wanted. You don't even study." And I'd say, "Mr. Sidey, I've got chores to do when I go home. I don't have time to do my homework." And he'd smile and say, "Eugene, don't exaggerate. I know how many brothers you've got and I know how many cows you've got. Don't forget, I worked on a farm too." You couldn't snow him at all.

Even though he was a Scottish Presbyterian, he knew the Catholic holy days of obligation, and if we went to church before school he wouldn't count us as late for that day. But if we were late and hadn't gone to church he could tell just by looking at us. Then after school he'd give us a stern lecture on honesty. He'd say, "You know the agreement we've made. Even if it's only verbal, it's binding. Now don't let this happen again." Walter Sidey was a good teacher and a good man. He believed strongly in the rights and freedoms of the individual. And I'll always remember him for that.

Summers were the best times when I was young. My older brothers would be helping on the farm or working for local farmers if there were jobs to be had, but we younger kids just played and had fun—once we'd done the chores. One of our favourite pastimes was to go swimming in the quarry lake, which was about a mile-and-a-half away, straight west from where we lived. To get there we would walk along the railroad track. We'd go in the morning and we wouldn't come back until late afternoon. At the quarry, we'd make a fire and cook our food. Sometimes we'd raid the gardens of the Italians who worked in the quarry. Each family generally had a small plot of land – some were as big as ten acres – and they had big gardens, sometimes an orchard, and maybe a cow and some chickens. They didn't mind our raiding the gardens as long as we didn't take too much. In fact they kept an eye on us for our mom.

I know my mother worried when we were at the quarry. People told her how dangerous the lake was – some kids had drowned there. But we always promised to be careful. And I guess she was glad to have us out of sight and sound so she could have a little peace. On a Saturday or a Sunday, when we passed the bunkhouse – it was a boarding house where some of the Italian workers whose familes were still back home lived all year round – they'd always warn us in broken English to be careful. And they'd count us on the way there and count us on the way back.

Sometimes town kids would be at the quarry and they'd challenge us to a fight. I remember one time when a bunch of town kids cornered us and told us they were going to whip our hides. There were black kids and white kids in the gang and we were pretty scared. But just in time, Jessie Henderson, an older black man, came along and saved the day. He told those town kids to leave us alone and get lost. I still see him occasionally. He must be eighty-five years old by now.

On winter evenings we'd fight over who would get to listen to the crystal set. You couldn't get much volume on those early radios so there were headphones. All of us wanted to listen at the same time but there was only one set. We would listen to WJR out of Detroit. There was a beautiful farm program and we'd listen to the hockey games and the baseball games, the Red Wings and the Tigers. But my favourite was the Lone Ranger. "Hi-Yo Silver." I loved it, this masked man who fought for good things and his devoted sidekick, Tonto, who always called him *kemo sabe*. Later we told the joke that one time the Lone Ranger found out that *kemo sabe* really meant "You son of a bitch" and he shot Tonto and took off on his own. It actually means "faithful friend."

Our nearest neighbour was a Major T.B. Balfour who'd been an officer in the First World War and who'd fought in the Boer War.

I remember what a thrill it was when he bought a battery radio with those big old speakers on top of it. This meant we could all sit around and listen at the same time to the same program. Sometimes the radio would conk out halfway through whatever program we were listening to because the battery had run out of power. This was before any of us had electricity.

I was a pretty active kid despite the fact that I had my share of health problems. I'm partly colour blind and I was born with a heart murmur and even when I was a little kid I was partly deaf. They called it convenience deafness, but it didn't become convenient until much later. After I became a politician I could tune out meetings – this proved handy in the Cabinet – or pretend I didn't hear something when I had but wanted the person to repeat it so I'd have more time to think. I'm now completely deaf in one ear, in part I think because of working near noisy farm machinery as a boy and a young man, but I also had the glands behind my ear swell up as big as a goose egg. And I had a bad hernia from the time I was about four and half years old until I was twenty-one. I wore a brace, or truss, until I could afford an operation to correct the condition.

Most of my brothers and sisters had health problems and still do. My brother Martin, for instance, had a tear duct problem and a thyroid condition. Tom had chronic asthmatic bronchitis. I blame most of it on the fact that we were poor and there wasn't universal health care like there is now. Sure, some of our problems were inherited, but I can see the difference with my own three daughters. My oldest daughter, Terry, had ear problems which she probably inherited from me. Thanks to medicare she can hear like a fox. I think most of my family's health problems were made worse by our being poor. We ate enough but we didn't always eat properly. And we were scared to go to a hospital for anything because it cost so much. Anyway, the nearest hospital was in Windsor, which was about an hour away. My mother had a linament – an old remedy that was handed down from before the white people came. It was made out of turpentine and eggs and cream and a bunch of other things mixed together. We used it on cows udders and that sort of thing. Sometimes she used it on us, but you had to be very careful with it because it was so powerful. It was primarily used for doctoring cows and horses.

My ailments didn't stop me from playing hockey and baseball and lacrosse and getting into fights. When I was about eighteen years old and playing senior hockey I took a very clean body check and broke my collar bone off on an angle that drove it right into the muscle (I was all muscle then, not like I am now). So I had to have surgery done on it. Our family doctor was a salty character named E. D. Hutchison who'd been a First World War doctor. He wasn't the surgeon – that was Dr. Frank Adams – but Hutchison was the one that took the stitches out. The suture looked just like a crooked little railroad track. When Dr. H. saw Dr. A's stitches his first remark was, "God damn Frank must have been drunk. Look at that cut he made on you. He didn't need to make a cut that long and leave a scar like that." The two doctors were good friends, too.

Dr. Hutchison was the one who'd delivered me on July 11, 1924, and afterwards he commented to my mother, "Just imagine if he'd been born tomorrow! A papist on the twelfth." July 12 is Orangeman's day when they celebrate King William's victory of the Battle of the Boyne in 1690. If I had been born on the twelfth they probably wouldn't have registered me for that day.

One of my happiest memories of childhood is of the thrashing bees that would happen at harvest time. Farmers didn't generally have their own machinery in the 1930s. So when it came time to thrash the grain a man would come with a custom thrashing machine – either a steam engine or an oil pull, which is an engine that burns half oil and half kerosene, and go from farm to farm. And all the neighbours would come with their teams of horses and it would be a great big community operation. You'd have all the local ethnic groups and all the different religions working together. The men would help with the thrashing and the women would provide the food.

I was just a little kid watching this big monster machine. About every fifty revolutions of its great fly wheels it would let out a big belch of black smoke and go boom. The most exciting thing of all was to ride up on the platform where the operator stood when he drove it. You could look right down into the

machinery and see the gears and chains turning and pulling –
what a noise it made!

Each farmer would cut his own grain and stook it to let it dry
in the sun. Then when the thrashing teams came they'd drive
the wagons into the field and load the stooks onto the wagons.
When each wagon pulled up to the thrashing machine there was
one man who we called the spike pitcher who'd climb a ladder up
to the top of the load and, with the farmer who drove the team of
horses and the loaded wagon, fork the bundles of grain into the
feeder conveyor of the thrashing machine. The thrasher operator would watch this carefully to make sure the bundles went in
straight. If you had two bundles sitting crossways on top of two
sitting straight they could plug the machine, and it was a hell of
a job to unplug it. Of course, sometimes bundles "accidentally"
got crossed so they could have a rest break.

There were two meals served at thrashing bees, a big meal at
noon and a big meal in the evening. Often the men would work
late to try and finish a particular farm and then they'd be even
hungrier and eat more which meant more work for the women.
Except for the man who operated the thrashing machine there
was never any money that changed hands. It was a wonderful
feeling, kind of a carnival atmosphere.

Today, I suppose it would be looked on as a kind of commu-
nism. People then simply considered getting together to help
each other the natural thing to do. If a barn burned down there'd
be a barn-raising. And when it was time to butcher hogs or beef
or whatever, the local butcher would run the show and everyone
would gather to help out. They'd go from farm to farm. That was
simply the way things were done. We worked like a bunch of
socialists and nobody got paid to do it – and it wasn't limited to
thrashing. For instance, the people who lived along a particular
stretch of road would look after it – grade it and so on – and in
winter there'd be whole gangs of men shovelling snow.

I think it was in 1939 that we finally got electricity. My great
uncle on my mother's side, Uncle Joe Kelly who'd been a train
engineer, died and left my mother one thousand dollars – quite
a bit of cash for that time. Her brothers were jealous because

she was the only one he left money to, but she was the one who needed it the most. My mother used the money to fix up the house. She replaced the rotting window frames and put on imitation brick siding. I remember the workmen used copper nails, which disappeared with the war because copper was needed for the war work. And she had the house wired for electricity. No wall switches in most rooms like you'd have today, just chains hanging down in the centre of the room from the fixture. It was cheaper that way. I think wiring the house cost about a hundred and sixty dollars.

It was a godsend, that electricity, especially once we'd put in the water cistern and got running water. We helped my older brother Bernard put in the cistern and an electric water pressure pump before he went into the air force in 1940. And we helped my brother Ed, who was a plumber, put in all the galvanized piping and our first bathroom.

The water from our well was as hard as the hubs of hell, as they used to say, and you couldn't use it for washing. But the cistern would catch the soft rainwater that fell on the roof. You can imagine what a difference running water meant with so many kids. Before we'd had a bath only once a week in the washtub by the kitchen stove – and we did chores in the barn every day, so we must have stunk pretty bad. Of course it didn't make that much difference because we all smelled the same. My mother used to say for years afterwards that she wouldn't have missed the electricity as long as she could have had running water.

Years later, when other people talked about the "good old days" as if the thirties had been a fine time, my mother would simply say, "I don't remember them." And they must have been much more difficult for her than they were for us. At this stage of my life I never paid very much attention to what was going on in the great world outside Anderdon Township. The only foreigners we knew were Americans, who seemed much better off. They owned all the summer cottages along the Detroit River and Lake Erie and they commuted from Detroit along the road by our place. When they raced by our house we used to say, "There go those rich Americans putting up the dust." But now I realize that very few of them were what we'd call rich now.

Most of what I knew of Canada I'd learned in school – history and geography, the names of explorers and the provincial capitals – but the lesson that meant much more to me was one I learned from one of our neighbours, a Frenchman who worked as a carpenter and a farmer. One time he said to us, "Some day you kids will have your own flag. Some day the constitution she will come home where she belongs. I won't live to see that, but some day the crown head she will roll." He meant that we would be truly an independent country. It gave me a hollow feeling even as litttle kid to think we didn't have our own flag. Little did I suspect that I'd participate in both the Flag Debate and bringing home the constitution.

2

Part-Time Farmer

The Second World War came along the summer I turned fifteen. That meant the first year of the war was also my last year of high school. All of my older brothers had quit school at age sixteen or earlier and gone to work, and that was my plan too. If it hadn't been for the war I'd have likely followed right in my brothers' footsteps. Instead, I took a slightly different tack.

Some government recruiters came to the high school that year looking for students with mechanical aptitude – they needed people to replace those who'd joined the army to fight in Europe. Mr. Sidey recommended a bunch of us, but only five ended up going: Jim Deneau, Cliff Eggleton, Walter Bebbington, Bill Wade, and myself. Jim Deneau and I were the only farmers; the other three were town kids. All five us were sent to Windsor Walkerville Vocational School to take an emergency wartime course in tool-and-die making.

We went to school from three-thirty in the afternoon until eleven-thirty at night; it was a four-year course crammed into only seven months. This meant we had to live in Windsor because it was too far to commute and we didn't have any time to waste.

The five us pooled our resources and rented an apartment in a house that belonged to one of the caretakers at the vocational school. We got nine dollars a week for going to school, which seemed like pretty good money in those days. We each threw our money into the pot to pay the rent and buy food and we always had money left over at the end of the week. We took turns cooking and buying the groceries. I'd learned to be a pretty good cook helping my mother but I really missed her home cooking.

Only my oldest brother Bernard had been accepted into the service. I remember Ed was particularly despondent when he was declared physically unfit to serve. He felt like he was missing out on a great adventure. He and my other two older brothers, Martin and Tom, who were also declared medically unfit, remained at home during the war and helped support the family. Ed got a job at the Ford Plant in Windsor, so my mother had income from him and income from the family farm – and Bernard even sent home some of his air force pay from overseas.

This was the first time I'd ever lived away from home and up until then I'd hardly been to the "big city" at all. It was a strange place – a completely foreign way of life at the time. The others thought they knew their way around better than me so they used to try to lose me in the great metropolis of Windsor. When we'd get off the bus after school they'd run down alleys and across vacant lots and leave me behind, hoping to lose me. But usually I was sitting in the apartment waiting for them when they got home. I've always had a natural sense of direction. You don't fool me too easily.

The school was also a new experience for a lot of the teachers. Many of them had been brought in from their jobs in industry and had never taught before. But they knew their trade and they taught well. Some of the teachers became good friends and they've remained supporters of mine to this day. Getting to know these people meant a lot to me. I began to learn about the way city people think.

City people then had a complete misunderstanding of the rural way of life. They had no idea how poor we were or how hard we worked. They thought because we came from the country we were rich because we didn't have to pay as much for food – in those days people spent a much higher proportion of their incomes on food than they do now. But I marvelled at their houses and all the conveniences, because at that time if you'd moved all the farmhouses into the city, you'd have had a big slum. On the other hand, as farm kids, Jim and I had some advantages – we learned fast because we had grown up working and knew tools and heavy machinery better than most kids. We both became quite good machine operators.

We used to enjoy aggravating the city students in a harmless way. Sometimes we'd go to the noon movie and we'd pool our resources to take a cab. Since the cab cost about fifty cents and the bus ride was ten cents each, we came out even. But if it was a sunny day we'd spend an extra dime and tell the cab driver to drive by the school, because we knew that around noon a lot of students would be there sitting on the front steps. We'd tell the cabbie to pull up by the steps for a moment so we could wave to our city friends. The detour cost an extra ten cents but it was worth it just to hear those kids yell "Rich Farmers!"

After we graduated from the course, all five of us wanted to join the service, but like my older brothers I was medically unfit. So while my four friends all joined up and went overseas, I stayed home and worked. That meant that only one of my mother's five eligible sons went to war. I really envied my friends at the time. And they all made it through without a scratch.

So I went to work in various shops. My first job was at Bendix Eclipse in Windsor, but not as a tool-and-die apprentice – I ran big production machines, which I didn't much like. Then I moved home and got a job in the main machine shop at Bruner Mond. After that I worked on the Repair Gang, which took me to various other plants and to the huge limestone quarry that was then the main source of much of the plant's raw material – and still is today.

As it turned out, I never did become a full-fledged tool-and-die maker but I gathered a great deal of knowledge about different trades and about a different kind of working people, which helped me later in public life. I always knew more than any other

Cabinet minister about how things worked and how things were put together. I could read blueprints and when I looked at a plan I didn't have to pretend I knew what I was looking at, like some politicians.

I also learned about unions since some of the shops I worked in were organized while I was there. That was when unions were still not tied with a political party – which is how they should be today. Now you're discouraged from being anything but a New Democratic Party member when you're in a union, which I think is wrong. I believed then and I believe now that every person should be free to vote their conscience, as God intended them to.

The first union I joined was at Bruner Mond – Local 89 of the UAW/CIO. It was a full union and when I quit working at the plant I got an honorary withdrawal card. I used to prize that quite a bit during election campaigns because most of the people who run – including the NDP – have never been union members. As a result of my early experience I've always had a strong rapport with union people and later I always got a lot of their votes that would otherwise have gone to the NDP. Without them I would never have been elected. I guess you could say that I was the working man's and the working woman's Liberal.

In the summers I generally quit working on the Repair Gang and helped with the farm and sharecropped on rented land – which was what I was doing in the summer of 1942 when my brother Ed and I decided to go West. I was eighteen and Ed, who was still working as a machine operator at Ford, had just turned twenty-three. It was August and we had no tomatoes that year so there was a lull in the farm work.

During the war it was quite common for men from the East to go out to the Prairies to help with the harvest because there weren't enough hands to bring in the crops. They were sent as part of a federal government program and there was a big appeal – radio ads and newspaper ads, and posters – asking you to volunteer for these "harvest excursions." The government even paid your ticket. Whole trainloads of people went West and men were dropped off all the way across the Prairies. It was considered important enough that you could get a leave of absence from your factory job. As Ed and I would find out, in those days the people out West didn't call us Eastern bastards; they welcomed us with open arms.

So Ed got leave from the Ford plant and we headed west. We decided to go to Alberta because that was as far as you could go and that way we'd see more of Canada. It was the first train ride I'd ever taken.

Ever since I was a little kid I've loved trains. My uncle Joe Kelly was a train engineer and that was going to be the job for me. My brothers and sisters and I used to go down beside the tracks that ran through our farm – they were only about a thousand feet from our house – to watch the trains go by, the old Canada Southern Railway (later known as the Michigan Central). They still had steam engines in those days and the engineers would always blow steam and toot the whistle as they passed. We'd throw rocks at the big, black engines and the fireman would often throw coal back at us. That was part of our strategy because it meant we got more coal off the train. Then we'd walk along the tracks with a basket and pick up the lumps that had fallen off or been thrown off and take them home. Free fuel.

People don't realize how fast those old trains went. Some of the engineers used to compete. One I knew told me they could have run the train between Windsor and Toronto in three hours, if they'd been allowed. They could make those steam locomotives go one hundred and forty miles an hour and just make them sing. Not far from where I lived we had the fastest curve in North America. All the way from Fort Erie to Essex there's not a curve and then at Essex there's a great long curve where the trains slowed all the way down to eighty miles an hour on their way into Windsor. They just pounded the hell out of those big heavy rails. Actually some of the trains then were faster than they are now. In those days the railroads weren't as experienced at making the red tape that slows them down as they are today.

Anyway, this trip West was the first time I'd ever actually been on a train, though I'd imagined myself in the engine cab or in the caboose many a time. The train ride from Windsor to Toronto wasn't too bad – I was so excited I didn't mind the fact that it was crowded – but at Union Station in Toronto there wasn't an empty seat on the train to Winnipeg. We sat on those hard coach benches, no bunks or pillows or anything like that, and there was no food on the train, so the smart travellers brought big boxes of provisions. The only places we got off the train were in Sudbury, long enough to walk around the platform, and in Winnipeg to change trains. It took us two days to get to Winnipeg and another day and half to get to Calgary, which meant we'd gone almost four days and four nights without enough food and with no proper place to sleep or wash. Ed had quite a rough beard when we got off and we must have looked more like two criminals than two fine young men you'd hire to help with the harvest.

Before we'd come out West we'd been given one piece of advice. That was to make sure we didn't work for a farmer who was originally from Ontario. They told us, "He'll be a son-of-a-bitch to work for." So I asked how we could tell an Ontario farmer from a Westerner and they said, "He'll wear a straw hat," something a real Westerner wouldn't wear. A real Westerner would wear a stetson – like the one I often wear now, only not green – or an old felt hat.

The first farm we went to was near Carstairs, which is just north of Calgary, and sure enough, the guy who ran this farm wore a straw hat and he was from Ontario and he was an s.o.b. He had a beautiful farm and a wife who didn't do any work. His hired man had joined the air force and it was that man's wife who did all the cooking and housekeeping while the owner's wife just sat around all day. I'd never seen that before: a lady of leisure.

Needless to say, we didn't like it much there. They fed us stew three times a day – morning, noon and night – which gets a little monotonous, and the four of us stayed in a little bunkhouse that was so cramped you could hardly move. The top bunk I slept in was so close to the ceiling I could barely roll over. The Ontario farmer was always spying on us to make sure we were really working, and he never talked to us or ever brought us water in the field. We lasted five days.

This time we were sent to High River, Alberta, Joe Clark's

home town. Of course, Joe would have only been a little kid at the time. Later, at the end of our stay, my brother went to visit Little Joe's father, who was the editor of the local newspaper; Ed went because Mr. John Marsh, the editor of the *Amherstburg Echo*, knew Mr. Clark and asked us to look him up. They had a nice half-hour discussion. I let Ed go alone because I had no more interest in visiting newspaper editors at that time than in going to the opera. So I didn't come close to meeting Joe Clark until much later.

Near High River we worked for a Scotsman by the name of Hart; George Hart. Now he was one of nature's gentlemen. He was tall and he wore a felt hat with holes punched in it and he had one of the longest bodies I've ever seen. He wore such long suspenders that it looked as if his pants and shirt would never meet. He smoked a pipe and he had a sense of humour, too. When we'd been there about a week he said to us, "You know, I nearly didn't hire you two." And I said, "Why, Mr. Hart?" because I knew we were working hard and doing a good job. He told me, "Well, if you hire two together and one gets mad and quits the other one always goes with him. So you lose two." Then he said, "If either of you had smoked, I wouldn't have hired you for sure." And I said, "What the hell has that got to do with it?" "Well," he said, "if you smoked and wore a belt" – both Ed and I wore belts – "you'd spend half your time either rolling a cigarette or pulling up your pants. I'd hire nobody like that." I guess that's why he wore suspenders. He figured it saved him the right to smoke.

George Hart was a wise man. He knew how to make people work: he treated us well and fed us like kings. I'll never forget our first breakfast. There was porridge and eggs and bacon and potatoes and toast and then there was steak and apple pie. I thought, "These people must have their meals all mixed up. They're nuts here." But that turned out to be the normal breakfast grub. And in the middle of the morning someone would come into the field with a little pick-up truck that had sandwiches and coffee and tea and milk. Then they fed you another big meal at noon and another snack mid-afternoon. The final meal of the day was at nine at night. So that was three meals a day and two snacks in between. They actually fed you five times a day.

Mr. Hart was a custom operator on a grander scale than we had back home since the farms in Alberta were too big and the farmers too few and far between. He went from farm to farm to do the thrashing. He had only about nine teams of horses and a crew of about twelve men, including one spikee and one field pitcher. The rest of us drove the teams that pulled the bundle wagons, loaded the stooks onto the wagons with three-tine pitchforks, and fed the grain into the thrashing machine. Our team of twelve could load and thrash between fifty and sixty acres a day.

We worked all day and then we went to bed. The day would start about 4:30 A.M. We'd get up and run to the barn to feed the horses. Then we'd have breakfast and hitch the horses up to the wagons and we'd be sneaking up on the stooks of grain by first daylight, before the sun was even up. We'd work all day long until almost dark.

One day toward the end of our stay I told Mr. Hart I wanted to take a half day off to walk over to the mountains. There they were every day when I looked up from working, so beautiful and seeming so close you could almost touch them. "That's going to be a long half day," he told me, "because you're eighty miles from those mountains." So I never did walk there.

We worked forty-two days with only one half-day off during the whole stretch. By the end of it I was so strong I could have beaten a grizzly bear with a lilac switch with one hand tied behind my back. That summer they had a beautiful crop – sixty to sixty-five bushels of wheat to the acre – and the stubble was long, over a foot high. In the mornings when you walked through it your pantlegs always got wet from the dew. And the ground was so soft and gentle that you could drive those rickety old grain wagons and work horses across a field and not hear a sound.

By the time we finished the harvest it was October, but before we headed home we went to Banff, so I did get to see the mountains up close. Then we headed back to Windsor. When we got back we each had one dollar. We'd earned eight dollars a day and we'd spent all the money we'd earned and it didn't matter a bit. It was an experience I'll never forget. I learned more about Canada than money could possibly buy. I saw more clearly than ever that there isn't a hell of a lot of a difference between people. The differences are mostly in their minds. And ever since I've always had a special feeling for the West. Maybe that explains why I've always been more at home out there than most of my fellow Liberals.

After we returned home I continued to help run the family farm and to work at Bruner Mond. Growing up on a farm during the Depression hadn't scared me off of farming. Quite the opposite. My goal in life was to be a rich farmer. And I would have been, too, if I hadn't got into politics.

During the war my older brothers Martin and Tom were full-time farmers, running the old home place along with a couple of other farms. Martin had bought a farm and the three of us rented a hundred and twenty acres across the road. So I became a sharecropper in my spare time and I needed equipment. I bought my first new tractor in 1942 and it cost me fifteen hundred dollars. This was not the first tractor I'd known, but it was the first new tractor I'd owned. Back in 1937 or '38 we'd had one of those row crop Farmall 12s, tractors that look a bit like a giant tricycle, only with two little wheels in front. I was only thirteen and when I drove it I thought I had the world by the tail. But now, when I got my first new tractor, a Farmall H, it was like I'd moved from a prop plane into the jet age. The new tractor had rubber tires instead of steel wheels, fenders, a padded seat, and even a muffler.

Naturally in 1942 I didn't have the money and no one in the family could lend it to me so I had to take out a loan. It was the good old Canadian Imperial Bank in Amherstburg that was kind enough to lend me the money. At this time my mother was still paying back the money my father had borrowed back in 1931. The bank manager was just as gracious as bankers always are—made me have two co-signers for the note. I was eighteen years old and my poor mother had never missed a payment on my father's loan and that was how much he trusted me to repay them.

Pretty soon my brothers and I were doing a lot of custom work for farmers in the area. Each of us bought our own machinery: we each had a tractor, one of us a cultivator, and one of us a combine – and so on. So our equipment didn't overlap. We owned all this farm machinery, or rather the bank did, and we worked hard, but we didn't make much money. We should have been buying land then, not machinery. In those days you could buy good land for around a hundred dollars an acre. When I finally got around to buying land it was five times that.

We had our big chance in 1946. My brother Tom and I wanted to buy three hundred acres from the old Briggs estate. This was a huge estate in our area that had been owned by the Briggs family of Detroit, the ones who owned Briggs Stadium (now Tiger Stadium) where the Detroit Tigers still play. At this time the Briggs were selling all their property in Canada and they were asking $16,000 for the three hundred acres. Imagine.

Well, we had quite a family discussion. Tom and I were all for mortgaging the family farm in order to make the down payment, but Ed was against it. He was predicting another, worse, depression now that the war was over and he predicted we'd lose everything. While we were trying to make up our minds, some people smarter than us went ahead and bought it. They were new Canadians who didn't worry about losing what they didn't have, whereas our family was still locked into the old philosophy of poverty and of not taking a risk. The willingness to take risks is one of the reasons why immigrants have made such a contribution to this country. The people who bought it still have that farm.

The saddest part is that, as it turned out, we could easily have borrowed the money from someone else. Later, when I told our old friends the Pettypieces about wanting to buy the farm they gave me hell for not asking them: they would have loaned me the money, no problem. Now, if I had bought that farm in 1946 I would probably never have become a politician. I'd have been too busy. And too rich.

I didn't buy my first farm until 1952. I bought it from Sam Travica, a Serbian who'd come down to Essex from Northern Ontario. He was a big, kind, muscular man with black curly hair who at the time ran The Anderdon (now the Anderdon Harbour Light Tavern), a hotel and tavern that sponsored our local softball team. After a game we'd often go to Sam's place for a beer and on this particular Saturday evening we were sitting around telling jokes and talking and Sam overheard me saying that it was my great ambition to own a farm. Afterwards he took me aside and said, "Why don't you buy my farm?" He had about one hundred and twenty-five acres, also from the old Briggs estate, just behind the hotel, running away from the river. "Well," I said, "I'd love to, Sam, but I don't have no money." And he said, "I didn't ask you if you had any money."

So I bought his farm for no money down – one hundred and twenty-five acres for $26,000, which was a fair price in 1952. He didn't ask me for any money until five years later when he got sick. Then I got a Farm Credit loan to pay off the mortgage, because he held the mortgage himself. He died a couple of years later from cirrhosis of the liver. So I bought the farm and I gradually worked on it and improved it while I continued to do custom work with my brothers. It didn't have a house on it. After I got married I bought a house in Leamington and my brothers and inlaws and I moved it the thirty-five miles to the farm and rebuilt it there. We took it apart brick by brick and put it back together on the new site, which was just behind The Anderdon. I grew winter wheat and soy beans and grain corn. I also did custom work, growing peas and sweet corn for Green Giant. We ran their first mechanical sweet corn picker and we worked crazy hours because Green Giant was very conscious of having top quality corn and the corn is best early in the morning, before the heat makes the sugar return to the stalk. So we'd start about two-thirty in the morning and stop for about four hours in the real heat of the day. The rest of our time we'd spend either sleeping or repairing the machine. I always used to tell people that if you steal corn make sure you steal it early in the day before the sun comes out too hot.

Later I grew tomatoes on contract for Canadian Canners, the old canning factory in Amherstburg. It's closed down now after eighty years of operation. Tomatoes require a lot of work. Nowadays the companies have developed strains with tougher skins that can be picked by machines, but in those days it was all hand-picking. Every picker had a hamper that they had to carry themselves – most of the picking was done by women, mostly recently arrived Italian Canadians who were our neighbours. There were none of the big bulk wagons that you have now. During the harvest season we had to have a lot of hired help and we worked twenty-four hours a day, right around the clock, picking the produce in the daytime and hauling it to the factory at all hours. Depending on the canning schedule you might have to deliver a load at two in the morning. The people who picked were paid so much a hamper and they kept track of how many hampers – it was an honour system. And they didn't demand payment until Christmas. Many of them used the money to help put their kids through college.

The farm was one of the main reasons I got into federal politics. First of all because it led me to join the local co-op and then get involved at the provincial level. But it also gave me an understanding of the unfairness in the marketplace, which was something I fought against from the time I was first elected to Parliament.

I tried to keep this farm going right up until I became Minister of Agriculture. But even when I was just a member of parliament it became a problem. Of course, I had my schoolyard friend Edmond Matte working for me but I couldn't spend much time on the farm and, when I did, it was a rare day that I didn't get interrupted with some constituency problem. In spite of this I kept trying to run the farm as if I wasn't in Ottawa. And I remember when I was appointed to the Cabinet, my wife Liz finally said to me, "Either be a full-time politician or a full-time farmer. You can't be both." That's when I quit farming except for straight cash crops that don't require so much attention – wheat, soy beans, and corn.

Apart from working, there wasn't much to do in Essex County in the 1930s and early '40s except raise hell. There was no television and we didn't have our first radio until 1940. So politics was one of our main forms of entertainment and practically everybody got involved, whether or not you were of voting age.

It was natural that my brothers and I would be interested. Politics ran in the family. Other than the Bible, practically the only books in the house were political books – *The Municipal World, County Government* – and one or two books about Canada. My father had been reeve of Anderdon Township and warden of Essex County and my mother had served a term on the local separate school board. My father had been the only Irishman on council; the others were all French. He used to ask the French Canadian voters why they put an Irishman in as reeve, and they told him it was to keep those other guys honest.

Up the road from where I lived was an old hall where the township council held its meetings. It was also where the nomination meetings were held before the elections. A council of five members was elected every year – four councillors and the reeve. The nomination meetings were always held in December, always on a Saturday. And they were done the old-fashioned way. Nominations began at twelve noon and lasted until one, but the meetings would go on for hours, sometimes as late as 6:00 P.M. Latecomers would sit at the back of the hall on the woodpile or hang on the windowsills. When it got cold, the big wood stove would be lit and when it began to get dark, they'd light the oil lamps.

The incumbent councillors sat up on a small stage raised about a foot and a half above the audience. Between twelve o'clock and one o'clock anyone who wanted to could get up and nominate a candidate for council or for reeve. Afterwards the current reeve would give his report covering what the council had done over the preceding year. Then the meeting was opened to speeches from the floor. People would get up and complain about the weeds, or the dust, or the condition of the roads, or the drains. It was kind of an annual community meeting of the whole of Anderdon Township, French-speaking people and English – including Italians and other more recent immigrants.

I believe the first township meeting I went to was when I was about twelve. The reeve then was a great big Irishman named Fred Pettypiece from the same family who were good friends of ours. Even the poorest kids in the township could get up and ask questions at these meetings and Reeve Pettypiece would answer them just as seriously as the biggest taxpayers. One time when I was still a youngster I got up and asked him why he wouldn't build a baseball park or a community centre for us. He told me the township didn't have enough money, but what stands out is that he answered my question and didn't make fun of me because I was a kid. I learned early that if you don't stand up and ask, you'll never get an answer. I guess you could say those township meetings were my early training for raising hell in Lester Pearson's caucus in the sixties.

As far as I'm concerned this was democracy in its purest form. There isn't much of it left now because people aren't as interested today. Why? Because a lot of the functions of local and municipal governments have been taken over by the province. In Ontario a lot of blame for this has to lie with the provincial Tories. Much of our local democracy disappeared when they took authority away from the township councils and the county councils and formed regional governments. When they did that they created a bigger bureaucracy and put the citizens further away from the people they elect. And that's a bad thing.

In the old days, the nominations sometimes got pretty exciting; I remember one that even got violent. The former road superintendent of the township was running for reeve against the sitting reeve. They were both French Canadians and the sitting reeve had fired the road superintendent for no good reason except to put one of his political friends in the job. So the challenger got up and made a speech. He said, "I had a dream last night and in it there was a two-headed snake" – at this point he turned and pointed to the man who'd fired him, the sitting reeve – "and both the snake's heads had this man's face." Well, the reeve jumped out of his seat up there on the stage and grabbed his rival and the two of them got into a wrestling match. They had to break it up before the meeting could go on. The thing that amazed us was that the road superintendent had a college degree – which was very rare in those days – and he still got into a fight. I thought, "What a terrible thing for an educated man." That proved to me that even an educated person could be human and get mad.

The next week when we read about the meeting in the township paper, the *Amherstburg Echo*, there was almost nothing about the fight at all. The reporter was John Marsh, who always covered the Anderdon meeting because he said it was more lively than the ones at Amherstburg and Malden. John wrote that there was a "disturbance" and then he'd just copied out the minutes and reported what all the candidates said. Nowadays it's just the opposite. What you read in the newspapers is often twice as exciting as what really happened.

The township election was always held on New Year's Day or the day after and people would vote no matter how bad the weather. It was important to them. If the snow was too deep for their car, they'd journey to the polls on horseback or by cutter or on foot, even through a raging blizzard. Apart from nomination meetings and election days people seldom saw more than their closest neighbours during the winter, so everyone got involved.

I really didn't plan to get into politics myself. It just happened. Although I suppose it was natural for a Whelan. It happened in December 1945 at a separate school board meeting. I was twenty-one at the time and I was single and still living at home. I was still farming in the growing season and working in the winter as a machinist on the Repair Gang at Bruner Mond. But I had some time on my hands and I'd occasionally go to my old elementary school to attend the school board meetings, even though I had no kids. My only qualification was that I was a Catholic.

The chairman of the board at this time was a fellow named Gaspard St. Louis. He was a neighbour of ours and I'd known him since I was a little kid. Anyway, he got up at the meeting and told everyone he was quitting the school board. Then he said, "And I nominate Gene Whelan to replace me." No one in the room could have been more surprised than I was. My first reaction was, no, I don't want to be on the board. But right in front of the meeting he gave me such a speech about Canada and serving my community. I imagine he sounded a lot like my father when he lectured my brothers on the importance of public service. He certainly hit a nerve and so I agreed to stand.

The vote was right there that evening and I was elected and they made me chairman. Just like that.

It wasn't exactly a heavy responsibility. There was only one teacher and at most forty-eight students at any one time over eight grades and our board had one meeting a month. My biggest achievement during my term of office was to have a well drilled in the schoolyard. Before then, one of the children had to go each day to a neighbour's house for water. So everyone thought it was a great thing that the pupils now had fresh water every time they wanted a drink – even though they had to pump it by hand.

In 1952 I got elected to township council. By this time the old township hall had burned down and we were using what people called the Patrons' Hall. It was bigger than the old township hall because it had been built by the community as a gathering place for entertaining and socializing.

Again I had no warning and no intention of running but at the meeting that December two people nominated me: Stan Odette, a French Canadian Catholic and Ivan Jones, a Welshman Latter Day Saint. Odette was a very active Conservative who'd known my father but he certainly had no evidence I shared his convictions. Up until this time I had no political stripe and had never belonged to a political party. People didn't know what I was politically. I didn't know then, myself; it wasn't an issue.

Anyway, I was elected to township council and four years later, 1956, I ran for reeve against the incumbent, Alvin Vermette. I went straight for the top job rather than running for deputy reeve, and this rubbed some people the wrong way. They said it was wrong for a twenty-eight-year-old kid – not dry behind the ears – to run the township. I won that election by twenty-seven votes out of a total of three thousand and both the head of the local Liberals and the head of the local Conservatives voted for me. Even so, some resented how young I was and they promised they'd get me next year. But after that my majority only increased every time I ran.

Some of my supporters came to our house the night I won.

A few of them were from McGregor, a French district partly in Anderdon Township. When the fellows from McGregor came in they immediately noticed the crucifix on the wall and expressed surprise. They said I should have told them I was a Catholic, that I would have got more votes from their area. But I replied then as I would today: "You don't have to know a person's religion to know his politics. It's really none of your business. It's whether or not I do a good job." The next year I ran again for reeve and I won McGregor by a bigger majority. So apparently it made a difference to them.

During almost the whole time I was on council—from 1952 to 1962—I continued to live at home with my mother and my two older bachelor brothers. Before I was married, my mother often worked as a sort of unappointed township secretary. Many people remembered her from her switchboard days and when I wasn't home she'd take all the messages about township business.

More and more I was helping look after my younger brothers and sisters. Ed went out West in 1946, Bernard was married with a family of his own, and Martin and Tom were busy farming. I was the middle child and I wasn't married and a lot of the responsibility fell to me. I was closer to the younger kids, too. We'd grown up together. What happened to Bryce—which I've already mentioned—and what happened to Gertrude was hard on me and hard on my mother.

Gertrude was a brilliant kid. She'd graduated from high school before she was sixteen and wanted to go to work right away but there was no place would hire a girl so young. So she took a special course to be a secretary and then she got a job in the Windsor Post Office and for the United Co-operatives for a while—that's when she had her first nervous breakdown. I think she had trouble coping because she'd moved up so fast, ahead of her age. She was in and out of homes a couple of times and, in 1950, I think, she took her life in the psychiatric hospital in St. Thomas. She had been there for over two years. That was very rough on my mother.

Thank God, Helen and Henry did okay. Helen was a nurse. She wanted to be a doctor but there was no way we could afford that, so she went into the Hotel Dieu in Windsor where they paid you five dollars a month and gave you a place to live. Because she wanted to do it so much I said to her, "I'll pay your way," and I did help her out. But I realize that she had to give up a lot of things. She didn't go to dances and so on because it would have meant buying a dress and she didn't want to ask me for the money. She did graduate work in surgery at the Royal Victoria in Montreal and was supervisor in the operating room at St. John's Hospital in Detroit before she eventually moved to Phoenix, Arizona, where she lives now.

Henry never liked school much and as soon as he quit high school he went into apprenticeship as a pipe fitter – a plumber and high-pressure steam fitter. He took practical training courses after he'd quit school. He did fine until not long ago when he fell off the back of a lift truck at the Ford Plant in Windsor where he was working. It gave him an aneurism and he hasn't worked since. You could say that my family has had its share of troubles.

During my tenure as reeve, I particularly remember one township council meeting when we were about to hire a police chief. I knew there would be a petition from a number of people telling us who to hire and before the meeting I talked the situation over with our township lawyer, Al Kennedy. I've always remembered the advice he gave me. He told me that in a democracy you listen to petitions but you have to make up your mind yourself. That's what you were elected to do. If you're going to be governed by petitions then you don't need elections.

That night the Patrons' Hall was full of people. And one of the part-time policemen – his nickname was Nap which was short for Napoleon – walked in with a Sam Browne belt strapped outside his suit coat and a gun stuck in the holster. He looked pretty funny, but I was careful not to embarrass him in front of the crowd. I called him over to where I was sitting and I said to him, "Nap, now get that gun off and get the hell out of here because you'll start a riot and probably shoot yourself in the toe." An older councillor called Austin "Pappy" O'Brien – we called him Pappy because he was a sharp thinker – was sitting right beside me when I said this. Pappy took a puff on his pipe and said, "Napoleon, you look stupid. Get out of here." That was the last we saw of Nap that night.

When the petition was presented, it had four or five hundred names on it, but the ones who'd organized it were afraid to come out and say so. So they got an innocent fellow to bring it up, a new Canadian who didn't realize what was going on. I looked the petition over and then made a very short speech. I said, "We'll hire the person who is most fit for the job and if you don't like the way we do it, then you can fire us all at the next election." That was the end of that. (That police chief, whose name was Eric Hooper, stayed twenty-five years and only retired just recently.)

At this time I was also getting involved in a number of farm organizations, which turned out to be a training for politics on a grander scale. My first involvement was with the local co-op, the Harrow Farmers' Co-operative, and with the Ontario Wheat Producers' Marketing Board. Eventually I ran for a position as a director of the United Co-operatives of Ontario and of the Ontario Federation of Agriculture. It was through these organizations that I really got to know Ontario and Ontario farmers. As a result, by the time I got to Ottawa I probably knew Ontario agriculture as well or better than any politician there.

I got involved with the local co-op because I wanted to see a new grain elevator and an improved feed mill and I wanted better services for our local farmers – including gasoline and oil distribution. After I got involved we built the new elevator and a feed mill, as well as new elevators in McGregor and Harrow. Anyway, if you were a member of the local co-op you could run for the board of the United Co-operatives of Ontario. The federation of co-ops in those days was a wholesaling and buying giant. They bought in tremendous volume and sold to their member co-ops. Even today they do roughly 30 percent of all the grain business in Ontario. They buy from farmers and they sell to the trade both domestically and for export. But there's more competition now.

Almost from the beginning I fought to get the Co-op more involved in the total complex industry of agriculture. I wanted them to expand and diversify, to run supermarkets in big cities, as the Alberta Co-op now does in Calgary and Edmonton. I particularly remember one time when the board was contemplating buying a distillery, there were a couple of board members who were anti-alcohol. I got up at the meeting and said, "You don't have to drink it to sell it. It's better selling it than drinking it and the grain will only be sold to someone else who'll make the booze. Alcohol is made from the products of agriculture and there's no reason why we shouldn't be making money from agriculture." We lost by one vote.

But my ideas didn't stop at agricultural industries. I saw no reason why we shouldn't make a good acquisition if an opportunity came along – one time we almost bought a refinery in Port Credit, including some oil leases in Alberta. (We were already buying over 50 percent of the refinery's output.) We lost that by one vote as well (and the oil leases turned out to be worth a fortune). Maybe people thought I was too uppity in pushing for these kinds of things. But I've always wanted to go for the most and the best. And I've always been impatient with people who can't see past their noses.

I was also on the board of the Ontario Federation of Agriculture and its meetings (like the Co-op board's) were held in Toronto. We used to stay in the King Edward, which wasn't posh then, like it is now and Toronto wasn't such a lively place then, either. People in my area don't like Toronto any better than the people out West. We always called it Hogtown, too, not because it had so many pigs but because it hogged everything, all the financial world and so on. It still does.

One time when I was reeve I asked our township lawyer, Al Kennedy, what we'd have to do to create a separate province in southwestern Ontario. It's such a rich area and I knew it could be self-sufficient. Al gave me practically the same answer I got when I asked the same question of Bora Laskin many years later when he was still a professor at the University of Toronto and before he became head of the Supreme Court. (Laskin was then a well-known Liberal and we'd invited him to talk to our caucus committee on the constitution. I was the only non-lawyer on the committee. Coming from southwestern Ontario I'd always thought it was unfair how the provinces could withdraw from the federal system but that a region like mine couldn't. Even then, the provinces thought they had total authority over their citizens, whom they often referred to as their children.) Anyway, on this occasion I said to him, "Mr. Laskin, tell me how could I create a new province." And he said, "Gene, there is only one way you can do it – and don't forget I'm from northern Ontario and I don't like Toronto any better than you do – and that's by bloody revolution." Then he said, "But you look like the type that could lead a bloody revolution and if you're successful, I'll draw up the constitution for your new province."

If the provincial legislature was in session I'd often go down after a day of meetings to take in an evening sitting. I'd had no experience of parliamentary carrying-on and I remember I was quite shocked at the way the members behaved – they used to argue and yell and fight verbally with one another. A lot of those night sessions were very poorly attended and I used to think this was terrible – all those people shirking their responsibility. It wasn't until I became an MP myself that I realized that members usually had legitimate reasons for not being there – they were probably in their offices working.

If certain people were going to speak in the legislature I'd go to hear them – Premier Leslie Frost, the great white-haired father, or Farquhar Oliver, the Leader of the Opposition, or old Ross Whicher from up in Bruce County. These men were great orators. Leslie Frost was a big man and he could really hold the floor, but I liked Oliver the best (and remember, this was before I became a Liberal). He was an even bigger man than Frost and he really used his hands expressively when he spoke. To me he was one of the outstanding leaders Ontario has had.

My work with the United Co-operatives led to my involvement with the Co-operators Insurance Association, the CIA. Many years later, when as a Cabinet minister I met foreign leaders – ministers of agriculture and prime ministers, and so on – I used to love to tell them I'd once worked for the CIA. They'd all do a double-take – especially the Russians – and then I'd tell them, yes, I'd worked for the Co-operators Insurance Association of Canada. It always got a good laugh.

When it was founded in 1949 the CIA was 51 percent owned by the United Co-operatives of Ontario. It's now the second largest general insurance company in Canada, something most people don't know, and it sells all lines of insurance from car insurance on up. Before I became a director of the CIA, I was a part-time insurance agent in Anderdon Township. It was a way to make a little extra money while I was trying to farm – and trying to meet my bank payments. I had licences to sell both life and casualty, but the bulk of what I sold was auto insurance.

After a while it seemed a natural thing to see if I could get elected to the board of the CIA. And I did. I was getting good at winning elections. I was reeve of Anderdon Township and I was on several boards at the same time. That was how I got my broader training in agriculture and in politics. And that was why, when I surprised myself by getting elected to Parliament, I had such strong support from all regions of Ontario. I'd listened to the elders of the various organizations and I'd learned. And even though I'd raised a bit of hell, I'd gotten their respect. My former colleagues were always proud of the fact that they'd helped this young whippersnapper get elected to the position of Minister of Agriculture for the whole of Canada, and seen him eventually appointed President of the World Food Council.

As time went by, I wasn't satisfied with just being reeve. I was thinking about running for warden of the whole of Essex County – just as my father had done away back in 1918. The warden of the county isn't elected directly; he's elected from their own numbers by all those who sit on the county council, which includes all the township reeves and deputy reeves – thirty-seven in all. In 1962, when I announced that I was going for warden, a man named Ferguson decided to run for reeve of Anderdon in order to stop me. Ferguson was a Conservative and I think he suspected that if I became warden I might run federally as a Liberal. This wasn't the first time I'd had serious opposition, and I'd never won an election by acclamation. But this Ferguson fellow fought hard – and he resorted to some questionable tactics.

He used to buy beer for voters. He'd go into a tavern in

Amherstburg, or McGregor, or Rivière Canard, and he'd buy
beer for everyone in the room. Then he'd get up on the table
and make a speech. He bought a lot of beer but he didn't get
many votes. I whipped him easily – in fact that year I won the
election as reeve by my biggest majority ever.

One of the things I learned during my seven years as reeve of
Anderdon and my one year as warden of Essex was how to build
political roads. By this I don't just mean how to reach out to
every group, every race, and so on – although that was always
my style. I also mean real roads, the kind you cover with
asphalt. (During much of my tenure as reeve I was also the
chairman of the Essex County Road Committee.) And as much
as anything it was the roads I built during the year I was
warden that got me elected to Parliament.

I used to say to the voters, "If you want good roads, we'll
get you the best. We'll run the most honest and the most competitive tender system and we'll get you the best price. We'll
put in the sidewalks, the sewers, and the water mains – but we
all have to help pay for them." Just paving roads was a big
thing in those days. In summer the dirt roads got so dusty that
every house would be full of dirt. So everyone was in favour of
better roads – especially the housewives.

Each township financed the roads by issuing debentures and
it's a sign of how good an administration we ran that there was
always a waiting list for our Anderdon debentures. One of the
reasons was that we had a township clerk, Mr. L.J. Mailloux,
who kept his mouth shut. Some of his peers talked too much. If
you bought a debenture in Anderdon it wouldn't automatically
become gossip all over the township and the county, travelling
up and down every concession. Why we had people coming
from neighbouring townships to buy our debentures. I always
felt Mr. Mailloux was responsible for keeping me out of trouble
as reeve – he was well educated, bilingual and honest.

As chairman of the Essex County Road Committee in the
late 1950s, I went on a wild road-building program. We paved
roads and we built bridges and we improved drainage. It was
a time of very high unemployment in the area so it had quite
an impact. We widened every road and moved every municipal

drain and every country ditch off the road right-of-ways, and we replaced every rusty iron bridge with a new concrete one. We built more roads in five years in Essex County than the province had in thirty-five years. And we got the province to pay half the shot.

Jim Allan was then the provincial Minister of Highways. At an annual Ontario Road Convention he told us he'd match the counties and the townships dollar for dollar for every mile of permanent hardtop road they built. So I went home and sold my county council on the idea and we issued millions of dollars of debentures. Allan hadn't told us how to do it and he probably figured we wouldn't be able to raise much money. After I'd gotten the council's approval to issue the debentures we just went down to Toronto and told him how much money we'd raised to improve the roads, and he said okay. And when it came time for the province to pay up, he swallowed hard and forked over. I'll always remember Jim Allan for that. He may have been a Tory, but he was a fair person. And he kept his word.

Political roads are just as important as those hard-surfaced ones. It's how you build them that counts. When you widen roads you have to cut into someone's property. If you put a curve across the corner of a farm there's a way of constructing that curve so that the curve is smooth and so that the relationship between the road committee and the farmer is smooth, too. Then you don't get into a fight and you don't have to expropriate.

I learned this lesson very early, and when I built roads I always made sure the property owners got a good deal. We'd sit down with them and explain what we wanted to do and we'd offer them a fair price for the land we needed. And if any part of what we needed was useable after we'd finished, we'd sell it back to them for a dollar – so they'd actually come out ahead. Never once did we have to go to court; so we spent less money and less time than a lot of people and we didn't make any enemies – except maybe the lawyers, who didn't get much work.

Building all those roads was good for the county and it was good for me. On every road construction site I always made sure there was a nice big sign saying something like: "This is an Essex County Road Project," and then in big bold letters my name as chairman of the roads committee and the name of the warden and the county engineer, Roy E. Lee. When I ran for Parliament in 1962 my name was all over the county before I'd put up a single campaign sign – and this time the sign said, "E.F. Whelan, Warden," which didn't hurt one bit. That was another way in which those roads I built turned out to be political.

3

How I Scared My Little Self

In 1959 I became a Liberal and I met my future wife Liz. As it turned out, the one thing led to the other.

I was still reeve of Anderdon Township in that year and John Wintermeyer was running for the Liberals against Leslie Frost – Old Man Ontario, as he was called. Wintermeyer didn't stand much of a chance. The provincial Liberal Party in Ontario had fallen on hard times since the days of Mitch Hepburn and federally my riding (which had previously often voted Liberal) was pretty solidly Conservative: Dick Thrasher had won it by a hair in 1957 and by a big landslide in the Diefenbaker sweep of 1958. So in 1959, provincial Liberal candidates of any kind were pretty hard to come by.

Up until this time my only official association with the Liberal Party had been in 1957 when I'd canvassed in Anderdon Township for Bob Clark, the unsuccessful federal Liberal candidate in Essex South. I hadn't joined the party but I guess the word had gone out that Reeve Whelan, the road-building madman of Essex, was a Liberal supporter. And, since the provincial riding of Essex and the federal riding of Essex South had roughly the same boundaries in those days, anyone who was as politically active as I was had a good base to run on. I'm sure that's why the Liberals approached me. They must have figured that at worst I wouldn't embarrass them.

Sometime before the election was called, I got a letter from a man from Kingston named Bill Henderson who was a provincial organizer for the Liberals, asking me to run. (Bill later became a Supreme Court judge.) Then Mr. Henderson paid me a visit—I guess he wanted to check me out in person, see what kind of a candidate I'd make. Afterwards he wrote me a beautiful letter, which I still have, urging me to run and inviting me to come to Toronto to meet the leader. So a few weeks later I went and I met John Wintermeyer in his suite at the Royal York Hotel. He seemed a very serious, very conscientious man; I liked him and I agreed to run. Which meant I had to join the party. I remember how pleased my mother was when I told her. Most of the Kellys were Liberals and always had been.

I was sure I had a chance. As reeve and as chairman of the county road committee and with my activities in various farm organizations, I was well known. I also knew that before the 1957 election the federal seat had been held for the Liberals by Bob Clark's father, Murray, for twenty-two years. And Bob had only lost that one by 325 votes. Looking back, I think if we'd had a proper campaign organization we would have won the 1959 provincial election. As it was, we came damned close—and surprised just about everyone, including ourselves.

The nomination meeting was held in the auditorium of the Catholic school in Essex. There were three, maybe four, candidates for the nomination but my only serious competition was Eddie Watson, the reeve of Mersea Township and the former warden of the county. He and I were pretty close friends and the whole affair was pretty friendly. There were only two or three hundred people and I won the nomination, no trouble. No one thought we had chance, so there wasn't all that much at stake. But Eddie Watson didn't work for me during the campaign, so I guess he wasn't too thrilled. With his help in the eastern part of the riding we just might have won.

My campaign manager was a lawyer from Kingsville named Bill Clark. His brother Bob was the one who'd run in 1957. Bill was a handsome fellow and a strong Liberal who loved politics. After I was nominated, I spent some time at Bill's law office plotting strategy and planning the campaign. Since we didn't have any money, we did a lot of plotting and planning.

It was in Bill Clark's law office that I first met Elizabeth Pollinger, who was working there as a legal stenographer. I only knew her to say hello, until one time during the campaign when we were attending a meeting in Harrow – a political rally. My car was in Windsor being fixed and either Bill Clark or his wife Marion asked Liz to give me a ride after the meeting to pick up the car. On the way to Windsor, Liz and I stopped and had something to eat, and I mentioned casually that I'd like to take her out after the campaign was over. She didn't show much interest. It was definitely not love at first sight, but we did find out that we had a lot in common: we'd both grown up on farms and we'd both worked at many different sorts of jobs.

During the campaign, Liz typed all my speeches and she heard some of them, too, because I practised them in Bill's office. She must have been appalled at my grammar. Even though her first language was German, she never made mistakes in English as I did – in fact when she was in grade five, only a year after coming to Canada, she came in second in a spelling contest between the four schools on Pelee Island. Beyond that one car trip, though, Liz and I didn't get to know each other during the campaign. We were just eyeing each other at that point.

Our total budget for the 1959 campaign was $1,400. Bill wrote my speeches and gave me lots of encouragement. It's hard to believe, but in those days I was scared to get up on a platform – Bill would have to coax me to get me up there, in part because of my stammering. In fact, it wasn't until after I'd been elected to Parliament that I got enough confidence to begin to speak well in front of big audiences.

On election day, I knew we were doing better than anyone had expected when I ran into my Conservative opponent, Bill Murdoch, in a little village called Gesto in Colchester North.

And Bill said, "Gene, I know elections and I think you've got me beat." I just laughed because I never dreamed it was going to be even close.

As it was I lost the election by 1,001 votes but, considering the situation, it was almost like winning and we were jubilant. I remember we had a big party at my mother's farmhouse and a lot of the workers came. The place was jammed. That was the only beer I bought for anyone in the campaign, too. We had a slogan then and we still do: "Win or lose, we drink the booze — but not before." It was a wonderful feeling having all those people support me, people I'd known and people I'd met for the first time during the campaign. The same people became part of my campaign "machine" in 1962. And Bill Clark was the master mechanic. We'd done damn well and the whole campaign had only cost us a bit more than a thousand dollars.

The winner, Bill Murdoch, I'd known for the fifteen years he'd been the provincial member and we'd become friends after I got to be reeve. We certainly stayed friends after the election. In fact, the morning after, we happened to be in the same restaurant in Amherstburg — Vic Neddon's Coffee Shop — and were sitting on stools side by side at the counter having a cup of coffee. We were chatting happily away when somebody who knew both of us came in and said, "Well, you two sons of bitches." He thought we'd had some kind of pact, that we'd rigged the vote. If you really knew me or Bill, you'd know that was out of the question. But that's what it looked like to him. Bill and I had a good laugh about it. Bill was the MPP for Essex South for another four years and he was a good member, too, but the Toronto Tories never treated him fair. He got to be Speaker, but he should have been in the Cabinet.

The main thing I learned from the 1959 campaign was the importance of having a good organization. I also learned that people don't like it when you make certain sorts of statements during a campaign. For instance, in one of my speeches I'd criticized Bill Murdoch's wife for being an enumerator, which meant she got paid during the campaign. People didn't like that. So I learned never to criticize a candidate's wife. They will come to her rescue by voting against you. And it's okay to make fun of yourself, but be careful how you do it with the opposition. In that campaign we made some cartoons of Bill and made him look silly. People didn't like that much, either.

After the election, Liz Pollinger and I went on our first date. I'd gone out with women before but it was never anything serious. My mother thought I was going to stay a bachelor like my older brothers Tom and Martin. It's true I was thirty-four years old when I met Liz, but I didn't want to rush things. And for a while it seemed as though we weren't fated to get together.

The first time I asked her out was soon after the election. I asked her to go with me to hear Sammy Davis, Jr., at the Elmwood in Windsor – which was a very popular nightspot then. At that point she was more interested in Sammy Davis than she was in me. But the week before we were to go, I got a bad cold and Liz got appendicitis and had to go the hospital. Because of my cold I couldn't even go into the hospital to see her, so I sent her some flowers and on the card I wrote: "What some people won't do to stand someone up."

But there was more. The day Liz got back from the hospital I drove out to see her at the family farm outside of Kingsville. But by the time I got there, she'd left to take her nephew to the hospital. I thought, "That woman has a thing about hospitals." Her nephew had fallen in the barn and broken his arm. So I visited with Liz's parents and waited, and while I waited it started to look like rain. So I went out to shut my car windows. That's when the Pollinger dog bit me. Maybe I should have taken the hint and given up on the spot. But I'm a stubborn man.

Not long after, I took Liz to a dance at the Leamington Arena where Guy Lombardo and his Royal Canadians were playing. I've never been much of a dancer, but I like good music. It was supposed to be a quiet date but, between us, Liz and I knew most of the fifteen hundred people there – Liz knew one half and I knew the other half – and people kept coming up to us to talk. The next day everyone in Essex County must have known that Gene Whelan had been out on a date with Liz Pollinger. We might just as well have put it in the paper. At the dance we laughed a lot and talked a lot and had a fine old time. So we decided to keep seeing each other.

I used to visit Liz at her family's farm. I don't think her parents approved of me at first because I wasn't German – they were German from Yugoslavia. And at first they were concerned because they were told that I drank a lot. They had me confused with my younger brother, Henry, who was then working as a pipe fitter at the Ford plant in Windsor. Liz's Uncle Joe worked on the same gang and he knew that this Whelan loved his beer. But I drank very little in those days. (I still don't drink much – except the occasional glass of fine Canadian wine.)

Eventually Liz's parents came around. It helped that I was Catholic since they were strong Catholics, stronger than the Whelans, for that matter.

Both Liz's parents worked awfully hard. It hadn't been easy for either of them. Her father Frank had come to Canada in 1929, leaving his wife and two daughters behind in Filipovo, Yugoslavia, which is near the Hungarian border. Liz would have been about nine months old when her father left. She didn't see him again until she was nearly ten. So at their reunion in 1937 he was a stranger to her.

Like so many immigrants in those days Frank Pollinger expected to find work easily in the New World. He was a skilled bricklayer and plasterer but he hadn't banked on the Depression. He arrived in Canada just before it hit – and it hit him bad. The first place he went to was Saskatchewan and he got a job working for a farmer outside Regina. But the farmer couldn't pay him so he ended up on welfare in the city. If you were on welfare in those days you had to work and he spent his first winter in Canada digging a sewer on Quebec Street in Regina. He later told me it got so cold and the ground was frozen so hard that the pick axe couldn't move more dirt than a piece the size of your finger. He worked all day long in the bitter cold and all they paid him was a place to sleep and some food. Years afterward I could never go to Regina without thinking of my father-in-law and his terrible first winter in Canada.

After another terrible winter, this one on the souplines in Toronto, he eventually found a job working as a hired man for a farmer on Pelee Island, a German Mennonite named John Wiebe. Since Frank was a strong Catholic, this would never have happened back in Yugoslavia or in Germany at that time. The other hired man, Mike Krestle, was a German Lutheran from Romania. They were all living together and working together, a Catholic, a Lutheran and a Mennonite, whereas in Europe they wouldn't have spoken to each other. That's one of the great things about Canada.

In fact, John Wiebe helped both men start up on their own. In 1937 he helped them borrow the money they needed to buy two teams of horses, two sets of disc harrows, two walking ploughs, and a corn planter so they could plant corn on a government farm. Those were farms that people had lost during the Depression and anyone could rent them out and plant on them for a season. The farm they worked was on Pelee Island – the southernmost part of Canada, out in the middle of Lake Erie. By 1937 both men had managed to save up almost enough money to send for their families – about seven hundred dollars. But they needed a thousand, so they each borrowed three hundred dollars from the bank. So it took Liz's dad eight years of work to round up enough money to bring his family to Canada.

My wife remembers her trip from Yugoslavia to Canada vividly – the train ride from Filipovo to Cherbourg, the trip across the Atlantic on the *Duchess of Richmond*, and the train ride from Quebec City to Windsor. Like her father, she expected the Canadian streets to be paved with gold. So she was confused and disappointed when she got to Pelee Island where the roads were mostly paved with gravel and mud.

I think "Grandpa" Pollinger, as we always called him after our kids were born, partly blamed the Tories for separating him from his family for so many years – that is, for causing the Depression. Many people in our area could never forgive the Tories for the Dirty Thirties. The R.B. Bennett government came to power just after it hit, promising to do something, and when the government didn't, Bennett took the blame. Whatever his feelings about Bennett, Grandpa Pollinger certainly became a staunch Liberal; he was one of my strongest supporters.

When I met Frank and his wife Katharine they were running a prosperous dairy and vegetable farm. They were both very industrious people and during the growing season about Frank's only relaxation – if you can call it that – was going to market in Windsor every Wednesday and Saturday with his produce. That gave him a chance to visit with old friends and make new ones. When he started to help me campaign, all those people he knew turned out to be a great political asset.

I proposed to Liz that Christmas. I was supposed to go with her to midnight mass on Christmas Eve, but it was cold and wet and rainy and I was out with Walter Ranta delivering good-will baskets to the needy in the township and stopping off for the occasional tipple. By the time I'd finished my rounds, there was no way I was going to drive to Kingsville. So I phoned up Liz and told her I wouldn't be there until the next day. She went to midnight mass herself.

The next day I came for Christmas dinner. All of Liz's family was there: her older sister, who was also born in Yugoslavia, and her younger sister and brother, both born on Pelee Island after the family was reunited. After dinner I got Liz alone and I proposed. I offered her a great big diamond ring and she accepted. By this time, I guess she knew what to expect.

Liz and I got married in the spring – April 30, 1960. She was thirty-two and I was thirty-five. Liz didn't particularly want a big wedding but it had been a long time since my mother had a wedding close to home (Ed had got married out West and Helen in Arizona) and Liz's parents, being European, wanted a big affair. So Liz was overruled.

The church was just packed – St. Jean de Brébeuf in Kingsville. My old friend Father Mike Dalton married us but there were two extra priests at the ceremony – Father Tom Kelly, a cousin of mine from Amherstburg, and Father James Martin. When Liz saw these extra priests she didn't know what to think. It was too much for her and she cried all the way through the service. By the time we were ready to sign the register she'd stopped crying and Father Tom said to her, "I've never seen a bride cry so much." That was all it took, and she was off again.

The reception was at The Anderdon Tavern, Sam Travica's place. He had died by then and his widow Mary was running it. So the reception was right next door to where we would soon be living. The party went off without a hitch and we made it to Florida and back on our honeymoon without further incident. Liz must have been relieved.

After we were married we lived in a rented house not far away from The Anderdon. Everything in that house needed fixing and the floors slanted. After our first daughter, Theresa, was born in November 1961, I developed this very efficient technique for keeping her happy. Whenever she cried I'd just give the baby buggy a push and, because of the sloping floor, it just rolled back by itself. We were there for only a few months.

Early in 1962, as I've mentioned, we moved a house from Leamington onto my farm and fixed it up nice. So in the spring of 1962 I was playing with my daughter and planning my next crop. I was ready to settle down, raise a family, and grow old and rich. I'd just been elected warden of Essex County and I thought I'd had my fill of big-time politics. I'd promised Liz I wasn't going to again seek a higher office after my term as warden ended. I guess you could say that I've always been better at keeping my political promises to the voters than I have at keeping my political promises to her.

As a newborn Liberal, I was on a committee in 1961-62 to search for potential candidates for the federal constituency of Essex South. We knew Diefenbaker was in trouble nationally, what with the falling dollar and the big split in his Cabinet over allowing nuclear weapons in Canada. Farmers were having a hell of a time and unemployment in the riding was over 20 percent. The 1962 election was Keith Davey's first election as campaign director (Walter Gordon was campaign chairman) and one of his gimmicks was the Diefenbuck, a dollar bill with Dief's head instead of the queen. Dief no longer looked like the great saviour from Saskatchewan. But the sitting member in Essex South, Dick Thrasher, had lived up to his name and thrashed the Liberals in the 1958 election by 6,104 votes. So it still seemed like a pretty sure thing for the Tories.

The search committee interviewed eighteen people we thought would be suitable. We talked to leading farmers, lawyers, teachers, professional people. Not one of them was willing to seek the nomination. They all thought it was a lost cause. It looked like there'd only be one person running for the nomination, a

Mr. Moore who was an insurance agent from Leamington. He was a nice enough man, but in my opinion he would have been just a token candidate. After the last potential candidate turned us down, I got mad – at this point it was only about ten days to the nomination meeting. So in a fit of rashness I just called up the local radio station (CJSP in Windsor and Leamington) and told them, "I'm going to seek the nomination." My wife heard about it first on the radio, which she didn't think was very fair. But it wasn't the last time I made her mad.

The nomination meeting was to be held in Leamington at the other end of the riding. It was supposed to be Moore's territory. And to make matters worse it turned into a stormy night, thunder and lightning and the lights went out – but no one left. The good thing was it was also Liz Pollinger's home territory and her whole family and a lot of friends were at the meeting working the crowd. By the time it came time to vote, people who'd come to support Moore had changed their minds and they voted for me. As it turned out, I won the nomination by a big majority, but I might not have won at all without Liz and her family and friends.

Just like as in 1959, we started with no money in the bank – nothing except enthusiasm. When Senator Dan Lang – who was in charge of campaign finances for the federal Ontario Liberal Party – came to my name on the list he just put a big black line through it, whack. He said out loud to himself, "That guy can't possibly win" and he didn't give us a god damned penny. I got to know him later and whenever I saw him I'd always say, "Dan, you bastard, I'll never forgive you for what you did then." He'd just laugh.

The people who were at the hall when I was nominated became the core of my campaign organization. Bill Clark agreed to act again as my campaign co-ordinator. And his father, Murray, who'd been the member for so long in the thirties and forties, became a close adviser. And of course there were some experienced Whelan campaign workers from the last time. It was a beautiful time of year – the election was called for June 18 – which helped our spirit.

The women in the campaign were particularly active. Fern

Clark, Bob Clark's wife and the person who'd organized the Essex South Liberal Women's Association, played a big part, as she was also to do in 1963 and 1965. (When I became a minister she ran my constituency office for a while and she later became president of the Ontario Liberal Women's Association. We didn't always see eye to eye in those later days, but she was a wonderful worker and a wonderful Liberal.) The women made red-and-white hats with "Whelan" on them and decorated the six-quart produce baskets they used to carry our literature when they were out canvassing. They did a lot of the footwork –knocking on doors, contacting people. There were about sixty of them and they could canvas a whole town in one evening.

Unlike in 1959, we kept close track of what the voters were thinking. We may not have had much money but we had a very sophisticated polling system in that campaign–a grassroots Gallup poll, you might call it. This was before Goldfarb and Gregg and that crowd started to take over Canadian elections and run the candidates' lives by putting them in nice neat packages all tied up in a bow. We just told our campaign workers to go out and listen to what people were saying and to mark it down. And we did quite a thorough canvas, finding out who was for us, who was against us and who was sitting on the fence. We sent them to the barber shops, the beer parlours, the grain elevators, the feed stores, and the supermarkets. The barbers were the best. After polling the barbers and their customers we had a pretty good idea how close the election was going to be.

We got people involved in that 1962 election who'd never been mixed up in politics before, people whose families had been in Essex County for generations and new Canadians. We involved French and English and all aspects of the community.

All my experience in farm organizations, my profile as warden, all those roads we'd built and all those signs with my name on them–it all helped. The road-building program was at its peak and the signs were nice and big. The opposition tried to get us to take them down, but there was nothing they could do. Later the provincial Tories picked up my idea and now you see signs on every building project.

Liberal Party headquarters didn't think we had a chance of

winning but Prime Minister Pearson did make a swing through the riding. It was the first time I met him and I liked him right away – and I continued to like him even after he didn't make me agriculture minister when I thought I deserved it. He had that ability with people. The part of the visit I remember best was when he stopped in Kingsville, which was Bill Clark's home town and my wife's home town. The national campaign organizers wanted all the local Liberals out for the PM's visit, even the school kids. The local public school board was dominated by Tories, and they said no, but they didn't have control over the separate schools.

The Catholic grade school in Kingsville was run by Father Mike Dalton, the same priest who'd married me and Liz. Mike was a big, tall Irishman who'd been overseas in Europe during the Second World War. He was the only officer in the Essex Scottish Regiment that wasn't wounded at the battle for Dieppe, and he'd been in charge of part of the evacuation. He was a good friend and, just like me, he loved a good joke. Mike is retired now and lives in a Catholic home for senior citizens in Court-land, Ontario. The home is mainly for Hungarian Canadians and he likes to say he's the only Irishman in the world who has a Hungarian accent.

Anyway, when Mr. Pearson arrived in Kingsville we walked him down Main Street and when we got to St. Jean de Brébeuf church there was Father Dalton – but no kids in sight. I introduced Father Mike Dalton to Mr. Mike Pearson and they chatted away. I could see they were getting along fine, but I was starting to get worried. Then I saw Dalton give some kind of a signal and out of the church basement came about seventy-five boys from grade seven and eight. They were all about the same height and they just surrounded Mr. Pearson and Father Dalton. Pearson looked pleased and started to talk to each one, asking their names as he went around. One after the other each one of them said his name was Mike. Well, it wasn't long before Pearson realized that Father Mike Dalton had set him up; he'd told all the boys to tell the Prime Minister that their name was Mike. When Pearson figured this out, he just howled with laughter. He always loved a good joke. I remember one time in caucus when I had him laughing so hard I thought I'd killed him – but I'm getting ahead of my story.

During that 1962 campaign Liz and I were invited by the Mennonite community near Leamington to come to their strawberry festival. There weren't very many Liberals there at the time and we were surprised by the number of people in the hall – there must have been eight hundred – and the organizers insisted that we go up and down every table and meet every one of them. I found this difficult to do because I've never liked bothering people when they're having a good time. But I did what they asked and I met every single person in that hall.

They asked me to give a short speech, no more than five minutes, which was fine with me, since in those days my problem was getting speeches up to five minutes, not keeping them short. Then they announced that Mrs. Whelan would get up and say a few words in German – they knew she was German-born. They hadn't even warned her, but she did fine. She outdid me in the shortness department and spoke for only about thirty seconds, saying something like, "I think my man is a good man. If you think so too, then vote for him." When she finished, the crowd just applauded like mad. On the night of the election we carried the Leamington-Mersea district, which is heavily Mennonite. It had never been won by a Liberal before.

As I said earlier, Liz's father also proved a big help in this first federal campaign. He was a real enthusiastic campaigner. It wasn't just that I was his son-in-law. Like many new Canadians, he felt very strongly about democracy, about having the right to vote. He prized the fact that he could participate in politics – in the political process. He'd fought against the Germans in the First World War and he'd lived through Yugoslavia's brief constitutional monarchy that was soon replaced by dictators. But in those days in Essex South everyone took their politics more seriously than they do now. It used to be nothing if we had a 90 percent turnout at the polls in township elections – in my final election as reeve of Anderdon we had a 92 percent turnout. And in federal elections we had turnouts as high as 80 percent or more. I recently read about a school board election in British Columbia where they had a 20 percent turnout – and the most recent Alberta election had barely 50 percent – which shows how times have changed. Grandpa Pollinger could never have understood people not exercising their democratic right.

Frank Pollinger was my right hand man when I was campaigning through some of the rural parts of the riding, particularly in the townships around Leamington and on Pelee Island where he'd lived. He spoke about four different languages as well as English: German, Serbian, Croatian, and Hungarian. If you speak one Slavic language, you can generally make yourself understood in the others. And there were lots of Slavic people in the riding – Poles, Serbs, Croatians, Ukrainians, Czechs, Slovaks, and so on. He'd speak to someone in their own language and he always got right to the point. He'd say something like, "Are you with us or against us?" If they were against us, he'd say right away, "Let's not waste any time here." We'd cover a lot of people in that way. We covered pretty near the whole of Essex South every election.

I remember the first all-candidates debate. As well as Dick Thrasher for the Tories, there was a guy named Cervin for the New Democratic Party (which had just got its new name) and Jack Backer for the Social Credit. It made it a little easier that the debate was in my own area, at the Verdi Club on Texas Road. When it came time for the questions from the floor someone asked me about turkey imports. That was an issue at the time because cheap imported American turkeys were undercutting Canadian birds and the Ontario turkey growers were going broke left and right. The import issue has always concerned farmers – with good reason. Anyhow, I'd been on the phone to Ottawa that morning asking questions on the same subject, so I had my facts and figures fresh in my mind. When someone asked the turkey question, I just spouted them off like a computer. And those farmers (and everyone else there) thought, "God, he's great." Thrasher, on the other hand, paid no attention to this sort of thing and he'd been a member for five years. So I guess I made him look pretty bad.

We knew the vote was going to be close and it was. We knew from our grassroots Gallup, our barbershop polls, that we'd peaked too early. About a week before the election we figured we were ahead by about fifteen hundred votes, but by election day we figured it was more like a thousand. In the end we won by 988 votes which meant our poll was pretty accurate for a bunch of volunteers without a computer in sight – or a Goldfarb.

I don't think Dick Thrasher could quite believe he'd lost at first. He never came over and congratulated me on the night, or afterwards, although we actually were pretty good friends – fighting friends – and remained so. He would run against me in 1963 and in '65. At least he didn't seem to be bitter, which often happens.

Of course, it's impossible to give everyone their proper credit in an election, but some of my workers in 1962 really stand out in my memory. Fern Clark, Jack and Don Paterson (who was elected MPP in 1963) were really a big help in Leamington. Willis MacIntosh and Ewald Wiebe from Mersea, Tony di Menna from Gosfield South, Ed Fox from Ruthven, Starr Hamel and Paul Rieger from Pelee Island, Jerry Pouget from Harrow, Bill Naylor from Essex, Pat Beneteau and E.T. "Red" La Framboise from Amherstburg, and Frank and Doris Smith, to name a few. Then there was the whole Kelly clan and my brother Tom. All of these people, and many I haven't mentioned, really did a lot and made a difference. Maybe it was just the overall spirit that we had. We took it seriously, but we had fun. People could sense that.

We had no idea then that we'd be fighting another election in ten months. That second one wasn't so much fun because Liz was laid up in the hospital. She'd fallen off a chair in the kitchen and hurt her back. She was pregnant with Sue at the time and we were all worried that she'd lose the baby. Everything turned out fine – although Sue was a month late in coming – but Liz spent seven weeks in traction in the hospital.

Just to show you how desperate people sometimes get in politics, some people in the opposition tried to use this to their advantage. They spread the rumour that Liz was laying low in hospital because she didn't approve of my running. They said that was the real reason why she wasn't with me on the campaign trail. We turned that around, though. We had a radio broadcast from her hospital bed and later we had a victory photo of me and Liz taken in the hospital room. We needed every vote we got in 1963 because we only won by 769 votes. In that election the Tories threw everything they had at Essex South, figuring I was the weak link in Liberal Windsor – they left Herb Gray and Paul Martin alone and swore they would get me.

But in my first election, in 1962, everyone had written us off. Even my friend Paul Martin, who'd been the Liberal member for Essex East since 1935 and had survived the Diefenbaker sweep in 1958, told the party I didn't have a chance. And even though I knew I had a chance, I was still pretty surprised that I'd won. And then I got scared. First surprised – and elated – and then frightened, afraid I wouldn't be able to do the job. I felt like that character Red Skelton used to play, the one who would often say, "I scared my little self." Well that's what I did on election night, I scared my little self.

Anyway, a lot of others must have been surprised I'd won, too. Over two thousand people came to our victory party, which was unheard of. I guess they wanted to see for themselves.

There was a terrible storm the evening of the election just around the time the polls closed – an early summer storm with hail and wind. It did a lot of damage in the riding, especially in the Leamington area to the tomato fields and the young corn. It was a very bad time because it was too late to plant again. So I got up early next day, after staying up until four in the morning to celebrate, and went out to inspect the damage. You might say it was a very early lesson in the life of a member of parliament. The farmers wanted some relief aid and so one of the first things I did when I got to Ottawa was go into Mr. Pearson's office and demand some money. I think we got them some, too.

Unlike 1959, in the 1962 campaign we spent a good deal more money than we'd raised and there were bills to pay, about nine thousand dollars worth. We were in debt. It doesn't sound like much with people spending hundreds of thousands as they do today, but it was a lot to me at that time. So I went to see my friend Walter Grondin, the bank manager whom I'd known since I was kid. His father even used to cut my hair after I decided my mother wasn't good enough at it – and when I could afford to pay someone else. Whenever I'd borrowed money I'd always paid it back. And I'd done all my banking with his branch of the Canadian Imperial Bank. Of course, he was a Conservative, which may have had something to do with what happened.

It was the day after the election when I walked into his office to negotiate a loan. Walter said, "Ah, Good morning, Gene. How are you today? And what can I do for you?" and I told him I needed to borrow some money and how much. I'll never forget what he said next: "Sorry, Gene, I can't let you have it. Your credit is no longer any good. You're in politics now." I'd just been elected to one of the most responsible positions in the land and this pipsqueak banker was telling me I couldn't borrow nine thousand. I said, "Are you serious Walter?" He was.

I was really stunned. As a result of winning the election I no longer qualifed for a Farm Credit mortgage on our house, and this seemed like the last straw. When I came out of the bank I didn't know what to do. I knew that one of the worst things that could happen was to carry debts in public life. If you were in debt then certain people could try to exert influence on you by offering to donate a little money to help you out. I was determined to stay honest, but I had this big debt. Finally I decided to go to Senator John Connolly who was the chief fundraiser for the Liberal Party. I told him my problem and he said, "Well, we haven't got any money either." Everybody thinks that political parties have bundles of money, but it isn't true.

So Senator Connolly and Senator Dan Lang made arrangements for me to see C.N. Phipps, who was a vice-president of the Canadian Imperial Bank in Toronto. In his office in the old Imperial Bank building he had on his desk every transaction I had ever done with the bank from my first loan for my first new tractor – which showed I was a good credit risk – and his first question to me was, "What's your problem?". When I'd told him, right there on the spot he offered to call Walter, but I said, "No, don't call Walter, call George Cuthbert at the Sandwich branch in Windsor. I'm not doing any more business with Walter's branch." So Phipps did and I transferred my account to the Sandwich branch and got my loan. George Cuthbert later told me that was the first time he'd ever got a call from head office in Toronto ordering him to loan someone money.

But I never did forget what my old friend Walter had said: "Your credit is no good. You're in politics now."

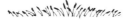

4

Raising Hell

I'd scared my little self and gotten elected to the House of Commons, the highest government in the land, and when I arrived in Ottawa, I was still worried about whether I'd be able to do the job. I was impressed by all those bureaucrats with their horn-rimmed glasses and their college degrees. And practically all my fellow members had gone further in school than I had – I hadn't got past grade eleven, and I didn't talk too good. In those days I was embarrassed about my bad grammar and my lack of education, but it didn't take me long to discover that, except for the letters after their names and their smooth way of talking, these people were just the same as me. And when I saw some of the messes they got themselves into for lack of good plain common sense I began to believe that this young farmer might just have a thing or two to teach them.

There were a lot of new boys like me that year because, although Pearson hadn't kicked Dief out, he had him on the run. The Conservatives were returned with a minority government while the Liberals had gone from forty-eight to ninety-nine

seats. Two of the new boys were John Turner and Donald Macdonald. Those two later became famous but at that time they
were nobodies, just a couple of young lawyers who'd run away
from St. James Street and from Bay Street. The most famous
new Liberal by far in 1962 was a fellow named Red Kelly. At that
time he was a star player with the Toronto Maple Leafs – and
those were the days when the Leafs were good enough to win four
Stanley Cups. I got to know Red pretty well because right after
the 1963 election we shared an apartment with another new M P,
Larry Pennell from Brantford.

Larry and Red and I roomed together for about a year and our
apartment was luxurious compared to my earlier living quarters in Ottawa. In the fall of 1962 I had lived in a rooming house
over near St. Patrick's Cathedral called the Presbytère. It cost
seven dollars for four nights and was run by two old ladies who
locked the door at eleven o'clock and put the chain on. And they
weren't too pleased if they had to let you in after hours. The
place was clean enough all right, but five of us shared one bathroom. Then I stayed for a bit at the Lord Elgin Hotel where I
had a room so small it was like a jail cell. At night I often dreamt
that the mattress was going to curl up and smother me.

Red Kelly was one of the nicest guys I've ever met and one
of the cleanest living, too. He almost never smoked or drank –
except on his birthday. Then he'd have a drink of Irish whiskey
and smoke a cigar. He was like a saint compared to me, but we
got along well. It may have helped that he was also an Irish
Catholic and that he'd been raised on a farm – a tobacco farm
near Simcoe, Ontario. We had things in common. I remember
him describing working with his father, walking behind a horse
and a cultivator in his bare feet, shorts, straw hat, and no shirt,
cultivating tobacco.

Larry and I had twin beds in the single bedroom and Red
slept on the studio couch – it was a fold-down thing that didn't
even have a mattress and with just a sheet for a cover. It had
those hard cushions with the buttons on them. In the morning
when he was doing his exercises – push-ups and chin-ups and so
on – I'd often see the line of circles down his bare back where the

buttons had left their mark. He was a member of parliament and he was still playing hockey, so he had to keep in shape.

He told me just how hard it was being a hockey player, the training they put you through and all the attention from the media. He talked about the youngsters, the hell they went through trying to make the team – some of them threw up on the ice, they were so nervous. You may wonder why he'd want to make it even more difficult for himself by being a member of parliament, commuting between Ottawa and the various places he played. One time he arrived back in the middle of the night from a game in Montreal because the FLQ had threatened to bomb a train trestle and his train had been delayed. But he'd seen becoming an MP as a great chance, just as I had. He had a strong sense of public service. He was a very human, very concerned person who always played fair – in sports and in politics. If there'd been a Lady Byng Trophy for members of parliament, he'd have won that one, too.

I don't think anything in hockey had prepared him for the rough way he was treated as a member of parliament. A lot of members were jealous of him and resented him for being a hockey player – a jock. And at first they didn't take him seriously. But he worked hard and he had a way of rolling with the punches. If he got mad he almost never showed it; he stood his ground. If you read the speeches he made in the House you'll find that they were as good as anybody's and expressed a lot of feeling and intelligence.

I remember just before the 1965 election he was trying to decide whether or not to run again and he asked me what I would do and I told him I'd go to Mr. Pearson and ask him, "What is there in the future in politics for me?" And then I'd go to Conn Smythe, the owner of the Leafs, and ask him, "Mr. Smythe, what is there for me in hockey?" And whichever of the two promised me the better future, that's where I'd go. I guess he followed my advice, because Pearson wouldn't promise him anything and he gave up politics soon after to concentrate on hockey.

A lot of people criticized Keith Davey for recruiting Red Kelly in the first place; they said he wasn't qualified. But I took just the opposite view. He was a fine man and a fine member and I think he set a wonderful example, especially for kids. Here was a real superstar of the sports world, someone whom young boys and girls idolized, who wanted to be member of parliament. He gave politics a better image just by being Red and being there. Red and I are still friends and he made a special trip to Ottawa in 1982 for a surprise party to commemorate my twenty years as an MP.

I wasn't such a gentleman as Red was in my early days on the Hill. Once I got over my fears and my feeling of being inferior, I began to raise a little hell. In this I'd had as good schooling as anybody. They told me, "Backbenchers don't have any power," but it was more a case of lots of backbenchers not knowing how to use their power. Or being too timid. Backbenchers have a lot of power if they're brave enough to pound on doors and make some noise. If you do, you can get the ministers and the bureaucrats to pay attention. Many backbenchers, the longer they sit there the more polite they become, hoping that eventually they may become Cabinet ministers. They're afraid of offending somebody and not getting promoted. That's the paradox. I wasn't that polite, and for a long time it didn't look like I'd ever make parliamentary secretary, let alone Cabinet. But I pounded on some desks and on some tables too, and I got things done. Once I got to be a minister, I often wished the backbenchers would make more noise. There were so many issues over which they could have pounded the hell out of us. I wouldn't always have liked it, but I would have listened.

I guess I used to be considered one of the most active backbenchers on the Hill. My experience in local politics helped. So many smart young people get elected to Parliament who've had almost no practical experience of politics. They think they know poor people, but they've never been poor themselves. They think they understand the workers but they've never loaded hay or worked on an assembly line. That's one of the few things I had against Trudeau. He'd had experiences all right, and he'd travelled a lot more than I had when he first came to Ottawa. But he'd never dug an outhouse hole or forked manure or worked in a factory. It's a subject that concerns me today – and not just about MPs. We give our kids all this education – they go to school for years and years – but we don't give them much experience of life. That's the way I felt when I met many of the smart new boys on Parliament Hill in 1962. I thought, "These fellows don't know sheep shit from putty. They don't know what's going on."

One of the first bits of hell I had to raise was in order to get a better seat in the House. The man I'd defeated, Dick Thrasher, had been parliamentary secretary to Mike Starr, Diefenbaker's Minister of Labour. And that had had a great impact in our area, which was a very working-class one. When I thrashed Thrasher, he immediately got a job in Mr. Diefenbaker's office as a special assistant. So he was still in Ottawa quite openly keeping an eye on me and just waiting for the next election, which we all knew wouldn't be long in coming. At his nomination in 1963, he made a point of saying of me, "I watched him – that was my job." When I made my 1963 campaign speeches I'd say, "You, my friends, are the most fortunate citizens in Canada. For the last ten months you've had two members of parliament for Essex South. One working and one watching." It used to get a good laugh.

Anyway, because Thrasher had had a fairly high profile and was still "watching," I knew it would be no good at all to be sitting way back in the corner with the Ws. (The House seating was assigned alphabetically.) So I went to Mr. Pearson and I said, "You know, Mr. Prime Minister, you can't put me where W says I should be. If I'm going to have any chance of holding the riding in the next election I'm going to have to have a better seat in the House." And I explained why. So he moved me down into the third row with the Cs and Ds. Since he didn't want it to look like favouritism he moved another W with me, a lawyer from Toronto named Ian Wahn. It caused quite a rustle in the backbenches. No one could figure out how Wahn and Whelan got to be way up there in the front rows. And it drove the clerk of the House crazy because when he called the vote he called it by the seating plan. We kind of ruined his rhythm.

In those early years, when I was still a new boy on Parliament Hill, I used to have breakfast regularly with a group of other first-time MPs. There were usually five of us. Joe Greene was a lawyer from Renfrew South who was elected in 1963 (he ran for the leadership in 1968 and made far and away the best speech at the convention). Larry Pennell, with whom I shared the apartment, was also a lawyer – from Brantford, Ontario. He was made Solicitor General after the 1965 election. Sherwood Rideout was a train engineer and the former mayor of Moncton, New Brunswick (his son George is actually the mayor of Moncton now). Finally there was Dr. Jack Davis from Vancouver, British Columbia, with a string of fancy degrees after his name. He'd been a Rhodes Scholar and had a Ph.D. in chemical engineering and a master's degree in business administration. I was most impressed and intimidated, at first. (Jack became Minister of Fisheries in 1968.) Then there was me, the only farmer. We did have a sixth member for a while, Harold Stafford from Elgin, a friend of Larry and another lawyer.

We made something of an odd group, but we got along well and helped each other out. Larry was the leader: we all liked and admired him. He didn't smoke and he didn't drink but he had a great sense of humour. He was one of the ones who helped me get over my initial awe of Ottawa. He used to say, "You've got an inferiority complex and you've no reason. You're just as good as the rest of us." After a while I got so I believed him. Also, I probably wouldn't have been made parliamentary secretary to Jack Davis in 1968 if I hadn't gotten to know him through our breakfast club. And much later than that, when I was running for the leadership, Larry Pennell's son wrote me a wonderful letter offering to help in any way he could. So those morning meetings and our horsing around not only had a lasting effect on me, but brought a lasting benefit.

We'd meet almost every morning in the parliamentary restaurant. We liked it because it's much quieter than the cafeteria and we could sit in a nice alcove all by ourselves. Mornings it was especially sedate with just a few old senators reading their newspapers and the crazy five of us off in a corner having a grand old time. We'd discuss what had happened in the House the day before or what had gone on that week in caucus, and we'd joke about the people who had the power, and we'd dream out loud about what we were going to do when we took over the government. I guess sometimes we made a fair bit of noise, because at one point the senators complained to the Speaker; we just made twice as much noise after that. I believe Al MacNaughton was the Speaker then and he came and asked us what we were up to. We told him we were just having fun, so he laughed and didn't do anything. I suppose we were a bit like schoolboys.

Some mornings Paul Martin used to join us for a cup of coffee. As well as being a renowned parliamentarian he was quite famous as a cheapskate and by sitting with us he could always get away without paying for his coffee. When the waitress came by to take his order he'd always say, "Oh, just a cup of coffee, please." They all knew him and they wouldn't bother making out a new bill; they'd just laugh and let old Paul have a free cup. If he'd sat by himself he would have had to pay. Some of them told us afterwards that when Paul had first been elected in 1935 he used to leave a ten-cent tip and he was still leaving the same tip thirty years later.

I didn't much like making speeches in the House of Commons when I was first elected; I was still learning the ropes and in those days the House of Commons used to scare me. So I watched the old pros like Paul Martin, and Jack Pickersgill (then House Leader), and Tommy Douglas, the leader of the NDP, and of course old Dief – they were the masters of Parliament. In 1962 the Liberals like Paul and Jack who'd survived the Diefenbaker sweep were just itching to get back in power. They hated being in the Opposition. Pickersgill had it drilled into us that it was practially sacrilegious to miss a single day in the House and the key Liberals made us backbenchers believe that the government and the country was going right to hell under the Tories. They were just waiting for their opportunity to bring Diefenbaker down, and if someone had given the order to charge across the aisle and attack the Tories, I think we would have done it and tried to physically destroy them – the feelings were that high.

Even my friend the gentle, docile Paul Martin became a raging tiger. I remember as clear as if it was today a speech I saw him give – not just what he said, but how he said it. The Tory Government benches across the way were yelling wildly at him and the Opposition was cheering him on and by the time he was finished he was standing nearly halfway across the aisle screaming: "This government must go. This government must be destroyed before it destroys this country." His mouth was about six inches wide. He was totally unlike the gentle Paul I thought I knew.

I loved to watch Jack Pickersgill in the House. Sometimes he got Pearson into trouble because he could be devilish as hell. Pickersgill's way of dressing added to his reputation as a crafty figure. He wore a sort of a coat that hung loose – it looked something like a cape – and this wide-brimmed black hat. He reminded me of Black Bart, a bandit in the silent movies I saw as a kid. In the House they used to say he only wore one blue serge suit that got shiny with use. He probably had three or four the same, but it seemed like he had only one.

He always wore suspenders and he'd hook his thumbs under them and stretch them out so far we were sure they'd break. In the House, when he made a real good hit against Mr. Diefenbaker, or when he asked a zinger question, he'd snap his braces and slide down under his desk until he'd pretty near disappear under the table he'd get laughing so much – all you could see was his head. You'd wonder if he was going to disappear completely. He was laughing at the Tories and laughing at himself, too. I liked him very much. I also thought he was a hell of a good minister.

The House of Commons could be entertaining, but the real power of a backbencher is in the caucus. And Pearson's caucus was really rowdy. There were some wild free-for-alls and we definitely spoke our minds. I'm sure Erik Nielsen and the other Tories had a wonderful time eavesdropping. I'm not surprised old Erik couldn't bring himself to stop listening in – it must have been the best show in town. I thought the fuss the Turner Liberals made recently when Nielsen admitted he'd listened in was a bit ridiculous. Some of the people making the fuss would have been the first to listen in on the Tory caucus if they'd had the chance.

We could speak our minds but you've got to understand that a party caucus is not a democratic institution. I found that out at my very first caucus meeting in late June 1962, the first occasion on which the newly elected Liberal MPs met to plan strategy for the coming session that would be Diefenbaker's last as Prime Minister. I thought I was going to have a chance to cast my vote on what the caucus would do, but I had the wrong expectation entirely.

All ninety-nine Liberal members were there and most of the Liberal senators, and I'll never forget what the caucus chairman, Lionel Chevrier, said when it came time to decide the issue. He said, "This is a democratic institution. We don't vote here, we take a consensus of those who've spoken." I'd never heard of such a thing. Consensus – what a load of putty. I should have stood up and yelled at him right then that he was a hypocrite, that you couldn't have democracy without a vote. That was an important lesson for me. I realized then and there that the only way I was going to make a difference was to express my opinion at each and every caucus. I saw that if you were quiet and polite the Prime Minister was never going to hear you and the Cabinet ministers weren't going to pay attention. So I resolved that they were going to hear a lot of expressed opinion from me on what the Opposition should be doing. And I didn't stop making representations when we became the Government. I spoke at almost every caucus – some of the old boys must have thought I was a real pain in the ass.

Pearson used to let the caucus be so free that sometimes they'd pretty near come to fisticuffs. There was the time when Judy LaMarsh had done something or other – she was Minister of National Health and Welfare – and the caucus was fighting mad. They wanted Pearson to fire her and they really made a hell of a fuss that day. Even the senators were aroused. I'll never forget Senator David Croll, with his great shock of grey hair, holding up his hand with his thumb sticking out and his two fingers bent back and lecturing Pearson. He said, "Mike, you're not enough of a son of a bitch to be Prime Minister." He meant that Pearson didn't have the toughness to fire someone when he or she needed to be fired. I admired David Croll, even if he was a senator – he'd been a hard-working elected M P, he was a hard-working senator, and he's still working hard for the party. Croll was right about Pearson, too.

I didn't really tangle with Judy LaMarsh until after the 1965 election, when she'd become Secretary of State. In her new job she was in charge of culture, so she was the one I went to for funds to start a museum of black history in Amherstburg. The museum was the idea of a local black man, Max Simpson, whose ancestors had come to the area on the Underground Railroad during the Civil War. Max was well respected locally and I supported his idea. My file must be about two inches thick with the letters I wrote to Judy, but I could never convince her. It wouldn't have cost her much then and it didn't cost me much later when I finally got the money after I was a minister. But as far as Judy was concerned, Amherstburg was just the end of the line. She didn't realize it is one of the most historic towns in Canada. Actually, I liked Judy well enough, but she could be mean. She held a grudge and let that interfere with the way she worked with you afterwards.

Pearson may not have listened to the caucus when we wanted him to fire LaMarsh, but one of his great strengths was that generally he did listen to his backbenchers. One time I even got him to change the way he was giving his speeches. I'd been in Kitchener, at a wedding that was attended by mostly new Canadians. Some of them were relatives of my wife and they knew I was a member of parliament – this would have been about 1963 – and a few of them came up to me at the reception and asked me what kind of man Pearson was and I said to them, "What do you think he's like?" They said, "By the way he talks on television and the radio we think he's a snob." And I said, "What do you mean?" And they said, "He uses words we don't understand. He talks over our head." So I said, "I'll tell him next Wednesday in caucus." They just laughed because they didn't think I would and they assumed that even if I did, it wouldn't make any difference.

The next Wednesday I went to the caucus meeting and I waited for the part when it's open to general discussion – when anyone can raise anything that's on their mind, generally on political matters. And I got up and said, "Mr. Pearson, I spent last weekend in Kitchener, Ontario. That's a very ethnic community – one-third of the people there are something like me: though they may have education they don't understand the English language that well. And they told me that they think you're a snob because you speak with words they don't understand. So I would suggest, Mr. Pearson, that when you're making speeches in future, use plain language." I'll never forget what he said in reply. He said, "I can't get away with using s-of-a-b like you can, Gene – but I'll do my very best."

So he went back to his speechwriters and he said, "Maybe Whelan has something," and they did change his speeches, so much so that about six months later I got up in caucus and said, "Remember that representation I made about your speeches? Well, my friends in Kitchener say you're coming across fine now. They're understanding you better all the time." Pearson just laughed. But he did have a tendency – like a lot of politicians who are fairly well educated – to forget that in Canada the great majority of the population never went to university and have no understanding of those big university words. Trudeau had the same problem to some extent – but not as much. We used to lecture him about it, too.

One of the worst fights we had in caucus was in 1963 or 1964 over the issue of a proposed pay raise for members of parliament. By then we were the government, but we were in a minority position, so it was a touchy question. I remember that the Ottawa members were all against the raise. That made me mad. George McIlraith was one of these (at different times he was Minister of Transport, House Leader, and Minister of Public Works). He had a law practice in Ottawa and he kept it up while he was a minister. When there was a vote on the Hill they'd give old George time to walk from his office so he could vote. And of course he didn't have to rent an apartment or buy a house – and he had a minister's salary. It was a lot different from trying to cultivate corn and tomatoes five hundred miles away, which I was trying to do, yet at the time Ottawa members got the same living expenses as the out-of-town members.

A backbencher's salary was only $8,000 then, and we got a small annual expense allowance of only $2,000. My first year in Parliament had cost me $6,000 more than I took in – on top of the $9,000 campaign debt I had to carry – and I was very strong in favour of raising our pay. So I got up in that caucus meeting and told a story about the time back home when they were debating whether to raise the pay of the township council – this was at a nomination meeting in Malden Township, the township next to Anderdon. Robert Atkin was reeve and my uncle William Whelan was the chairman of the meeting. He ran those meetings with an iron hand. Anyway, I told caucus about this particular occasion when my uncle Will got up and asked Bob Atkin, "Is it true that you have raised your own wages 25 percent in these tough economic times?" (This was during the Depression.) The reeve was a tall man, probably six-foot-four when he stood up to his full height, but as my uncle spoke Bob sat hunched in his seat. Then he stood up and he turned to Uncle Will, and he looked down at him and at the audience and he said, "Yes, Will, that's right." (The raise was from $100 to $125.) And he sat down again. Then my uncle shot back, "Is that all you've got to say in these hard economic times when you raise your salary by 25 percent.?" So Bob Atkin stood up a second time and he looked around at the audience and he said, "Will, a man would be a damn poor shitass couldn't raise his own salary."

As I hit that punch line, Mr. Pearson was sitting resting his head on his hand with one elbow on the table and when he heard the joke he went to slap his forehead and his elbow fell off the table and he nearly fell off the chair laughing. The whole caucus went into bedlam. The Railroad Committee Room where we used to meet went crazy and that afternoon the Cabinet met and we got our raise in pay. Afterward George McIlraith was heard to say, "These guys are the richest they've ever been and this is no time to be raising their pay." That really made me mad. (George was one of the cleverest political ministers I observed as a backbencher; he either ate his notes or burnt them and he never kept a letter – and he wrote very few.)

I spoke my mind in caucus and I guess some people were afraid of me. I used to blow my stack when the wind-baggery of puffed-up people got too much to take. Some press and others even said that Pearson was scared of my thunder – maybe he was. It's true that if I didn't think the Prime Minister knew what he was talking about, I'd say so. I'd say "Mike, you don't know what in the hell you're talking about." Or "Mr. Prime Minister, that's a pile of that stuff we spread on the fields in Essex South to make the crops grow." I remember what I said in caucus when Pearson introduced his Royal Commission on Bilingualism and Biculturalism after the 1965 election. I said, "Biculture? What breed of bull is that? I've heard of agriculture and horticulture, even floriculture and aviculture. But biculture?" (When I was first elected to Parliament no one had told me I'd be expected to become bilingual. Later, when I understood the reasons behind the policy that resulted, I supported it wholeheartedly.)

Smart politicians listen to what goes on in caucus. Paul Martin was one of those. When he'd been away from the Hill he'd always call me up to get my reading of what had been going on. I said to him one day, "Paul, why do you call me?" And he said, "Because you're the wisest politician in the caucus." He'd watched me, and he was aware I was on five committees and that I knew pretty near every member of the House of Commons by name even though I hadn't been there that long.

When I was first elected, Paul Martin had been pretty good to me – although once he became a minister again I often wanted him to do more for me and my riding than he did. He'd helped me learn the ways of the House and the ways of the Hill, and he often asked my advice on political matters because, even though I was a new boy, he knew I listened to what the people were saying. He was very considerate, too. Once we were on the Government side he didn't put on airs as did some of the other ministers. For instance, he would share his private train car with you. He'd load it up with people from Windsor, students at Carleton and Ottawa, and so on. And later, when he and I travelled home regularly by airplane, he'd make sure to give me a ride to the airport with him. We've had our differences over the years but we've remained good friends to this day.

Of course Paul was a great politician and a fine constituency man, so I used to have great fun teasing him. One time he couldn't be home on the weekend and a priest in his riding was celebrating an anniversary – forty years as a priest in that parish – so he asked me to go and stand in for him, to bring Paul's best wishes and greetings. He told me that he would be in New York at the UN but that he and his wife Nell, who loved baseball, were going there early so they could take in a game. I told him, no problem, and I went to the dinner and I did my thing.

When he got back, he asked me, "How did things go?" And I said, "Well, I don't think you're going to be very happy with what I did." And he said, "What did you do?" And I said, "It was partly because of what you did." And he said, "What do you mean?" And I said, "I didn't know you were sending that telegram so I got up and spoke before they read it out. I said, 'Paul and Nell are sorry they couldn't be here but they're going to a ballgame in New York,' and then the master of ceremonies got up and read out that stupid telegram you sent which said you deeply regretted you couldn't be there because you were on 'government business.' It sure made me look stupid. I guess I sort of messed things up for you."

Paul knew me pretty well, and he didn't know whether to take me seriously or not, but I didn't give anything away. So he called all sorts of people who'd been at the banquet and with each of them somewhere he'd work into the conversation, "And how was Gene's speech, by the way?" Everyone he talked to would say something like, "Oh, he made a short speech, nothing special." Finally Paul called Bernie Newman, the provincial member in Paul's riding and a good friend of mine. And Paul went through the same rigamarole and Bernie told him I'd made a nice little speech. Paul just wouldn't come out and ask. Then he called Bernie a second time and he kept beating around the bush until finally Bernie asked him, "Paul, what's the matter with you? This is the second time you've asked me what did Gene say. What did Gene tell you he said?" So Paul came out with it; Bernie told me later he nearly fell off the chair laughing. Of course, I'd done no such thing. For about two weeks after, Paul didn't have too much to say to me. But he recovered. And I'm sure he laughed about it later. He had a wonderful sense of humour – although he wasn't generally funny in public.

I didn't make many speeches in the House but I made lots in the caucus. That's where I learned to be a better debater. It didn't win me many points back home or with the Press Gallery, but I did make my point with my colleagues and with the Cabinet ministers.

What I did do often in the House, even after we were on the Government side, was to ask questions. When we were first elected and in the Opposition we were trained in parliamentary procedure by Paul Hellyer, who was then Minister of National Defence. Paul gave us little classes on how to ask questions. The main thing was to keep it short and clear. He told us we should be able to get the question over in thirty seconds. But you'd almost never just get up and ask a question. For one thing, the Speaker, Marcel Lambert, would always call you out of order. For another thing, you'd get a lot better answer if you gave the minister notice of the question you were going to ask.

One of the best of Diefenbaker's ministers for answering questions in the House was George Hees; he was the Minister of Trade and Commerce. Old George loved to give you a good answer. I used to go up to his office and tell his executive assistant that I was going to ask a question of George, and this guy would even help me word the question to make sure it made sense. Now that was the way to do things. And it's still done that way in the British Parliament. In the present day, with television and without the requirement to give notice, it's turned into a circus. It's like some sort of stage show instead of a question period. In my early days, the only time you didn't give notice was when a question was urgent, and you'd apologize to the Speaker and tell him your question was of great concern to the people of your riding, and usually he'd let you ask the question. Of course, lots of times it wasn't that urgent; it was done by members who were lazy.

Asking questions was a good way of getting attention from the press. If the press liked your question, then they'd write about it and your constituents would hear about it. Maurice Jefferies was the *Windsor Star*'s Ottawa correspondent in those days and I always used to give Maurice notice of my question as well as the minister. He was a fair reporter, in my opinion.

Once we were on the government side, if you wanted something as a backbencher there was a procedure to follow, a gentlemanly procedure of escalating threats. First you'd go to the minister – either see him personally or write him a letter. Then if the minister turned you down, you'd first warn him that you were going to bring it up in caucus where he would have to defend his decision in front of the whole group. If that didn't work, you'd carry through on your threat and take it to caucus. Sometimes even that wasn't enough and you'd actually bring it up a second time; you'd say something like, "This is the second time I've brought this up Mr. Prime Minister, and I don't intend to bring it up here again and I want you and your minister to do something about it. If you don't, I'm going into the House and I'll bring it up there. I've given you fair warning."

In my case, most ministers didn't want to let it get that far. They knew that I was a stubborn s.o.b. and that if I felt strongly about something I'd take it to the limit. Jack Pickersgill, who took over from McIlraith as Minister of Transport in the first Pearson term, was one who never liked to let my pet projects get as far as the caucus. Pickersgill used to love my letters, too. He said they were generally to the point. I wrote all my own letters then.

Pickersgill and I had a system. If I wrote him a letter I'd get an answer back in two days. When I was a minister, I don't remember ever answering anybody back that quickly. One of my favourites was the letter I wrote to him about putting in lights at the Pelee Island airport, which was in my constituency. I'd recently been in the new Edmonton airport and seen one of those modern art murals on the wall there. A group of us stood around trying to figure out what the thing was. They told us the mural had cost $28,000, which was a lot of money at that time and then they pointed to a big blank wall and said the transport department was going to put a second mural on it. So when I got back to Ottawa I wrote Pickersgill a letter. In it I told him, "You're going to have a big problem on your hands. People in Edmonton are going to have nervous breakdowns trying to figure out the first mural and they'll require a doctor's treatment or maybe even have to be hospitalized – so instead of paying for another mural and all those health costs I humbly suggest that you put in some lights at the Pelee Island Airport. The lights I have in mind for the airport cost only about $25,000. So you'll even save a bit of money."

In a couple of days I got a two-line letter back saying simply that lights would be installed at Pelee Island airport. Nothing more. What Pickersgill did was to take some lights from an airport up north that was on the DEW line and wasn't much used anymore. They just packaged them up and shipped them to Pelee Island. Pickersgill would do anything to avoid having me go after him in front of the caucus. One time he told the whole caucus, "If I was up for a charge of murder I wouldn't let any of you lawyers defend me, I'd get Whelan to speak on my behalf. He can argue better than any of you."

I wasn't all confrontation. I was a combination of a mean old bull and a little lamb. I could paw and stamp the ground and make my charge, but I could also be as sweet and nice as could be. I knew that the most important person in a minister's office was his personal secretary, and I always made a point of making friends with them. When I was elected, old Murray Clark (who'd been the Liberal member up to 1957) had told me his secret of how to get things done in Ottawa. He said, "Don't worry about the ministers themselves. The way to a minister's ear is through his private secretary." I took his advice: I paid attention to the secretaries and told them on the phone, "I don't want to talk to the minister, I want to talk to you – you're the one who runs the office anyhow." I even bought some of them presents and treated them like important people – which they are. So later, when I'd call up and ask, "Whatever happened to that letter I wrote your minister a week or so ago?" I knew my letter would be on the top of the minister's pile the next morning.

I have to admit that I wasn't always so subtle. When I first roared into Ottawa in 1962, I had a funny idea about how much I could get done right away. After all, I was a backbencher and we were in the Opposition. One day I charged into Mr. Pearson's office in the Centre Block and handed his secretary, Mary Macdonald, a list of things I wanted done in my constituency, from solving all the local farm problems to rebuilding all six harbours in the riding – Wheatley, Leamington, Kingsville, Colchester, Amherstburg, and Pelee Island. (I got all of them fixed up over time.) It was a long list. And I said, "Mary, this is what I want." She was very polite but she must have been ready to burst out laughing. "What gall," she must have thought. Then, just like I was a minister, I said, "I'd like to use your phone." She didn't crack a smile, she just handed it to me. Later we used to laugh about it together, this new boy with his long list of demands and not taking no for an answer.

By the time something big came along I'd learned the ropes on the Hill. I knew how to sweet-talk the secretaries and bother the ministers and bully the caucus. And I knew when to go all the way. That's how I got my private member's bill; it took me five years and, as far as I know, I was the first backbencher ever to successfully amend the Bankruptcy Act. I know in his book, *Straight from the Heart*, my friend Jean Chrétien boasts about how in 1964 he got his private member's bill passed to change the name of Trans Canada Airlines to Air Canada. But I changed something much more important in my opinion – although the change to Air Canada was important in a symbolic way.

From the minute I arrived in Parliament I spent my time looking out for farmers' interests. I knew the farm issues and I knew the farmers' concerns. And, as you'll remember, I've always had a rather keen interest in the banking profession which at this time began to translate into an interest in finding a way of protecting farmers from bankers.

My father,
Charles Bernard Whelan.

I always wore a straw hat when
I was a little kid. It was good for
keeping off the sun, and also for
hiding behind.

The whole family got its picture taken just before my brother Bernard
went overseas. LEFT to RIGHT: Henry, Martin, Tom (hidden),
Gertrude, Bernard, Helen, me, Bryce, Ed.

Liz's parents, Frank and
Katharine Pollinger, still look
good quite a few years after
I met and married their daughter.

Liz and my mother, Frances
Whelan, were there to help
celebrate my first election to
Parliament in 1962.
The Windsor Star

It seemed like the whole town of Essex turned
out when I won again in 1963.

Liz spent the 1963 campaign in the hospital.

This picture with Prime Minister Pearson was a campaign shot we used in the 1965 election. Cathy was just a little baby. (Sue is on the left and Terry on the right.)

Paul Martin, the parliamentarian and diplomat, was always quite serious in public. But behind the scenes he had a great sense of humour.
Canapress Photo Service

Ray Worbetz, Bill McKeen, and Percy Trepanier led the 1963 celebrations in the town of Comber.

When Jean Chrétien was Minister of Indian Affairs
and Northern Development, Pelee National Park
Superintendant Harry Cooper and I gave him the
grand tour, including the tip of Point Pelee, which is
as far south as you can get and still be on the
Canadian mainland.

You can see that Jack Davis,
whom I worked for in 1968 when
he was Minister of Fisheries and
Forestry, didn't go in for much
decoration in his office.
Canapress Photo Service

These two pictures show my young family getting older. ABOVE: the family portrait we used in the 1968 election. BELOW: a picture taken with Pierre Elliott Trudeau on a visit to Ottawa after the election. (The girl on the right is my niece, Anne Griffin).

Mike Kerr Photography

I'm not much of a dancer, but in 1972 I had good reason to kick up my heels (here, in the town of McGregor).

After Pierre made me Minister of Agriculture he must have sometimes wondered what sort of bull he'd let out of the pen.

"Eat better, love more, vote Whelan." That was our campaign slogan in 1972.

In 1972 and '73 I was able to get flood relief
money for my riding.

In this picture it looks like I'm
trying to convince my first deputy
Syd Williams (on left) and
Ross Whicher, chairman of the
Commons agriculture committee,
to see things my way.
Canapress Photo Service

I don't know what John Turner
would have done without that
tab book that Simon Reisman
always prepared for him.
Canapress Photo Service

The gang of 1974 (the Cabinet after we'd gotten our majority back).
See if you can remember all their names.

From the button I'm wearing ("Don't Feed Me") you'd think
I was worried my old friend Keith Davey was trying to make me fat.
Canapress Photo Service

One thing I don't mention in the book is that the milk the Quebec dairy
farmers threw at me in 1976 had been watered down – which made
the insult even worse.
Canapress Photo Service / Russell Mant

Peterson, Vancouver Sun

"You'll thank me in the
long run, lady ... by raising prices
now I'm saving you a price
increase in the future ..."

Despite Trudeau's smile, you can tell he isn't
really enjoying the 1979 campaign. And from my
expression I seem to be thinking: "Are we
going to make it?" We didn't.
Spike Bell, M.P.A.

In 1980, campaigning with Trudeau was a lot
more fun than in 1979. Here I seem to be thinking,
"Yes, Pierre, it's in the bag." It was.
Spike Bell, M.P.A.

The day I met Princess Anne she was also wearing a green hat. And this photo appeared in the *Citizen* with the caption, "And where did you get *your* green hat?"
The Citizen, Ottawa

Once in a while I got all dressed up. Like the time Liz and I went to meet Prince Charles and Princess Diana. (Governor General Ed Schreyer and his wife Lily are the other people in the picture.)

I was very proud to be Honorary Colonel of 21 (Windsor) Service Battalion. Left to right: Lt.Col. G.E. Ryan, Lt.Col. R.D. West, me, Lt.Col. Hugh McMahon, Lt.Col. T. David Wearne.
The Windsor Star

I travelled so much on armed forces planes that 412 Transport Squadron presented me with a metallic green hat – it's attached to the stairs in this picture. (The fellows with me are Capt. Pat Dowsett (left) and Master Corporal Dennis Dove.)

I flew so often on small planes I figured I'd better take lessons so I could take over in an emergency. I never did finish getting my flying licence, but my instructor Boutris Abdelnour taught me well.

I've always liked to stir things up – in this case in the cause of the Canadian Chefs de Cuisine.

During my visit to the Inniskillin Winery this guy just popped out of the tank. I said to him, "Did you really drink it dry?" (Lincoln M P Bill Andres is in background.)
Denis W. Cahill

For the hundredth anniversary of the Holstein Association of Canada I had to fight to get permission to have cows on the Hill. It was even debated in Parliament. (Beside me are President Allison Fawcett and Grant Smith.)
Patty Jones

Beef builds better bodies. And makes you ferocious, too. (Beth Gehring is wearing the other T-shirt.)
Toronto Star/Ron Bull

The caption on this cartoon read: "You can eat it, drink it, bathe in it and dust with it. Kids and kittens are crazy 'bout it, too."

The beautiful young woman in this picture seems about to say to me, 'I'll trade you my carrot for your apple." (Her name is Shirley Yanek.)

I really surprised the press and everyone else when I lost more than 25 pounds for the Canadian Save the Children Fund Slim-a-thon weigh-in in 1979 – the International Year of the Child.
Ottawa Journal / Bill Grimshaw

I always took part in the annual
Roman Festival in Windsor.
Louie Scodeller is behind my
chair to the right and Augustino
Lopz to the left. Mrs. Eva Agnew
is sitting in front.

I turned the sod for the new
Canada Building at the Canadian
Western Agribition in Regina
with the help of Mayor Larry
Schneider (left) and Agribition
President Gerry Miller. (The
Agribition is something we built
from nothing to the largest
cattle show in Canada, and one of
the largest in North America.)

I didn't only worry about
agricultural exports. On this
occasion I represented the federal
government at the official opening
of the new coal terminal at
Prince Rupert, B.C.

In November 1980 I opened the
rodeo at the Agribition. They
gave me a nice horse to ride.

My private member's bill, which I first introduced in the
1962-63 session and then re-introduced after we'd won a minority government in 1963, was designed to protect farmers and
other primary producers in the case of bankruptcy. The bill was
actually an amendment to section 51 of the Bankruptcy Act, a
section that gave banks the first grab at the assets of food
processors in case of bankruptcy and left the producers – even if
they hadn't been paid – with nothing. My amendment would see
to it that the producers who'd sold their products to the processors would have first call on the money owed them before the
banks got their hands on any of it.

Pretty soon word got around the caucus that Gene Whelan
had this "sexy" private member's bill. And suddenly I found
that some of those cocky young lawyers I spoke about earlier
wanted to be my friends. They wanted a piece of my bill. Now,
I was smart enough to know that I hadn't a snowball's chance
in hell of getting it through if I tried to do it all by myself. And
I knew that the toughest thing of all would be getting it through
the Commons Committee on Banking and Commerce. So I
grinned and said fine when Herb Gray and Don Macdonald and
John Turner all said they wanted to come along for the ride.
They jumped on my old political horse because they saw it was
a good political horse to be on. They were just as interested as
I was in making a name for themselves. And in those days I
found John Turner a lot easier to take than I do now.

The best part of the fight was when we considered the bill
in committee and we called on some bankers to testify. If you
want to read something funny, go read the transcripts of those
committee hearings. You'll see just how little the bankers knew
about the Bankruptcy Act and about the agriculture business.

When we were preparing our questions we'd sit up all night
and Turner and company would coach me on how to question
the bankers who were to appear the next day. Since I wasn't a
lawyer, we figured I could get away with more. And we were
right. During the hearings, when it came time for us to do our
bit, I'd say to the chairman, Eddy Asselin, "Mr. Chairman, now,
I'm not a lawyer, and I don't understand all this complicated

banking legislation, but could one of the witnesses explain to me such and such?" And I'd usually get through about half my line of questioning before those smart bankers with their college degrees realized what I was doing. They found themselves saying some things that got us lots of publicity. They could not tell us, for instance, how much the banks stood to lose if the amendment went through. And they came across looking mean and greedy, which they are. It became quite controversial.

I sure found out that bankers are easy to attack. The little people don't like bankers and don't have much respect for them, so it's certainly something that the public appreciates – and the press knows it sells papers. Maurice Jefferies gave us wonderful coverage in the *Windsor Star* and we were in all the national papers. Farmer Gene against the big bad bankers.

Perhaps the greatest lesson I learned from this whole affair was how little bankers really know about what is going on in their own business. I'll bet you today that if you investigated the Big Five you'd find them making greater errors than the Western banks that recently went broke. Look at the mess the big banks got into with Dome Petroleum and with the East Coast fisheries. It's because they're so big that they can cover up their mistakes, like a farmer who uses manure to cover up the bad spots. They can take a forkful out of one side of the pile and throw it over the place where they've made a bad mistake so it doesn't show.

Some bankers came to really dislike me. They used to call me a god damned socialist, and worse. I can understand why they were mad – I made them look bad – but I think they're one of the most overrated groups of people I know. They believe they're the great untouchables, answerable only to themselves. When one of them would call me a socialist, I used to shoot back that they practised a form of socialism themselves – socialism for the few. I used to tell them that they should behave more democratically, that their money is from the people and yet they invest it as if it was their own. It's a socialist dictatorship they've got going, with the top bankers getting the special privileges of an elite class – for example, interest rates sometimes three or four or more percentage points below what the rest of us pay.

When my private member's bill left committee, I had a majority of the members on my side – including Tories and the NDPers. After I'd lobbied the Conservatives and I'd lobbied the NDP, I went to the caucus. I said, "I've got all this support on both sides of the House and the majority of the banking committee behind me and if you don't back me I'm going to make a great row in the Commons."

Soon after that caucus meeting I got a call from Walter Gordon who was Pearson's finance minister. Walter said, "Gene, Mike says we have to do something and I'd like to have a talk to you about your bill." By the time he'd finished talking I'd lost half of what I wanted. I had to compromise. My bill had started out to protect all the primary producers – of the forest, the mine, the sea and the farm – and what I ended up with was only the primary producers of perishable agricultural products. I know now that the banks lobbied hard to get the scope of the bill cut down. They argued that it was going to make their administration a little harder. But later when we asked them how much they'd lost under the amended section 51 of the act, they were ashamed to tell us, because their loss was so small.

So Walter Gordon and I made a deal and he sent the bill to the House as a Government bill. All this committee work and lobbying had taken so long that it was already 1965 and my amendment died on the order paper when we called the 1965 election. It was reintroduced in the next session and finally passed in April 1967, almost five years after I'd first started working on it. That's a real lesson for today's backbenchers: you can make a difference, but you've got to be patient and you've got to be stubborn and you've got to work hard.

Herb Gray, who worked with me on my private member's bill, had been elected along with me for the first time in 1962. Our ridings were next to one another and initially we shared an office in the West Block. In those days the backbench MPs had considerably less budget to run their offices (something that improved a great deal under Trudeau) and we were crammed into little cubbyholes. With our two secretaries we shared one small room – and there was only the one telephone between us. Herb and I got along quite well in those days – we used to make comments about each other's letters because we could overhear each other dictating them.

Herb was another one of those lawyers and from a strictly city riding – you could ride around it in half an hour on a bicycle. I'd known him for quite a while because as a junior lawyer in Windsor he'd been our legal advisor for the local Co-operator's Insurance. He was brilliant at the law and he seldom lost a case. When he walked up the courthouse steps, the other legal beagles were all ready to settle because they knew how good he was and how hard he worked. Herb and I had our disagreements when he became Minister of Consumer and Corporate Affairs in 1973, but I can certainly say that he always worked hard.

I've known Herb a long time but you could also say I don't know him at all – you never really got to know Herb Gray. He's a very private person. But I did know how to get him going when we shared that office. I'd just pretend I was dictating a letter about crooked lawyers in my riding or some such. My secretary Loretta O'Regan knew I was teasing, but Herb didn't. And he'd say, "You can't send that kind of letter." And I'd say, "Mind your own business, Herb. I'll run my side of the office and you run yours."

I also got along quite well with John Turner in those early days when we were trying to get my private member's bill through the committee; we worked together and laughed together. But this didn't last too long. In 1965 he was made parliamentary secretary to Art Laing, the new Minister of Northern Affairs and Natural Resources, and almost immediately we crossed swords over Pelee National Park, which was in my riding.

The subject was duck hunting, something that had been allowed in Pelee Park since it was established back in 1918 – in fact, the park was originally set aside in part as a place for duck hunters. Art Laing wanted to ban duck hunting in the park and I fought him on it and won. There's nothing wrong with duck hunting as long as it doesn't get out of hand. I can count on one hand the number of times I hunted them (and I could count on even less fingers how many I shot, too). I used a number of arguments with Art. I said that pollution was a bigger problem than hunting, for example. But my main point was that ducks are different from bears. A bear doesn't migrate like a duck does. So you can protect a bear and other mammals but you can't really protect a duck. You can pat him on the head at Point Pelee but when he gets to Ohio the hunters there will just fill him full of lead.

John Turner did Art Laing's dirty work on the duck-hunting question and I guess he got pretty tired of my defence of those duck hunters. He even came and toured Pelee Park, which only added to his bad feelings. As soon as he took off in a little helicopter to tour the park the fog rolled in off Lake Erie and the pilot had trouble getting back to land. I think that scared him pretty good and afterwards we teased him about it. All in all we caused him quite a bit of work, which is why he was kind of irritated with me for some time after.

One day shortly after the Pelee duck incident I was sitting in the parliamentary barbershop just finishing up a haircut when in walks John. He used to talk to me like I was some kind of football player. He'd call me Big Gene. "Hiya, Big Gene," he'd say, "How ya doing today?" Anyway, on this particular occasion I got the usual greeting: "Hiya, Big Gene." And we made some small talk while he waited for his turn. He never referred to our disagreement over Point Pelee. Anyway, I got out of the chair and he sat down and when I was barely out the door I heard him say to the barber, "I could kill that s.o.b. pest." He knew I was partly deaf and I guess he thought I couldn't hear him. Well, I turned around and walked back into the barber shop and said, "I beg your pardon, John? Would you mind repeating that so I can be sure I heard you correctly?" Then I walked out. He didn't have the nerve to say it to my face, and he didn't have much to say to me for some time after that.

One thing that always amazed me about John Turner was how much he sweared. It was okay for a farmer like me but I didn't expect this of such a highly educated young man. I guess it was his locker room slang. Or maybe he thought it impressed people.

It was also during these early days that I first got to know Jean Chrétien, who was elected to the House of Commons in 1963. We used to spend time together and became good friends, which we've remained to this day. When he first arrived in Ottawa, he spoke almost no English – but he learned fast. Lots of times we used to have lunch together because Jean said he wanted to practise. I'd tell him he could pick a better teacher. I'd say, "I don't speak it too good myself, Jean." Now I just laugh when people criticize the way he talks. I like to joke that he speaks bad English because he learned it from me. (Of course he can speak better or worse depending on the occasion.) You might say that Chrétien speaks Whelanese with a Quebec accent.

I didn't spend all my time raising hell on the Hill. I had a constituency to look after and I had a wife and a young family to attend to. Apart from anything else, this meant I did a lot of commuting. It was a good thing I loved trains, I spent so much time on them.

You'll remember that Liz was none too happy when I ran for Parliament. And she had pretty mixed emotions when I got elected: on the one hand she was glad and proud, and on the other she knew she'd be seeing a lot less of me. During the campaign we'd made a commitment that I'd spend more time in the riding than my opponent, Dick Thrasher. Dick had moved to Ottawa and nobody saw very much of him after that. He'd come home once or twice a month, that type of thing. So I made the commitment to be a full-time Ottawa member and to be home every weekend, and I said that my wife would stay in the riding and be my representative when I wasn't there. I would never advise anybody now to make that kind of commitment, because I've lived it and I know how tough it is.

One time a farm reporter from my area who'd worked for a while in the Press Gallery decided to follow me around for a week, to see what I did (and to see how hard I worked). His name was Ernie Bezaire and he was a rural reporter for the *Windsor Star* before it was bought by Southam and before it decided that it had no use for Gene Whelan. Ernie followed me around Ottawa, came home with me on the train, and followed me around the riding all weekend. By the time it was over, I think he was pretty glad to get back to his home in Kingsville.

In Ottawa he talked to a lot of civil servants and they told him they could always tell when I was coming by my heavy footsteps echoing down the hall – by which they meant I was making my weight felt as a backbencher. At the end of the week, he told me I looked awfully tired. "Well, you look exhausted," I told him.

Part of it was the commuting. Each weekend I spent twenty-eight hours on the train and had little more than twenty-four hours at home. I'd leave Ottawa about four-thirty on Friday afternoon and arrive in Windsor Saturday morning. Then I'd generally have meetings with people in the riding. And usually at night there was some function or meeting to go to – a wedding or a political gathering. Then early Sunday morning I'd go to mass and meet people at my home and then Sunday afternoon I'd catch the train back to Ottawa. When Parliament was in session, Sunday morning before church was the only time of the week I could really set aside for my family. I generally got breakfast ready for the kids, but even that was often interrupted by people calling or just dropping in. When this happened my wife would always say, "Saved by the bell."

As I've mentioned, my daughter Theresa – Terry – was born in November 1961, not long before the 1962 election, Susan was born in May 1963, just after the 1963 vote, and our youngest, Cathy, was born in October 1964, not long before the election of 1965. It got to seem as though whenever an election was called my wife was pregnant. In fact, people used to say, "Liz is pregnant again so another election must be coming." All in all I missed a lot of my kids' growing up. I was riding the train when I could have been with them.

I got used to the commuting, but I never got used to the expense. We took the train then because air passes hadn't yet been introduced and, as I've mentioned, we only got a small living allowance which didn't begin to pay the cost of maintaining two homes. (Our basic train fare was taken care of as part of our travelling expenses.) Coming back from Amherstburg I'd always get a sleeping compartment out of Toronto – if I could find someone to share it with, and I used to share with a Conservative member out of London, C.E. Millar. It was only two dollars more expensive than an upper berth. Even that extra two dollars was enough to break you in those days – we made so little.

When we were arguing in caucus over improving the travel allowance and getting free air passes, I used to say, "Why, we're still riding the train just like in 1867, just like Sir John A. And didn't Laurier say that the twentieth century would belong to Canada? Well how about bringing us MPs into the twentieth century by letting us travel by air?"

But the nice thing about the train was the comradeship, the sense of fraternity. It was always full of MPs from all parties and we were away from the pressure of Ottawa so we'd put our rivalries in the back seat, so to speak. There was always a club car at the back of the train and, since I went right to the end of the line – my stop was known as Fish Hook Centre – I got to know a lot of people better than I ever would have in Ottawa. The other thing I missed when we stopped taking the train was the comments of the trainman when he checked my free pass. He'd shout to the conductor, "One dead head all the way through." That's because I was going to the end of the line for free. But I was glad when those train days were over.

It's funny, you know, but in some ways I think I have a better relationship with my children than if I'd brought the family to Ottawa with me. When I was away from home I would talk to the girls every night before they went to bed – if I didn't they'd be real upset. Even when they were going to school, if I didn't talk to them the night before, Liz would always tell me that she could hardly do anything with them the next morning. They'd always come to the train station or airport to meet me or to see me off. They knew everyone at the Windsor airport and everyone knew them – they were cute kids. Sometimes they'd come to visit me in Ottawa and we had our summer vacations together. In some ways I have a very special relationship with my daughters. In my last couple of years in Parliament I had two of them living with me. Certainly if any of them decide to follow their old man and go into politics, they'll have few illusions about the political life.

We had so many people come to our house over the years, everyone from local farmers to Liberal Cabinet ministers to the great Mikhail Gorbachev, I think my kids learned things other kids don't learn so easily. Children are, in many ways, what you teach them. If you teach them to hate somebody because he's different or be afraid of what they don't know and understand, that's how they'll live their lives. But my kids got used to people of every colour and every religion and every language and they weren't scared of anybody. On the other hand, I certainly paid a personal price for being in politics – and I almost quit more than once.

In those early days, Liz was my unpaid riding secretary. She was looking after the three kids and looking after the riding, too. One time after all three of my daughters were born, with at least two of them still in diapers, she was getting forty or more calls a day. She'd take notes and follow things up and call people back and change the diapers. This was before I opened my joint constituency office with Don Paterson, after he became the provincial Liberal M P P. Liz was almost like a second member of parliament who was in the riding all the time. That was how she helped me keep my commitment to the voters.

Even when I opened the joint constituency office in late 1963 – in Harrow, which is right in the middle of the riding – Liz still got a lot of calls at home. Don Paterson and I paid for the office out of our own pockets – it was still a new idea and there was no funding from the party or the government. Now the offices are paid for out of the House of Commons budget. Don and I worked well together. We shared the cost and we shared the work. He'd refer matters to me and I'd refer things to him. We were pioneers in serving our constituencies.

The guy who ran our constituency office was Larry Wigle. He had one of the best Liberal libraries I ever saw and he just loved running that little office for us. It was the first job that he really had of any kind, I'm pretty sure, but he was a very determined person. He'd been crippled with polio as a child when he was five or six and was in a wheelchair and drove around in a hand-controlled car. I think Larry was about twenty-five when he started working for us, and he was perfect for the job. For one thing, he loved to talk on the telephone and, for another, he treated people well. After we closed the joint office – once my riding had been changed and didn't much overlap with Don Paterson's any more – Larry went to university and got a degree. Then he moved to Hamilton and joined the NDP – too much education, I guess – but we've still remained friends.

One of our main concerns in those days was immigration problems. Liz and I helped a lot of people. Everyone knew Liz was approachable and that she'd do what she could to help. And because she spoke German and understood Hungarian and Serb a lot of people from Herb Gray's and from Paul Martin's ridings would come to her for help. We have over four thousand files on immigration cases that we worked on.

At one point during the Pearson years, there was a big logjam in immigration – a backlog of thousands of people who wanted to bring their relatives to Canada or wanted to appeal a deportation order. And many were being turned down by bureaucrats or deported by bureaucrats without any hearing. So we formed a committee of caucus, all backbenchers, and told Pearson that we needed something better. Our proposal was an appeal board that would be cheap and quick. That was one suggestion we made that got picked up right away. Within a year we had a three-person board and anyone – lawyer or not – had the right to argue publicly before it. The first board was set up in Ottawa in 1967 and was made up of ordinary citizens from the various sections of the community instead of bureaucrats. Later, similar boards were established in other cities.

We noted that a lot of lawyers were taking money from people when they represented them before the board and were hardly doing any work at all – some of them would only study the brief for twenty minutes before they went into court. What's more, they weren't winning very many cases and too many people were still being deported. So I began to take a vivid interest in immigration cases – it was the court of last resort for them. Many people in my riding and the neighbouring ridings were affected.

I worked very closely with a young lawyer from Windsor by the name of Tony Cusinato, a very good lawyer who later became a very good county court judge. I'd refer a lot of people to him and often he'd handle the case himself, but sometimes I'd go to the Immigration Appeal Board in Ottawa and argue a case myself, and I won quite a few. Of the more than four thousand people we represented in many different ways, I reckon we won close to 90 percent. We fought hard on humanitarian grounds and we'd usually win, and not one of the people I fought and won for ever got into trouble or became a ward of the state.

Generally the summer recess was when our family spent the most time together, but 1964 was a bit different. That was the summer of the great Flag Debate with Parliament in extended session while we whipped ourselves into a frenzy over whether or not to give Canada its own flag. Since I couldn't come home, Liz drove the kids up to Ottawa in our old 1959 Plymouth and we rented a cottage on the Rideau River for the last two weeks of the session.

The Flag Debate was quite something. People really got worked up. I can remember Angus MacLean, a Tory from Prince Edward Island, giving a speech about what a tragedy it would be if they got rid of the old Red Ensign with the Union Jack in the corner – our great British heritage, and all that. He talked about how it was the flag we'd fought under in two world wars and how they'd buried soldiers in the old Union Jack, which in 1964 was still the official Canadian flag. He went on and on. But there was another, older MacLean in the House – Allan McLean – a Liberal from New Brunswick, and I can remember his speech vividly. He said, "I was in the war, too, and I was on the burial crew and all this talk about having the Union Jack to bury them in – that's a lot of nonsense. Why sometimes we couldn't even find burlap to bury them in, let alone the Union Jack."

But the best of all was Tommy Douglas' speech on the flag. He was still leader of the New Democrats then and he was one of the greatest orators in the House. He was parrying the argument that the Union Jack was a Christian flag, which the Tories were using as one of the reasons we should keep it. He said, "I should like to point out that the crosses in the Union Jack are not Christian symbols in the true sense of the word. They represent battle banners which were used: St. George's cross was first used in the Crusade when the kings and barons and knights of Christendom perpetrated murder, rapine and plunder in the name of Christianity; the flag of St. Andrew was first used by the Picts and the Scots in their wars against the Saxons; the cross of St. Patrick was on the banner of the Fitzpatricks when they conquered Ireland, and very few Irishmen will be crying for the cross of St. Patrick. Certainly it has never been adopted as Ireland's flag." Then he went on to talk about how Canada was not only a Christian country, but one where many faiths were equal. It was a hell of speech.

Although I didn't speak in the Flag Debate I was a strong supporter of the new flag, of a flag for all Canadians. I knew that many of my constituents didn't have any connection to the British heritage of Canada, for example, Grandpa Pollinger, who wanted to know why I didn't speak during the debate. As a new Canadian he was proud of his new country and wanted a flag that was his, not Great Britain's. And I remembered what our French Canadian neighbour had said to us when we were growing up: "Some day you kids will have your own flag and the crown head she will roll." There were times during the Flag Debate when it seemed quite a few heads would roll.

The debate lasted from June 15 to December 15, when we finally invoked closure. So in 1965 Canada finally had its own flag. Those of us who were for it have certainly been proved to be right. Even some of the greatest opponents at the time came to accept the flag and fly it and, in the years that followed as I travelled around Canada, I would see more and more flags all the time. It's got to the point where you see many more Canadian flags flown in our country than there are American flags flown in the United States. And they're supposed to be the great patriots and flag wavers.

As I've said, I didn't give many speeches in the House. I wasn't all that comfortable in that forum and I felt I could get more done by writing letters and making speeches in caucus.

And since there was no television then it didn't make as much difference back home as it now does. But there is one speech I almost gave that I wish I had. It was on the subject of the abolition of capital punishment, which came up in 1967 when Larry Pennell as Solicitor General introduced a bill to make the punishment for murder a mandatory life sentence except in the case of police officers or prison guards. This was for a trial period of five years and was later renewed. The House of Commons didn't actually abolish the death penalty until 1976, but there hadn't been an execution in Canada since 1962.

When I came to Ottawa I wasn't an abolitionist. I had no opinion one way or the other, although I did remember the last two people they'd hung in the old Essex County Jail who'd both been innocent; they'd hung them on circumstantial evidence and the mistake was only found out five years later when the real murderer confessed on his deathbed. In Ottawa I got to know quite a few trial lawyers and some of them had defended people charged with murder, and I noticed that to a man they were opposed to capital punishment, Diefenbaker included. They knew that if they did a bad job, an innocent person might hang and if they did a good job they could often get a guilty one off scot free. Also, they knew that the courts weren't always fair – if you couldn't afford a high-priced lawyer, you might not get the same defence. My friend Larry Pennell had long been opposed. I listened to him and the others talk and gradually I became convinced; I became a strong abolitionist.

When the bill was going to be debated in the House, I wrote a one-page speech and I sent it to Mr. Pearson – I told him I wanted to speak. At that time I used to walk every day past the plaque to Thomas d'Arcy McGee, the Father of Confederation who'd been assassinated on the Hill in 1868, supposedly by a Fenian because he'd angered the Irish voters. As a result I'd taken a bit of interest in the old guy and I'd found out we had something in common. So I used him as the centrepiece of my little speech. Here's what I wrote.

"Mr. Speaker, I only intend to take a few minutes to express why I am going to vote as I intend to. Every day, I walk past that spot on Sparks Street, on my way to the House of Commons, the spot that is marked by a bronze plaque to point out to the public the place where Patrick James Whelan was hung by the neck till dead in public view, for all to witness who cared to. The young man or boy, only nineteen years of age, was taken from this world in the most barbaric and medieval way known to man. This was done to this young man, why, I ask you, why? Well, I will tell you. Because he shot a Tory.

"Mr. Speaker, it is a horrible death, this hanging, and that makes me a one hundred percent abolitionist. Thank you."

What I didn't put in my speech is that there's considerable doubt Patrick James Whelan committed the crime. So it may well be that they hanged an innocent man for political reasons. I later heard the story that one of Sir John A's advisers came to him before the execution and told him the young man might not be guilty. So Sir John A asked the young man's name and, when he was told, he said, "Hang the Irish bastard."

I sent a copy to Mr. Pearson and he wrote back on it, "You must give this pregnant speech." But I never gave it. I never took part in the debate because there were already so many speeches scheduled that it just didn't make sense. But looking back, I wish I had.

Pearson called the 1965 election because Keith Davey and Walter Gordon told him he could win a majority. Before he made up his mind he asked each Liberal member to write him a letter; I wrote him to say he wouldn't gain anything by calling an election. I told him, "There'll be some of my colleagues who will tell you to go because they hope some Cabinet ministers will get defeated and they will get their turn in the Cabinet." I advised him against it, but I was one of the few. He wrote me a letter back and told me I was in the minority. He said, "There's only a few of you who are against the election and that's why I've called it." We'd only been in office for eighteen months and people weren't ready for another campaign. They should have waited another year. We ended up with only two seats more than we'd had before, so it was a big waste of time.

A lot of people criticized the Rainmaker after this and they made fun of his name, because he hadn't been able to make much rain on this occasion. But if you look at Keith Davey's overall batting average, you'd have to say he was a big league player.

But I never agreed with his decision to go to the Senate – and I told him so more than once. He asked Pearson to put him in there after the election when he resigned as national organizer of the Liberal Party. When I heard the rumour that he was going to go there, I wrote him to say I didn't think he should. I didn't have any use for the Senate then, and I don't today. A year or two before, I'd even presented a private member's bill to abolish the Senate – I've never been very popular with the senators since then – and they've never been very popular with me. One thing that has always burned me up is that the minute they're appointed, they're called honourable, while a member of parliament who's elected by the people doesn't have the right. If you're from the Commons, you become honourable only if you go into the Cabinet.

I thought it was a mistake for Keith to go. I thought he should have run for Parliament: he would have added a lot to the House of Commons. I told him he should pick a seat and run. "After all the time you've been sitting in your treehouse in the political jungle – sitting up there and watching what goes on and orchestrating from behind the scenes – you've got to know politics better than anybody. You should use that knowledge as an elected member." I thought he would make a fine minister. After all the times he'd told others of us how we could get elected, I thought he should accept that challenge himself.

I don't recall whether he ever wrote back, but I would kid him about it afterwards. Like most of them, Keith got to love the Senate. It's a wonderful club. And they pay you well to become a member.

Pierre Elliott Trudeau was one of the new boys after the 1965 election. But he didn't stay on the back bench for long. Pearson clearly had special things in mind for him because he made him his parliamentary secretary right away. Trudeau was a very quiet person although he had a reputation as a swinger. We both tended to work late and I would often see him leaving his office at ten-thirty or eleven at night as I was leaving mine. And lots of times in the morning when I met my friends for breakfast in the parliamentary restaurant around 8:00 A.M., Trudeau would be there too. So when people asked me if he was a swinger – especially later when he was running for the leadership – I'd say, "After those days he puts in, if he can swing then all the more power to him, because this old farmer can hardly swing himself into bed to go to sleep." Trudeau was older than I was, too.

We first got to know each other because he used to walk to work and so did I. That was the main way I kept in shape, that and running up and down stairs. In 1965 it was fourteen blocks to my apartment and, in cold weather especially, that was quite a haul. Back home when I went hunting pheasants on Pelee Island my friends couldn't understand how somebody leading the soft Ottawa life could keep up with them so well. It was because of the walking. I didn't get a car in Ottawa until I was a minister. That's when I started to gain weight.

Once Trudeau became justice minister in the spring of 1967, each time we ran into each other we would talk about all the letters I wrote him or the latest fight in the caucus. One time we had a problem in my riding with outboard motorboats racing on the Rivière Canard – Duck River. (It flows into the Detroit River only about a mile and half from my house.) There was a big Catholic church on the river and the priest used to call me up and raise hell about the boats racing there on Sunday and disturbing his mass. So I wrote to Trudeau to complain on the priest's behalf.

I wrote to the Minister of Justice because I wanted him to bring the federal law to bear. In the letter I mentioned that it says in the constitution that any stream you can float a log in is classified as navigable and that all navigable streams come under the jurisdiction of the federal government. The next time we were walking together after he got the letter, Trudeau said to me, "What section is that under?" He was a constitutional expert and he'd never heard of it. And I told him it was an old saying we'd learned as kids but I didn't know where to look it up. It is in fact in the constitution but not the way I learned it. We eventually did make them stop racing their motorboats, and after that Trudeau always referred to me as "Eugene from Rivière Canard."

After the 1965 election, Pearson made my friend Joe Greene Minister of Agriculture. I knew I was being considered for the job, but I didn't lobby for it. Greene, on the other hand, sat outside Mr. Pearson's office for four days. I wouldn't do that for all the gold in China. I would have liked the job, but I wouldn't beg for it. Joe Greene's behaviour puts me in mind of an old man, a neighbour of ours. He was a French Canadian, a very independent fellow, a skilled carpenter and a good farmer. He didn't have a big farm, but he kept it as neat as could be. If anyone told him to do something he didn't want to do, he'd say, "Radder dan do dat I go whittle myself a bill and go pick shit wit de hen in de barnyard." Well, I would rather have whittled a bill than do what Joe Greene did.

You may think I was kind of brash thinking I was ready to be Minister of Agriculture in 1965, but I really believe I was qualified. I'd been a hardworking backbencher for three years and through my involvement in the co-op movement and farm organizations and the Canadian Mayors and Reeves Association and the Canadian Roads Association, I had a pretty good grasp of the national scene and, unlike many new ministers, I would have known quite a bit about the department. I'd been a farmer and I knew agriculture.

Mike Pearson knew I'd like the job, but he never spoke to me about it. That is, not until the caucus Christmas party that year. I had just finished talking to my wife at home on the phone and I was chatting with a group at the party. I turned to one of them and said, "My wife is a great admirer of Allan MacEachen because of what he did as labour minister, but she can't understand why Mr. Pearson moved MacEachen from Labour to Health and Welfare." Then out of the blue sky I heard a voice behind my back: "And where does your wife think you should be?" It was the Prime Minister. I turned and told him exactly what my wife had said: "At home!"

Pearson took me aside and said, "I want to talk to you, Gene. I want to tell you something. I nearly picked you as Minister of Agriculture. But I couldn't make up my mind. And then we finally decided on Joe Greene because we felt he could handle himself in the House better than you could." And I said, "Gee thanks, Mike, even if Joe doesn't know a sow from a cow." And he said, "I feel better now I've told you." I replied, "Mike, I don't know how to tell you how I feel." But, you know, he was that kind of guy. It bothered him because he didn't make me Minister of Agriculture in 1965. (I later found out that one of those who was against my promotion at the time was my friend Keith Davey. Not long after, he commented to Doug Fisher, "He can't be a minister. He never even finished high school." Keith should have known better.)

It wasn't the first time Pearson had tried to soothe me when I was aroused. Usually he succeeded better than on this occasion. He was a wonderful diplomat – a much better diplomat than he was a political leader. He was very approachable. You could be mad as a hornet – just furious about what one of his ministers was doing or what the government was doing – and all you had to do was call Mary Macdonald up and tell her you wanted to see the boss. It might take a week or it might only take a few hours, but you'd always get in to see Mike Pearson. I'd storm into his office and Mike would be as nice and as sympathetic as could be and, by the time I got done talking to him, I'd wonder what in hell I went in the room for. He was as smooth as honey. And if he said he'd look into something, he would. He'd follow it up and get back to you. He was a great diplomat.

I wouldn't have minded missing out on Agriculture so much if Harry Hays had still been the minister. He was the former mayor of Calgary – that disappearing breed known as the Western Liberal – who'd been elected in 1963. Getting to know Harry was one of my most pleasant experiences as a backbencher. He was a great minister as far as I was concerned. He really listened to the backbenchers and canvassed our opinion. For example, he'd often have a bunch of us who represented rural ridings to breakfast at 6:30 A.M. – he always got up at 5:00 A.M. himself – and he'd go over draft legislation and ask us what we thought. He always kept us informed and he listened to our comments and made changes. In some ways I think he was a better Minister of Agriculture than I was. He certainly worked more closely with the backbenchers than I did – and I did it better and more than most of my Cabinet colleagues.

He was a successful cattle farmer and he was very proud of a breed of cattle he'd developed called the Hays converter. They called it a converter because it converted roughage into meat better than any other animal. It took him twenty-five years to develop that breed and now it's used all over Canada and in other parts of the world. Harry was a wealthy farmer who'd made his money first and then gone into politics. He was one of the smartest cattle breeders and exporters and auctioneers and men I ever knew.

I remember we were sitting in the parliamentary restaurant one day after he'd lost the 1965 election – by only a few hundred votes. (Only one Liberal has been elected from his riding since then – Pat Mahoney squeaked in in 1968.) We were talking over old times and Harry told me how he'd asked Pearson to name me his parliamentary secretary back in 1963. The reason Pearson didn't was because they decided it wouldn't do to have two Catholics working together. It wouldn't look good. Harry told me that was the first he knew I was Catholic – and that breakfast was the first I knew it about him. Then he laughed and told me he hadn't been to church in twenty-eight years. He thought Pearson's decision was wrong, but those sorts of considerations were still important then. (Pearson appointed Bruce Beer from Peel, who was a prominent Mason.) If you were going to put a Catholic in the Cabinet you practically had to call up the Cardinal to get his permission. But Trudeau didn't pay any attention to that. It ended with him.

Instead of agriculture minister I became chairman of the Commons agriculture committee. In those days the committee was the largest one there was – we had forty-five members. (I think the numbers are limited to fifteen now.) Every farmer and every MP who represented a rural area wanted to be on the committee, so you can imagine what fun I had as chairman. The Liberals didn't even have a majority on the committee. I learned to be a pretty good diplomat running those meetings.

As chairman I started something that is now done much more: I took my committee on the road. We were studying the operations of the Wheat Board and yet most of us had never been to the West and didn't understand the Canadian transportation system at all. (I had an advantage over most of them because of my trip to Alberta as a teenager to help with the 1942 harvest.) We went in the wintertime and all forty-four of my members went. Jack Horner was one. Jack and I got along quite well even though he showed no sign then of turning into a Liberal. When we got back, our committee recommended strongly that we should be improving the grain elevator system and the transportation system for grain – especially the rail lines through the mountains. They don't yet have double-tracking all through the Rockies.

The only other travelling I did between 1965 and 1968 was in 1966 when I went for the first time to the United Nations in New York. I had no idea then that one day I'd be the president of a UN organization. I was just curious to see the place and how it worked. Walter Gordon – who had by then resigned from the Cabinet – joked with me at the time that I was on a two-week junket to hob-knob with the pinstriped set – the diplomats – but to me it seemed more like a jail sentence. I didn't know anybody from New York and I went with only a few other MPs, including Fernand LeBlanc (a Liberal who's now a senator) and Ed Schreyer, who was then in Ottawa, but who later became Premier of Manitoba, then Governor General. I found the United Nations one of the dullest, most infuriating places you could imagine. People made speech after speech and I couldn't figure the point. When they were supposed to be mad at each other, you couldn't tell because of their polite diplomatic language. There was one guy who wanted to declare war, or something, and his country was so poor he couldn't have gone to war on a bicycle. I thought the whole charade was quite ridiculous.

When I came back Mr. Pearson asked me what I thought, and I told him I didn't want to go back because I thought the UN was the biggest waste of the time of mankind that I had ever witnessed. And he said, "What do you mean?" And I said, "If they'd really say what they think to one another, get it off their chests, it would maybe make some sense." And he said, "Well we can't use your kind of language there, but sometimes the diplomatic language we use is much worse. We say terrible things to one another." I saw quite a bit of the UN over the

years but my first impression didn't change much. Maybe the
UN would work better if it were someplace other than New
York, a poor place like Burkina Faso or Ethiopia. They would
probably do a lot more work. I used to say that if they had
some of their meetings in tents out in the middle of the desert,
maybe they wouldn't take so long.

Before I went to the UN, I'd complained to Mr. Pearson on
several occasions that he ought to take along MPs when he went
on foreign trips. I argued that we needed this great broadening
experience. At that time Jim Coutts was working in his office —
but he wasn't so important as he got to be later — and I pointed
out that he took that pipsqueak Coutts along when he could be
taking MPs. And Pearson replied, "Well, if you want to carry
my bag, you can come along too, because that's mostly what
Coutts does." And I said, "Sure, just ask me to go and I'll carry
your bag. They won't know if it's mine or yours, anyhow."
And Pearson just laughed. But I still think I was right about
the principle. I could make the same criticism of Trudeau. He
didn't take very many ministers or MPs along with him when
he travelled.

One of the funniest things that happened during Pearson's
last term was when a band called the Deep River Boys — black
musicians from New York State — was playing at the Château
Laurier in Ottawa. The week before, they'd been playing at the
Killarney Hotel in Windsor and my wife had been to hear them
play with a group of women from our Liberal women's riding
association. During the shows the band leader, Harry Douglas,
had a habit of walking in the audience and talking and singing
to the crowd. When he did this, the people there with Liz found
out he would be playing the next week in Ottawa and said,
"Why don't you go see her husband? He's in Ottawa and he'll
show you the Parliament Buildings." So when I came home the
next weekend she told me I'd better call Harry up and invite
him to lunch. And I did.

It was a Wednesday and in the caucus meeting that morning
we'd had a terrible fight about bringing Caribbean farm workers
to Canada on a temporary basis to help with the harvest. Some
of the MPs didn't want them to come because they were black

and because they'd be taking jobs that Canadians should be doing – even though Canadians didn't want to do the work. So we had a hell of fight and Pearson finally sided with me and said we could bring in the farm workers.

That afternoon the Deep River Boys came over to my office and I took them to the Speaker's Gallery to watch Question Period. They'd never been to Parliament before. From where we sat we could see the front bench quite clear, and there were Mr. Pearson and Paul Martin and Jack Pickersgill looking up at me and whispering back and forth to one another. I could guess what they were thinking. "What's Gene doing with a bunch of Caribbean diplomats right after this thing about bringing in their workers?" They figured I was up to some plot.

Later that day I took my guests to the parliamentary restaurant. It was a beautiful spring evening and we were sitting at the table chatting away when Paul Martin came along. And he said in his most friendly voice, "Well, hello Gene, how are you?" I knew he wanted to find out who these people were but I wasn't saying anything. And he said, "And who are your friends?" I said, "Paul, I'd like you to meet Harry Douglas from Jamaica." So Paul shook hands with them all, then said, "And what brings you gentlemen to Ottawa?" That's when Harry said, "Well, we're playing over at the Château Laurier." So I finally had to introduce them properly: "Paul, I'd like you to meet Harry Douglas and his quartet, the Deep River Boys, from Jamaica, New York." All Paul said was, "Gene, you're a terrible fellow." He and everybody else were convinced afterward that I'd planned the whole thing.

After I'd been passed over as agriculture minister I remember Paul Martin consoling me when I complained about not being recognized by the party or by the Prime Minister. He reminded me I'd only been a member six years and he'd been ten years waiting to be called to the Cabinet. He told me I shouldn't complain, that Mackenzie King walked past him every day to get to his place in the House and "it was seven years before the Prime Minister even knew I was there." That's one of the many good stories Paul left out of his book.

I hoped I'd have better prospects under a new leader and I was pretty excited in late 1967 when Pearson announced his resignation and called a leadership convention for the following April. I wasn't ready to quit yet. I wanted to be around for the fun and the new challenge – especially after Trudeau decided to run.

5

Trudeau

By December 1967, when Mike Pearson finally got around to announcing his retirement, it seemed as if everyone in the Cabinet was a candidate. The first to officially enter the race was the one serious contender from outside Ottawa – Eric Kierans, a former Quebec Liberal Cabinet minister who'd turned his attention to Ottawa when Daniel Johnson and the Union Nationale won the provincial election in 1966. Kierans was a nice man with an economic ego. He had economic theories that I never agreed with and once he became a minister – Postmaster General – he was bullheaded as could be. If he didn't get his way he was ready to throw in his chips or take his bat and ball and go home. At the 1968 convention he was not much of a political heavyweight.

The Cabinet under Pearson had never been noted for keeping its mouths shut, but in late 1967, when everyone was expecting the Prime Minister to retire, it leaked all over the place. (Cabinet leaks were something Trudeau tried not to tolerate – although he could never stop them completely.) Supposedly there was a joke going around the Press Gallery at that time that all a reporter had to do was stand outside the Cabinet room door on the third floor of the Centre Block and ask the first person who came out what had gone on in the meeting – and you'd have the whole story. They were all looking for attention, jockeying for position before the starting pistol was fired. Sixteen years later, in 1984, before Trudeau resigned, I wasn't one of those horses who left the gate before the race began. That's not my style. And I wasn't very impressed with the behaviour of the Cabinet in 1967.

In January, after Kierans declared, the rest of them lined up pretty quick: Paul Hellyer, whose great accomplishment was unifying the armed forces; Allan MacEachen, who certainly had the brains but wasn't willing to work hard enough – maybe he thought being Prime Minister would be easier than being Minister of National Health and Welfare; John Turner, who'd just been made Minister of Consumer and Corporate Affairs and was supposed to represent the future of the Liberal Party; Mitchell Sharp, the former bureaucrat who was then finance minister; Joe Greene, my former breakfast buddy, now Minister of Agriculture; and Paul Martin, who'd run for the leadership against Pearson in 1958 and figured it was his turn this time, even though he was almost as old as Mike. As it turned out, the two big guns were the last to declare. Bob Winters, who was Minister of Industry, Trade and Commerce, first announced he wouldn't be a candidate, then later changed his mind when he saw that Bay Street might get booted out of the party. The last to announce, except for Winters, was Pierre Trudeau, the dark horse from Quebec. Everyone had been expecting that the Quebec candidate would be Jean Marchand, who was older – and much more politically experienced.

I'd known Jean Marchand in the House as a backbencher and as a minister and I liked him. When the talk was that he would be the Quebec candidate, I went to him and said, "If you're going to run, Jean, I will support you." That's when he told me he didn't think he would go for it since he didn't believe he would be accepted in English Canada because of his strong accent. He didn't think he could win the election for the Liberals. I guess he'd had a rough time with the West as transport minister. But he was tough and a good administrator, though not as articulate as Gérard Pelletier and Pierre Trudeau.

Trudeau had become the darling of the press and, after his face-off with Daniel Johnson at the federal-provincial conference later that spring, had got the reputation of being someone who'd be tough with Quebec. In 1968 the reporters just loved him, and the people followed suit. But I'm told it wasn't that easy to persuade him to run. He had some serious doubts about whether he could do the job – or wanted it – and about whether he would be accepted. Marchand and Pelletier talked him into it.

For a backbencher, the big thing, of course, was which candidate you were going to support. Most of them came courting and making the wildest promises – you'd be minister of this and minister of that. Paul Martin wanted my support – he expected it, because we'd known each other so long, we were old friends, and our ridings were next to one another. I'll say one thing for Paul: he didn't try to bribe me with a Cabinet post or some other plum. But I'd made up my mind I was going to support Trudeau, and when I told Paul to his face he was none too happy.

I delayed going to see him about it because I knew it would be unpleasant. But he called me four or five times and finally I said I'd come over and see him. When I got to his office I didn't beat around the bush. I said, "You know who I'm going to support, anyway. I'm supporting Trudeau and I've made up my mind." So he asked me why and I said, "Because Pierre Trudeau can lead us to a majority government and I don't think you can. I don't think you have enough support from Quebec." Just like that. That remark about Quebec would have hurt him, too, because he was bilingual and from a French Canadian family and he claimed during his campaign that if he won we could still say that we'd kept the principle of alternation going – that an English leader should be followed by a French leader. Many people believed that Pearson was unofficially supporting Trudeau for that reason. They brought back the same nonsense about alternation when Jean Chrétien ran against Turner in 1984 – and it probably cost him the leadership. In 1968, it certainly helped Trudeau's chances.

As you can imagine, old Paul wasn't too happy when I said these things to him. And he tried to argue with me. He said, "Gene, out of the caucus I've got thirty-two members supporting me and a number of those are from Quebec." He was wrong and I told him so: "Paul you don't have any thirty-two. You've got five." I even told him who they were; I gave him the names, but he didn't believe me. Then I said, "Does this mean you were lying those times when you told me I was the wisest politician in the caucus?" "No," he said, "I meant what I said then and I mean what I say to you now. I want your support." Then I said, "You don't have a hope in hell of winning and I'm going to throw my support where it will do some good. I'm going to support Trudeau and I'm going to make a public announcement." Then he kind of begged me. He reminded me that we were both from Windsor and of how it would look if his own neighbour didn't support him. He cried at the end. It was a hard meeting.

I admit he made a pretty strong case, but I held firm – I'd made up my mind even though we were good friends and it was a very hard thing to do. Despite what I'd told him Paul still believed he was going to do well, that he could win.

As it turned out I was right and only five caucus members supported him. A lot of people had told him one thing and done another. It's often that way in politics. Some time afterwards he told me, "You know, you're one of the few honest politicians, if not the only one." Ever since, I've always had reservations about not supporting him on the first ballot. But I was like a bull and I was going to support Trudeau. I would have gone to Trudeau on a later ballot, regardless.

That was a trying time to be a backbencher. The candidates knew I'd been active in local politics and with the co-ops and the credit unions and the Ontario Federation of Agriculture, and I'd kept up all my contacts in rural Canada. So they figured my support was worth something. Once Bob Winters changed his mind and declared, I had Winters after me and Paul Hellyer and Joe Greene – practically all of them. But I stayed firm and supported Trudeau, not just because I thought he could win, but because he was different; he had that certain appeal. And there was one thing in particular I liked about him: like Paul Martin, he didn't promise me a damn thing.

Most of the others were promising the moon, but not the people around Trudeau. I remember I met with some of his staff to find out what I could do to help. Jean Marchand and Gérard Pelletier were there and I believe Pierre de Bané, who was later an M P and a minister and who, like me, got fired by John Turner in 1984. I told them I'd campaign wherever they thought it would do the most good and I agreed to write a letter to the delegates explaining my support for Trudeau. They knew there were many doubts in English-speaking Canada about this intellectual professor from Quebec and they hoped I could answer some of them. When I met with Trudeau, he just said, "Thanks, Eugene, for supporting me. Whatever you can do to help will be appreciated." I was one of the first English-speaking M Ps who joined his camp and I tried to persuade others. But I had more success with the delegates than with the M Ps.

Shortly after, I went with Trudeau to a delegate meeting in London, Ontario. I simply talked to the delegates and told them what I thought of the man; I was there to show I was supporting Pierre. At that meeting I knew right away that he would be accepted by the people. It was just a few delegates gathered in someone's house, but he made a wonderful impression. He seemed to have that natural attractiveness that can be so important in politics.

I still have a copy of the letter I wrote to the delegates in late March, just before they gathered in Ottawa. My basic point was that Pierre Trudeau represented something new and fresh – a change for the Liberal Party and a change for Canada. In the letter, I said, "I believe our whole governmental system needs a complete overhaul. I don't believe anyone is any better suited to do this than Pierre Elliott Trudeau."

I suppose I supported him in part because of the way he'd treated me as a backbencher when he was Minister of Justice. Not only did he answer my letters quickly, he paid attention to what I said in caucus. He'd always comment – often during one of those morning walks to work – on what I'd said afterwards and tell me whether he thought I was wrong or right. I never found him aloof or arrogant.

During the leadership race, I campaigned for him in about twenty-five ridings in Ontario, mostly southeastern and south-western Ontario. I'm sure I helped a lot because many people were suspicious of this intellectual swinger from Montreal – but they knew and trusted Gene Whelan. I told them what I knew about Trudeau, and how he'd treated me, and how hard he worked. They knew I was no citified swinger and they could see I got along with Trudeau just fine.

Before the convention some pundits were predicting he would win, but I had special inside information on that score. I was at the Serbian Businessmen's Association dinner in Amherstburg at the Lakeshore Tavern. Fedor Rajic and his wife were there and they'd brought with them a Serbian woman who read tea cups. She couldn't speak English and she didn't know who I was, but she read my tea cup. Fedor was a Paul Martin sup-porter and he knew I was backing Trudeau. Anyway, she looked at my leaves and said, "I see a throne, and perhaps there is a king on the throne. Ah, you are supporting someone for a higher position. The person you are supporting will be successful. And so will you. You will be rewarded for it." When Fedor heard this, he got terribly excited, so I asked him why and he said, "She's never wrong." After the convention was over he said to me, "Remember what I said?"

The convention began on Thursday April 4, 1968, in the brand new Ottawa Civic Centre. I worked from the moment the dele-gates arrived until the final ballot on Saturday. I talked to literally hundreds of delegates from right across the country. I knew many of them from farm organizations and so on. And I was able to persuade quite a few of them to support Trudeau. During the convention sessions I worked the floor, buttonholing people, sounding out their support, trying to persuade them to support my man – and also always trying to find out what the other camps were up to. The atmosphere on the floor was excit-ing – emotional – but friendly. I experienced none of the vicious-ness that took place before and during the 1984 convention.

I remember Ross Thatcher, who at that time was Premier of Saskatchewan and was leading the Saskatchewan delegation, coming up to me on the floor of the convention. He wanted to talk to me about Trudeau, to know why I was supporting him. I'd met Ross in Regina on a trip out West when I was chairman of the House of Commons agriculture committee; he knew my background and I knew his. I gave him my reasons and then he asked me, "But don't you have any reservations about Trudeau?" I said, "Yes, I have one." And he said, "What's that." And I said, "Well, I think he's a little too conservative." I was sure he'd say something like, "Oh my, that's terrible," but he said, "That's good enough for me." And he went back and persuaded most of the Saskatchewan delegates to vote for Trudeau.

I wasn't joking either. Trudeau was conservative in many ways. People often accused him then and later of being a socialist or too liberal. But I've always thought that was a great misconception.

There was a lot of nasty literature being sent around at that time, and later during the 1968 election campaign, claiming that Trudeau was a communist because he'd rowed to Cuba and visited China and written a book, that sort of nonsense. People would ask me about it and my patent answer was, "Look, I've studied the man, and take my word for it, most of the stuff they say about him is not true." The other camps used all this rumour and innuendo to try to get people to leave Trudeau and come over to their side. I guess some of them – like Judy LaMarsh – really hated him. I've never understood why.

The day before the speeches Mitchell Sharp dropped out of the race and threw his support to Trudeau. That meant it looked like a three-way contest between Paul Hellyer, Bob Winters, and Trudeau – with Trudeau in the lead and Hellyer ahead of Winters. No one predicted that Hellyer would make such a bad speech and lose so much support that Turner would end up coming third on the first ballot.

I liked Paul Hellyer, but he rubbed many people the wrong way – still does, I suppose. The nickname we had for him then was Charles de Gaulle, because he was stately and tall and he held himself aloof and thought quite highly of himself. He was a very bright man and he knew it, too. Once he became a minister he was full of ideas – not necessarily ones that related to his own portfolio. That probably irritated his Cabinet colleagues. He wanted us to build super cities in the wilderness in Canada – complete new cities with the safest environment you could have – instead of letting places like Toronto and Montreal and Vancouver grow too big. His dream cities would have such fine public transportation that you wouldn't need cars. Maybe he was too advanced for us. But his main problems were that he lacked political savvy, didn't have much of a sense of humour, and had a pretty big ego. That was obvious after he ran for the Liberal Leadership in 1968, then turned around and ran for the Conservative leadership in 1976 against Clark. But he was as approachable as could be, unlike some of the other Cabinet ministers.

One of the most emotional moments at the convention for me and for most of the delegates was on the first night when Pearson made his farewell speech. It was one of Pearson's best speeches – if he'd given more like it he might have got his majority in 1965. Many people were weeping openly. I don't remember shedding any tears, but I do remember my mixed emotions. People loved Pearson as a person. He was very warm – he didn't like to appear to be mean – and we liked and respected him as a man, but I had serious reservations about him as a politician and as a Prime Minister.

If you look at his record you'll see that he was actually tougher than he seemed. He fired many more Cabinet ministers in a short period of time than Trudeau. Trudeau could rarely bring himself to fire anyone. Pearson even got rid of his good friend Walter Gordon. Other times he was too soft – like that time the caucus wanted him to fire Judy LaMarsh. But I think Pearson will be remembered as a good Prime Minister. Remember he was Prime Minister under difficult conditions. He never had a majority and he had to use his great diplomatic skills to keep the House working – to make concessions and get concessions. You could almost say it was a form of blackmail government, but it worked.

History shows that he accomplished a lot of things. It was

Pearson who gave us a made in Canada flag. He developed and
expanded the health insurance programs and a lot of the other
social services. And he increased the federal contribution to
higher education – constitutionally a provincial responsibility –
to 50 percent. Actually, in some cases we ended up paying more
than a hundred percent. For instance, one time after Trudeau
became Prime Minister we paid 113 percent of the cost of post-
secondary education in New Brunswick (which meant that they
were paving parking lots and roads with some of the money
they'd claimed). But we made it possible for many more Canadians to have a higher education than would ever have been
possible if we'd left it up to provinces. Trudeau continued this:
we went from $26 million in 1963-64 to $7.4 billion in 1983-84.

Pearson saw what was happening in Quebec and he was the
first one to push bilingualism, even though he wasn't bilingual
himself, because he recognized the importance of Canada staying together. He was the one who recruited Marchand, Pelletier
and Trudeau in the first place.

So all things considered, he did a pretty good job. But I will
always remember what Senator David Croll said about him that
time I've described in caucus: "Mike, you're not enough of an
s.o.b. to be Prime Minister." If he'd been tougher, he might
have been an even better one.

My father-in-law wasn't too happy that I was supporting
Trudeau. He asked me why I wasn't supporting Winters and I
replied, "That Englishman?" And Grandpa Pollinger said,
"That's no Englishman, that's a German – Winters is a German
name." I thought he was wrong but I was curious to find out, so
I went to Bob Winters before the convention and asked him
about his ancestry. "Four generations German from Lunen-
burg, Nova Scotia, that never crossed bloodlines once," he said
proudly. Then I told him what my father-in-law had said and we
had a good laugh about it. That was the last good laugh we had.

Actually, I was scared to death that Winters was going to
win. He had some funny ideas. When he was trade minister I
used to fight with him all the time about free trade. He was all
in favour and I was all against. I thought he was going to destroy the greenhouse industry and the dairy industry and the

beef industry and the poultry industry all in the name of freer trade. If Winters had had his way, he would have destroyed much of Canadian agriculture. The odd thing was he had a lot of farmers supporting him, but he never spoke during the campaign about this pet idea of his. Which I don't think was very honest. I was amazed he wouldn't tell the farmers, but I made sure as many of them as I could corner knew, and I think I turned quite a few of them away from Winters and toward Trudeau. But leaders often don't reveal their ideas, their deep-down philosophies. And maybe if you're an open book, people don't like it. Certainly Trudeau was a very private person and in many areas you didn't know what he was thinking.

People forget how close we came back in 1968 to having a secret free trader as Prime Minister. Second time unlucky, I guess. Brian Mulroney sure never told us he was going to try to get all cosy with Washington and go after free trade with the Americans. It would have cost him votes. Canadians have never been free traders; they've always believed that their little country needs to protect itself from an elephant like the United States. But the current Liberal Party seems to have forgotten this in the current debate and they can't seem to make up their minds where they stand. The only thing they can agree on is that they don't like the Tory government, and that's not much to convince the Canadian people to vote for them in the next election. If I were still Minister of Agriculture, I'd certainly be making some noise. I'd be telling the Canadian people just how crazy and dangerous an idea free trade is. It's an idea that's popular with big businessmen whose industries won't be affected and with fancy economists, but it will hurt ordinary people.

When I hear the free traders talk about how they are going to create all these jobs and help the Canadian economy, I'm reminded of a story. It's about an old man who had a billy goat. One morning the man told his wife that he was going to market to trade the billy goat. He was gone all day long and didn't come back till late that night. And he still had the billy goat with him. So his wife said, "Well, you no account fellow, where have you been all this time and nothing to show for it? You've been gone all day and you've still got that stinking old billy goat."

"Now listen here, Martha," he says, "I was very busy all day." And she says, "What do you mean?" "Well, I traded that goat for a bicycle and I traded that bicycle for a wheelbarrow and I traded that wheelbarrow for a forge and anvil, and I traded that forge and anvil for a pig, and then I traded that pig for a calf, and then I traded that calf for a sulky, and then I traded that sulky for the goat." So she looked at him for a few minutes after he'd finished, looked at him as if he was crazy, and then she said, "Like I said, you just wasted all day long." And he replied, "But Martha, you don't understand. Look at the spell of business I did."

Those free trade negotiators are looking to do a spell of business. But when they're done, I expect we'll be left holding the stinking billy goat. This so-called free trade they say they're after is the most medieval horse-trading system imaginable. The free trade economists are all in love with the "free market" and with their holy commandment, the "law of supply and demand." In my books the law of supply and demand simply means that the biggest dog gets the biggest bite. It's one of the most vicious systems in the world and it's one of the things that has destroyed agricultural production in the developing world.

If we got free trade in agriculture – which I very much doubt will ever happen – it would mean the end of the marketing boards which provide some price protection for farmers. It would mean the end of agriculture in Canada. People forget that the Americans have a system of government marketing agreements and marketing orders that in many instances are tougher than any marketing board that we have. These orders set quotas and prices and all sort of things. They were brought in by Franklin Roosevelt back in 1937. Nobody in Canada has ever made a study of them – and in a negotiation they're much harder to get rid of than marketing boards. If you ask any of the people who are going to do the negotiating for us you'll discover that they're completely ignorant of these marketing orders and how they work.

If you had free trade between Canada and the United States, that would be the end of our primary producers. The dairy industry would go and the poultry industry would go – that's eggs, broilers and chickens. You can't produce chickens in Canada as cheaply as you can in Alabama or Georgia. And the hog industry and the beef industry would be in trouble too because it costs a lot more in feed to raise meat in a cold climate than in a warm one. And the death of these industries would have a spinoff effect on the feed industries because it's beef and poultry and hogs that eat the feed and make the feed grain industry prosper. And a lot of our vegetables and fruits – and all our wine – they'd be finished, too, with the cheaper American produce crossing the border. So much for the primary producers. Agriculture in Ontario would be completely destroyed.

Then the whole food-processing industry would be pretty near annihilated – meat-packing, canning, freezing. There'd be no reason for the big multinationals to maintain plants in Canada because it's a lot cheaper for them to produce their goods in the sun belt and then ship them up here. In my riding, the big Heinz plant in Leamington would be gone in no time, and with it thousands of jobs. And Heinz would just be one of many plants right across the country.

If we get free trade in agriculture, Canada will just turn into a great big national park for the Yanks to come play in.

Fortunately, I don't believe the Americans will ever agree to free trade. For all their free-market rhetoric, all they've been doing in the past few years, as far as I can see, is moving in the other direction. They've been eating away at GATT, the General Agreement on Tariffs and Trade, since before I left the Department of Agriculture. For example, they recently put new tariffs on Canadian pork, which is contrary to GATT – not to mention their tariffs on lumber, on potatoes and on raspberries. Individually these may seem like little things, but they all add up. The point is you can never have fair trade when a nation of 25 million is doing business with a nation of 250 million. We'll never have enough clout.

When I was a backbencher I used to argue with Bob Winters about free trade but at the 1968 convention he didn't even whisper about the subject.

The last day of the 1968 leadership race was also the last time I spoke to him. We had two related conversations, and that was it. The first was early in the morning. Every day I'd sleep about four hours and be at the Ottawa Civic Centre by seven or seven-thirty. Most of us didn't drink a drop during the convention – otherwise we'd never have made it through. So, there I was meeting people coming in the doors and giving them the good word about Trudeau, and Bob Winters came in the door, I guess to do a little last-minute campaigning. He said, "Good morning, Gene." And I said, "And how are you today, Bob?" And he said gloomily, "Well, it will all be over in a little while." He was sure he didn't have a chance to win. And I said, "Who knows, Bob, anything can happen at a political convention." And he said, "You won't have to worry about me because after today you won't have to write me any more nasty letters." I used to write tough letters to him when he was industry minister.

The second time I bumped into him was when it had come down to just before the final ballot between him and Trudeau and Turner. If Turner had dropped out and gone over to Winters, Bob might well have won. It revealed something about Turner's character, the fact he stayed in. All you have to do is play back the convention film where Turner is standing there saying, "No deals, no deals," to see what I mean. He looks like a scared rabbit in a corner. A lot of people admired him for doing what he did. Politically he was probably wiser not to throw his support to either one – one way or the other he'd have been criticized – but he could have just dropped out and not gone to either camp. I never really knew why he stayed in unless it was just for his own ego.

Winters and I were both getting ready to line up and parade around the floor with our respective camps and his mood had changed completely. He smiled his Bay Street grin and he joked, "I just can't wait until you write me another nasty letter." He thought he was going to win for sure. And I said, "Look around you, Bob" – at that time the Trudeau signs were coming up everywhere in the audience just like spring flowers – "look around. Can't you see? You can't win today. We have won this convention. I won't ever have to write you another letter." He never spoke to me again.

It made me sad. I could never take politics that seriously. I didn't mind him being tough with me; I was tough with him. But he took his loss awful hard. And he died not very long after.

The result on the final ballot was Trudeau 1,203; Winters 954; and Turner 195. Of course none of us imagined then that Trudeau would be leader for sixteen years.

After the convention, Paul Martin decided not to run again and Trudeau appointed him to the Senate. I ribbed Paul mercilessly about his appointment because I knew he didn't like the Senate any more than I did – and his views were quite well known. I had fun teasing him – and I knew he didn't like it there much, either. He told me one time, "I just can't stand this place." After being such an active MP he said it was kind of like going to sleep. He probably would deny he said that today. But I have to hand it to him: when Trudeau appointed him High Commissioner to London he actually resigned from the Senate, gave up his seat in the comfy club. That surprised a lot of people. Paul wasn't the only one who'd resigned, but it made him a pretty rare bird.

The 1968 election was different from the previous three I'd fought. Both parties had a new leader: Bob Stanfield had been chosen by the Conservatives in 1967. And there was Trudeaumania. I found it much easier campaigning in 1968. Trudeau was new, he was an unknown subject and he wasn't making many promises. People voted for him as a person – the image he presented to people. And it's worth remembering that most of Pearson's ministers stayed on and fought the election with him, so he had a very strong team. Unlike Turner in 1984 he offered every defeated Liberal leadership candidate a position in the Cabinet and I believe the only one who didn't stay was Bob Winters, who was just too bitter.

Trudeau came to my new riding of Essex-Windsor in 1968. There'd been a redistribution and the old riding of Essex South was gone. The eastern half including Leamington had become part of the new riding of Essex-Kent and the western half where I lived had joined up with a chunk of the city of Windsor. So I had more constituents and more urban voters. My riding was a microcosm of the country even more than it had been before. So I saw Trudeaumania in action.

Everywhere he went there were crowds of people trying to see him and touch him. And right to the end of his career he could always draw a crowd. I never understood the intensity of the emotion connected with Trudeaumania – but it wasn't phoney. A lot of people treated him as if he was a messiah. But I don't think it ever went to his head. In fact, I would think it was just the opposite. He'd be wondering why and what was all the fuss about, saying to himself, "I don't deserve this."

When it was all over, I'd won Essex-Windsor by 5,308 votes – my biggest majority so far – and Trudeau had won the country. So Eugene from Rivière Canard left his farm and his wife and kids and headed up to Ottawa yet another time. Trudeau hadn't promised me a thing, but I hoped for better than I'd got from Mike Pearson.

6

Hired and Fired

After the 1968 election Trudeau asked me to be parliamentary secretary to Jack Davis, the new Minister of Fisheries (which soon became Fisheries and Forestry). He just called me up on the phone and told me. My first response was, "Did you ask Jack Davis?" I was surprised that Dr. Davis would want to have an uneducated farmer like me as his assistant, even though we'd been good friends since our breakfast club in the early sixties. So Trudeau told me that Davis was the one who'd put my name forward. Then I said, "What do you want me to do that for? Why not put me in Agriculture?" And Trudeau replied that he wanted me to learn all I could about fisheries and forestry because some day he would put fisheries and forestry and agriculture in a single portfolio – all these great natural resources together. That was his idea at the time and I thought it was a damn good one. But he never did do it. In fact he never even managed to give Agriculture back the Wheat Board, despite the promise that was made to me by Keith Davey just before the 1974 election. When I ran for the leadership in 1984, I put the same ideas forward about making the three renewable resources – fisheries, forestry, and agriculture one portfolio. I would have done it, too.

After I agreed to be parliamentary secretary to Jack Davis, people would come up to me and say, "How come you're working with Jack Davis? You two are so different." And I'd say, "Well, Trudeau was running down the list of his MPs and he said, 'We've got to put Gene Whelan some place.' So he went down the list and said, 'Ah, we'll put Whelan with Davis. Davis has got education enough for both of them.'" But the fact was we got along well and worked well together.

It's true that Jack was a very educated man, but he wasn't very much of a politician. When I say Jack Davis wasn't politically smart, I've got to admit he wasn't all that politically dumb either. His main problem was that he didn't know how to tell anyone, even caucus members, to go jump in the lake without them feeling as if a shark had just eaten them up. He was blunt and very no-nonsense. Just the facts. He was like Sergeant Friday, the detective on *Dragnet*, who'd say, "Just the facts, ma'am." Actually Jack wasn't always as polite as Friday was. When it came to doing anything with the public, Jack Davis lacked finesse. He had a brain to think up ideas and a hell of a job in selling them. But he certainly knew his portfolio and he was good to work for because he made sure I knew it too.

I found him a very decent person and a very honest person. He didn't take himself too seriously, even though many of the civil servants treated him special. Whenever someone would call him Dr. Davis he'd take them aside later and say, "It's either Mr. Minister, Mr. Davis or Jack, but not Dr." He would never let them call him Dr. Davis.

One day in his office I asked him, "Jack, what does a Ph.D. stand for? What does it mean?" He was a very unassuming man with simple tastes; we always rode economy class, for example, and he never liked pictures on his walls. So he pointed to this bare wall and to the hole where a picture hook had been. And he said, "See that little nail hole where a picture used to hang? Well the whole wall is Chemical Engineering and a Ph.D. is that teenie little hole in the wall. It's only a little speck." Then he told me, "In order to get that degree all you have to do is know how to read and have a decent memory and be able write down what you remember. It doesn't mean you know a thing about practicality." Ever since then I've had a very exact understanding of the meaning of a Ph.D.

Davis used to take me to into all the departmental meetings and I'd go with him to all the Cabinet committee meetings – and he'd always give me all his briefing material. At the time, this behaviour was very unusual, although it is done more today. I've always thought that one of the reasons Jean Chrétien thinks so highly of Mitchell Sharp is that Sharp gave him so much responsibility when he was Minister of Finance and Chrétien was his parliamentary secretary. Jack Davis once told me, "You know as much about this department as I do." And I did. The problem was that at that time it didn't matter how much you knew, you didn't have a chance to show it because the parliamentary secretaries weren't even allowed to answer questions during question period in the House of Commons when their minister was absent. Donald Macdonald was Government House Leader at the time and he enforced the rule with an iron hand.

Macdonald was a bullheaded Scotsman – that's the best way I can describe him – and he was often impatient even with his own members. I can remember during the time he was a minister and I was only a lowly parliamentary secretary I'd sometimes come sit beside him in the House because I wanted to ask him a question. This was a normal routine for backbenchers who wanted a word with a busy minister. Don would be working on his briefing books, as most ministers did during long debates, but he wouldn't have the time for you. He'd be very rude and say, "Look, I'm busy and I don't have time to talk." What made me madder was that when an Opposition member came over, he'd put down the book and talk away.

He was a strong minister, however. When he was Minister of Finance after Turner resigned I saw him at his bullheaded best. I don't remember him giving in on any issue in Cabinet: he wouldn't budge even if it was suggested by the Prime Minister. And he had a temper. When he was crossed, he'd just fly off the handle and get very furious. But he probably would have made a pretty good Prime Minister because he was tough enough for the job. He'd have offended a lot of people, but then it's not uncommon for Prime Ministers to offend people.

Anyway, under Don Macdonald, we parliamentary secretaries were simply supposed to take down the questions in the House and refer them to our minister. This was true even when we'd received prior notice and had an answer all prepared, which was most often the case. Jack Davis complained to me about this: "You're wasting the House's time, you're wasting my time, and you're wasting your time," he told me. Finally he got so fed up that he said, "The next time somebody asks you a question in the House, you give him the answer. And if the House Leader says anything to you, you tell him to come and see me."

The questions that came up were from John Lundrigan, a Tory from Newfoundland. (I knew Lundrigan pretty well – he was a good poker player but he had a rough temper especially when he was losing.) Lundrigan had given me notice in advance, so I was well prepared, and when he got up in the House to ask his two questions, I just stood up from my seat and I answered them, bang, bang. I slaughtered him with my answers.

Well, the backbenchers on our side of the House all cheered because I'd struck a blow for them. And even some of the Conservatives cheered over on the other side. It was the first time a parliamentary secretary had ever answered a question. Then Lundrigan got up and asked a supplementary question and I hit him a second body blow and knocked him down to his knees again. The crowd in the House just went wild, applauding and laughing. But that wasn't the end of it.

After the tumult died down, George Hees rose and asked the Prime Minister a question – and Trudeau said he was very sorry but he didn't have the answer. So George shot back, "Well, why don't you let Gene answer the question – he seems to have the answers." At this, Trudeau made a step toward my seat and I made a step for his seat and the House just broke down. Even the people in the gallery applauded.

That incident changed the whole system for parliamentary secretaries, who had never before been permitted to answer questions. Trudeau told Macdonald to allow it in future, although it was still done at the discretion of the minister. Some of the secretaries don't do their homework and you can't trust them to answer.

Parliamentary secretaries are in a funny position – they're neither backbenchers nor ministers, neither one thing nor the other. And since it's seen as a stepping stone to Cabinet I guess some ministers are a bit afraid of these guys who are breathing down their necks, wanting to know everything about the department.

One change Trudeau made was that he told us all quite plainly in 1968 that we would be in for only two years: all the parliamentary secretaries would be changed after two years so that more backbenchers would have the experience. No one believed him, of course. We thought we'd either stay where we were or get promoted to Cabinet.

I couldn't believe how timid the backbenchers became under Trudeau and I said so more than once. Maybe they were still a bit mesmerized by Trudeaumania, but he seemed to cast a spell over the caucus: they became like little lambs. I recently came across a letter I wrote in February 1970 to Senator Richard Stanbury, the Liberal Party president. Dick knew I was discontented with the way things were going halfway through the first Trudeau mandate and he'd been trying to calm me down. In the letter I was brutally frank. I said: "I have never, since being a Liberal member of parliament, seen such a gutless caucus as we have at the present time and in general, with some exceptions, I have never seen a Cabinet which seems to care so little about the Members' representations." Dick wrote me a nice soothing reply and nothing changed. Since nobody seemed to be listening, I concentrated my forces on being the best parliamentary secretary I could be.

I have to hand it to Jack Davis. He got me to do more in that job than any minister I've known, including myself. (I never gave my secretaries as much responsibility as Davis gave me because I've never had one as capable as Davis had!) One of the great things about my two years working with Jack at Fisheries and Forestry was the opportunity to travel. Sometimes I'd travel with the minister and sometimes by myself on behalf of the minister. Either way, I was getting to see the country and getting to know places and people and problems that were completely new to me. I'd gotten to know Ontario pretty well, but in most of Canada I was a stranger. This was another way in which Jack Davis was exceptional. He really trusted me to represent him in any part of the country.

Jack may have been from British Columbia, but that didn't mean he kept B.C. for himself. In fact, some of my most vivid memories of that period are from my trips to the West Coast. In my two years with Davis I must have seen more of B.C. than do most British Columbians, including their own elected politicians. I visited almost every outport along the mainland coast and along the shore of Vancouver Island, every spawning ground, every fisherman's co-op, every fish hatchery and every government research station. I visited them by car or float plane or fishing boat. I used to be in British Columbia pretty near every two weeks.

We were changing the licensing program for B.C. salmon fishing and the main reason I was there was to explain the changes to the fishermen, answer any questions, and calm them down if they were mad. I've always believed in going to the people before they come marching to you.

On one occasion I flew by float plane to a small fishing port on the Vancouver Island – Sointula. I was told beforehand that it was a place that had been settled almost entirely by Finnish people and I was told to expect to see one of the best little fishing fleets on the coast, since the Finnish are renowned for their neatness and efficiency. When our plane landed it was low tide and I had to walk up a long flight of steps to the top of the wharf where I was met by this elderly man. To start a conversation I said, "I understand this area is predominantly Finnish. Are you Finnish?" He looked at me for a second and then he replied in a lovely French accent: "Yes, I'm finished. My name is Dupuis and I'm seventy-three."

On my trips to British Columbia I got a completely different impression of native people from the one I'd had living in my ignorance back East. I had Indian blood but I didn't know any Indians because there were none left in my riding by the time I was born. But the fisheries department had a special program to help native fishermen in B.C., so I met with native people on a number of occasions. I discovered that when they are given the wherewithal to make it economically they are as successful as any of us.

There's always a lot of talk about how Westerners feel alienated, and it's true that they start out with a prejudice against people from the East – even all the ones who've moved out there from Ontario, Quebec and the Atlantic region. But I never found it to be a real problem, not when I met people up close. A lot of it was the media: they had put it into peoples' heads that those guys on the other side of the mountains – those people in Toronto and Ottawa – were bad people. The press still does this in the West. Sometimes when I'd read a paper out there I'd wonder, "Gee, what country am I in here?" But I soon discovered that the wishes and wants of the ordinary person there weren't much different from anybody else's. That's true wherever you go in the world, for that matter. They want to make a decent living and have some form of security in life. It reminds me of that old saying: "Shoes on the baby and bread on the table." That was all these people wanted.

I met W.A.C. Bennett a few times during this time and I always liked him, even though we were quite far apart politically. Wacky Bennett was like so many of them, a disgruntled Easterner (from New Brunswick) who went West and always resented federal authority. But I think he did a lot to build British Columbia under tough conditions. And he was a good politician. He listened to the people. He was very ordinary when you met him: he didn't put on the dog. I particularly admired the way he handled the press – especially Allan Fotheringham, who was younger then but just as nasty. Bennett knew who he was perfectly well, but he always pretended at press conferences that he never knew Fotheringham's name. It was his way of putting him down. When Fotheringham wanted to ask a question, Bennett would always say, "Now who are you and who do you represent?" That used to just burn Fotheringham up and he used to write scathing articles about Bennett. Didn't prevent him from getting re-elected more than once, though.

At one point I travelled around British Columbia with the

members of the House fisheries committee, meeting people involved in the industry. At every meeting in every little town and city I went to I used to ask the people, "Who do you feel you're closer to, Ottawa or Victoria?" And every time, they said they felt closer to Ottawa, that Ottawa was more responsive, that we'd done more to save the spawning grounds and help the fishery. This amazed most members of the committee, especially the Western ones. I never had any problems in B.C., then or later. And I used to joke with the people I met, "You've got a beautiful province and you'd have so much more room if you could just iron out all the wrinkles."

As with many of the people I've worked with in public life, Jack Davis and I were fighting friends. We often disagreed, even though we were close, and occasionally he took my advice. Once we had a problem in the Maritimes. We found out that the fish-processing plants in Nova Scotia sent people to spy on the fishing boats coming in – they'd go down to the harbour with binoculars and telescopes. We realized what they were doing. They were looking to see if the ships coming in were low in the water – that meant they'd made a good catch. If the ships were loaded to the gunwhales, they'd rush to the phone and tell the boss to lower the price. Whenever the fishermen caught a lot of fish they couldn't get a decent price, so we knew we had a problem.

Jack Davis asked me what I thought he should do and I said, "Let's use the Fisheries Prices Support Board. We'll set a minimum price and if the fish plants won't meet it we'll buy it ourselves and then the fish plants will have to buy it from us because we will have stabilized a floor price." This wasn't exactly a marketing board, but it was similar in principle. I'd had lots of experience with marketing boards when I was farming and I knew how well they worked.

Jack went along with this idea and the system worked well because there was a large surplus of both fish-processing and cold-storage capacity at the time – and we never lost a penny on it, either. I never understood why they discontinued the use of the Fisheries Prices Support Board in this way.

While I worked with Davis we also started the Canadian Salt-fish Corporation and the Freshwater Fish Marketing Corporation

—both of them crown corporations operating on a principle similar to a marketing board. So these were my first experiences of setting up something like a marketing board, but they certainly wouldn't be the last. When I became agriculture minister, I was accused of all sorts of terrible things—of being a communist and so on—for wanting to put in more marketing boards, for wanting to protect the farmer and the fisherman from the crazy variations of price in a free market.

It's kind of surprising that Davis went along with the idea of supporting the price of fish in the Maritimes. It went against his economic philosophy and it shows perhaps that when it comes to a choice between good politics and bad economics, politics has a tendency to come out on top. Jack had some of the same funny ideas as Bob Winters about free trade. That was one of the things we'd argue about. Whenever he'd get on his professor's high horse I'd tell him I was going to establish a Hong Kong fishing boat just outside the twelve-mile limit off the coast of B.C.—a big factory ship—and pay the workers a buck an hour to process salmon and then ship it to B.C. This would give him and his constituents a first-hand experience of free trade. He and I both knew that would have been the end of the B.C. salmon-fishing plants, where the workers are among the highest paid fish-processing workers in the world.

Of course, not all my time between 1968 and 1970 was spent working with Jack Davis. I also had to look after my riding and make some noise in the peaceful Trudeau caucus. And I went on what was only my second trip outside North America as a member of parliament—to Lima, Peru. The first trip had been back in 1963 when I'd gone to Yugoslavia to a meeting of world parliamentarians. These trips were supposed to be a fair reward for being a good boy, which is why I didn't go on so many of them when I was a backbencher. I generally didn't get along that well with the Whip. When I went to Yugoslavia in 1963 the Whip was Joe Habel from Cochrane and in 1968 it was Jimmy Walker from Toronto. I would never beg them for trips like a lot of the guys did. And I wouldn't be good in caucus just so I could go away. But I'd been active in the world parliamentarians association since I was first elected to Parliament.

Back in 1963, someone had told Pearson that my wife was from Yugoslavia, so he made sure I went; it was her first time back to her grandparents' home in Filipovo. There was almost nothing left of what she remembered as a girl before the war. The town had had many German-speaking families but they were all gone – it was all Serbs and Slovaks – and her grandfather's house was different and trees that she remembered had been cut down. But we met President Tito and his wife at a big reception in Belgrade when we were going through the receiving line. When we got to Mrs. Tito I said to her, "My wife comes from Yugoslavia." And she immediately asked, "What year? When did you leave?" because if she left after the war that might have meant Liz was a Nazi. And my wife said, "I left in 1937." And Mrs. Tito seemed reassured. But Liz said to me afterwards, "You're just trying to get rid of me. You figured that Tito and his wife would keep me here as an illegal emigrant."

The Peru trip in 1968 was scheduled for the day after I was appointed parliamentary secretary so I asked Jack Davis if I should go and he said, "Yes, as long as you visit the fish plants when you're there." So Peru was a double learning experience for me. When I wasn't meeting with the international parliamentarians I was visting the fish meal plants and the harbours – and seeing the terrible conditions the people lived under.

When President Belaúnde opened the conference I couldn't believe all the soldiers and military hardware. I'd never seen anything like it – except maybe on television. There were tanks and military vehicles and soldiers on foot and on horseback – all fully armed. During this display I commented to some of the other members of the Canadian delegation, "The president of this country is a prisoner, a prisoner of his own military." They all told me I was crazy, but it turned out to be more true than I had guessed.

I simply couldn't get over the poverty in Peru, both in the city and in the country. I had never seen beggars in the streets before, and in the city dumps, when the big trucks came to unload garbage, literally hundreds of people would tear the stuff apart looking for food. And the houses they lived in weren't houses at all. Outside the city on sand dunes, the poor people had built little adobe huts. It would be an exaggeration to call them houses – or even shacks. At the time there were around 500,000 people living in these little huts along the coast. If it rained, the sand adobe bricks would have just washed away. It never rained – it was a desert – yet the people lived in fear of rain. It was a tragedy. And these were mostly people from the rural areas who'd come to the city hoping for a better way of life. I was also amazed to discover that the schools in Lima ran day and night because there weren't enough of them to handle all the kids. I'd never seen anything like that before either. If it weren't for the missionaries, many Peruvians – even today – wouldn't be getting an education at all.

The contrast between rich and poor made me sick. One night I went to a reception at a Peruvian senator's house. To get there we rode down this terrible street, full of poverty, but when we opened the gate in the wall and went into his house, it was like going into another world – a huge old villa with a courtyard garden and servants and candlelight. At the reception I got talking to the wife of the Israeli ambassador – she'd been there for a while and she asked me how I liked Peru. "Well," I said, "it seems okay, but I wouldn't want to live here. I couldn't live here because of the poverty. I would find it too depressing." "But you don't understand," she said. She was insinuating that the poor people were happy, that they didn't know any better. And I said, "No, I do understand. It's you who doesn't understand if you think these people are happy living the way they are." I found it hard to believe she would say that. I could remember as a kid seeing richer kids who had good clothes and good shoes and knowing I wanted to have some of that someday. Those poor Peruvians had dreams just like I did – but people like that Israeli woman don't want to believe it. It would make them too uncomfortable.

Later I discovered that her attitude is quite common among North Americans and Europeans (in which I include Israelis) who are living in poor countries. Fifteen years later – in 1983 – I had a similar conversation with a retired Canadian banker living in Mexico. He had even taken out Mexican citizenship. When he asked me how I liked the country – at this point I'd been visiting Mexico on and off since 1972 – I said, "I like the Mexican people very well, but I could never live here." And I described the poverty I'd seen, the conditions in which people lived – ten people in a small room, no electricity, no plumbing, nothing. And he said, "But they're happy." He had never lived poor, and I told him so.

The trip to Peru was the first time I became aware – in a direct, immediate way – of the seriousness of the problem of world poverty. You might say this visit planted a seed that was to take root and mature much later when as agriculture minister I fought to persuade Canada and other countries to do something about the developing famine crisis in Africa. But back in 1968 it just seemed like an isolated horrible thing and something I was glad to get away from.

The day we left Lima, President Belaúnde left too. The military staged a coup and a military government took over. They had waited until the representatives of the world's democracies flew away, because it wouldn't have looked too good if they'd made their move while we were all singing hymns to freedom and the democratic way of life.

In 1970 Trudeau kept his word and he replaced all the parliamentary secretaries – a practice he continued right up to the end. I wasn't too hurt, because he'd said he'd do it. What hurt was how the press described it. Some of the parliamentary secretaries returned to the backbenches and some were promoted to minister. My Windsor neighbour Herb Gray, who'd been parliamentary secretary to the Minister of Finance, was made Minister without Portfolio. That day, the headline in the *Windsor Star* read: "Gray Promoted, Whelan Fired." I thought that was pretty mean, but by then the *Star* had turned on me. It had been bought by Southam and since then the editorial board has always had it in for me. I'll never understand why.

This time the press hit me when I was down. I'd wanted a promotion and naturally I was disappointed when it didn't come. But I'd been disappointed before. So when the reporters from Windsor and other places came and asked me how I felt, I said, "Look, I've been elected to one of the highest elected positions in the land. I've worked hard and I've had fun being a parliamentary secretary for two years. Now it's someone else's turn."

Afterwards, some who'd suffered my fate got completely demoralized and lost their seats or didn't run in the next election. They
gave up. And I must admit I came pretty close myself. It didn't
help at all that people kept telling me what a good job I was
doing. Just before I stopped as parliamentary secretary, Charles
Lynch had written that I was a member of Trudeau's "Second
Cabinet." It was a nice compliment, but that was about it.

I have to give Trudeau credit for improving the lot of the parliamentary secretary. He may have limited the term to two
years, but he gave them more to do. Under Pearson, parliamentary secretaries really didn't have much authority, whereas
Trudeau's were generally better informed and more involved
with the running of their departments. Of course, some parliamentary secretaries liked the name more than the job. But if you
wanted the responsibility you were likely to get it under Trudeau.

In my view, parliamentary secretaries should have more
power still. I think their title should be changed to associate
minister and they should have the status of deputy minister.
They should be the second-in-command of their department.
Then you wouldn't get them taking the job for the name only and
you'd have stronger political control of the bureaucracy. I also
believe that parliamentary secretaries should be appointed by
the minister, not by the Prime Minister, though perhaps subject
to the Prime Minister's approval or veto.

The way the press behaved when I was fired in 1970 makes me
remember the way I felt when I first walked into the House of
Commons. I looked at this huge hall with all those reporters
looking down on us and I thought, "What the hell are those
people doing up there?" It put me in mind of an arena full of animals with the spectators above it all, laughing and jeering. I
believe it definitely has an effect on the way the press sees things.

Maurice Jefferies of the *Windsor Star* – who always treated me
fairly – told me once what it was like. He said, "Gene, I really
have to watch myself, sitting up there. We look down on you all
the time and pretty soon we start saying to each other, "Now,
aren't they a dumb bunch? And we start to feel superior. And
then we start writing that way." I think this is a terrible thing.

If I could I'd knock out the back wall of the House and put the press on the same level as the elected representatives of the people.

On the whole the press treated me pretty fairly, but I still believe they have too much power and often don't know what they're talking about. Looking back over my twenty-two years in Ottawa, I'd say that the Press Gallery began to change drastically after about 1974. Part of it was the arrival of television in a big way in the late 1970s. But it also has to do with the training of reporters. When I first arrived, the majority of press people I dealt with had started out as copy boys and received their education on the job. Now we're getting people out of university journalism programs. And who's teaching them? Often it's the people who couldn't make it as reporters on their own.

The other problem is that in the last ten years there have been fewer independent newpapers. Thomson and Southam now own most of the major papers in the country and most of the weeklies, too. I'm really scared about this attitude of bigness in the media. There's almost none of the personal touch left that there was when a family or small group owned the daily newspaper and the weekly. The same thing is happening with radio stations and television stations. We're fortunate in Amherstburg that our weekly paper, the *Amherstburg Echo,* is still independent. That's only because John Marsh wouldn't sell out to Thomson, only to someone who promised to keep it independent.

Of the Press Gallery reporters I knew, I think Douglas Fisher was the fairest and the most knowledgeable. Remember he'd been elected to the House of Commons for the C C F back in 1957 when he knocked off C.D. Howe, and he'd been a good member before he quit—he was still an M P when I was elected to the House. Doug can be tough, but I always read his column because it's usually pretty accurate; just once in a while he'd get nasty and I'd have to call him up and tell him what I thought.

But most of the press were pretty mean to me in 1970 and I didn't feel any better when I looked at Bud Olson, the man who was then Minister of Agriculture. He was a former Socred from Alberta who'd come over to our side, so I felt bad when he was given the job, even though I knew we needed ministers from the

West. At least he was an experienced member who'd cut his teeth in the House of Commons. Bud was a nice enough man, but as minister I thought he did some kooky things. I used to fight with him every week in caucus about what he was trying to do. I'd just tear right into him. But he didn't change his ways. By 1972 I had completely lost patience and was writing so many letters to the Prime Minister and to Bud Olson to complain that it's a wonder Trudeau ever made me agriculture minister at all. I pointed out that under Olson farm incomes had gone down and cheap imports were hurting Eastern farmers. I think I must have written Olson more letters than all the other rural MPs put together. But Trudeau wouldn't fire him, particularly not with another election in the works.

In 1970 it took me a while to get back into the role of back-bencher. I didn't have much stomach for the old fights in caucus, the old crusades for my constituents. While I was adjusting, however, momentous events were taking place. Probably one of the most controversial things Trudeau did was bringing in the War Measures Act after Pierre Laporte was kidnapped in October 1970. I supported him then and the vast majority of my constituents did, too. I didn't know the details beyond what was reported to us every week in caucus and perhaps if I had been in Cabinet I might have thought differently. But I doubt it. It's very easy to be critical in retrospect, but you certainly didn't hear much from the FLQ after that. I think terrorists have to be dealt with firmly.

The soldiers and the tanks in the streets reminded me a little bit of Peru in 1968. Some Cabinet ministers, including several from Quebec, had guards. But the soldiers handled it well. They built a tremendous amount of respect in the neighbourhoods where they were. Generally they had a bunch of little kids follow-ing them around and talking to them. They spent most of their time being diplomats – there was nothing else to do – and indeed they were some of the best diplomats for the government's pol-icy. (That's why I think it's wrong now that they're training the RCMP to control terrorists. It should be the military.)

The only party to oppose the imposition of the War Measures Act was the NDP. And I remember that Tommy Douglas gave a

speech opposing the suspension of civil liberties. I didn't agree
with him, but I admired his courage and his eloquence. He was
a little man, but he had a loud voice and he was quick on the
trigger – he'd been a preacher before. Despite our political differences, he was one of the politicians I most admired during my
years in Ottawa.

He had a great rapport with the people – they could always
understand what he was saying. He respected the people and
they respected him. He was a great humanitarian and not such
a rabid socialist as some people might think. Many of the programs he fought for, such as medicare, had been proposed by
Wilfrid Laurier's Liberals back around the turn of the century.
But Tommy's greatest strength was his ability to communicate
with feeling and with humour. He was sincere and he had a way
of saying things so that you remembered them.

When I knew him, they used to tell a story about when he was
running for premier of Saskatchewan against a Liberal named
Walter Tucker. Tucker was a big man and at one debate he said,
"Tom's so small, in one bite I could swallow him," and everybody
laughed because he just towered over Tommy. He was twice his
size. When Tommy got up to speak he said, "Walter, if you did
that and swallowed me, you'd be one of mankind's strangest
oddities. You'd have more brains in your belly than you've got
in your head." The audience just roared. I've heard that story
told many times.

Tommy and I used to send little notes to each other in the
House. We had a connection through my brother who'd been
in his CCF government in Saskatchewan, but I think he was
especially nice to me because he knew I was a real Liberal and
probably more to the left than he was on certain things. I used
to tease him about this. I'd say that he was more conservative
than I was: "The NDP has stuck with the same philosophy for
thirty years and you haven't changed it a bit. You're too rigid.
That's why I could never join your party." He'd just laugh.

During 1971 I came around slowly. By November of that year
I was more my old self when Trudeau's finance minister, Edgar
Benson, handed me my issue on a silver platter. He was an
accountant from Kingston, Ontario, and always seemed better

off than the rest of us. He brought in a budget that included a new tax on credit unions – and I went on the warpath.

The bureaucrats in the finance department had come up with this bright idea for an income tax change that would hurt both co-ops and credit unions. I guess the bureaucrats thought of co-ops and credit unions as big, rich organizations – fat cats. They didn't understand the strength of the co-operative movement and the credit union movement – the thousands upon thousands of Canadians, little people, who'd be affected by the change. This was something I absolutely had to stop.

First I wrote one of my patented letters to the minister, and when that didn't work I went after Benson in the caucus. I told him that this new tax had been thought up by experts who knew nothing about farming, co-ops, credit unions, or taxation. And I told him, "If you don't withdraw this measure, I'm going to raise a storm in the House." I had many allies on both sides in the Commons and I knew I could get quite a little tempest going. But Benson believed his bureaucrats before he believed me – maybe he didn't think I'd follow through.

So I made a speech in the House. I threatened to resign my seat over the issue. I attacked Benson for listening to civil servants instead of MPs. And I said, "I realize it is more difficult to get rid of a civil servant than a backbencher, because top civil servants are here forever and backbenchers come and go like the wind. But if we pass this legislation in its present form, when this backbencher goes, he will go in the damndest storm you ever saw." Thanks to my speech and my support in the House, Benson took the tax out of his budget. And they've never tried to reintroduce it since.

This episode didn't affect my friendship with Benson. We'd been friends since the first time I met him in the House of Commons. He was the type of politician who could lose a fight and not hold a grudge. Ed just said, "You fought a fair fight and you won your battle." I always admired him for that.

To win that battle was satisfying, all right, but I was still fed up with politics. After my attacks on Olson and my fight with Benson, I figured I was probably further than ever from becoming Minister of Agriculture. In early 1972, before the election had been called, I went to see Trudeau and told him I was quitting politics. I'd been a member for ten years and I said to him, "I think I'm just going to throw in the towel. My three daughters are still young and I haven't spent much time with them. My wife's raising them all by herself and my farm is going to hell. I'm going home." But Trudeau wouldn't let me leave so easily. He said, "Gene, we know that you can win your riding and we're going to need you in the next election." Then he gave me a big speech about Canada, what he thought of it and how much it meant to him, and how I had a little bit of duty, if not to him, then to Canada. He could have been giving the same speech my father used to give to my older brothers about public service and all that. I have no doubt that he was sincere. So I went home and talked to Liz. I know she was looking forward to seeing me out of politics so that she could lead some kind of normal life, but she swallowed her own desires and said, "Well, you can run once again."

I didn't, however, much fancy the idea of spending the rest of my life as a backbencher. I'd done about as much as a backbencher could. If you check the records of the House of Commons you'll see that not many members stay as long as I did without becoming ministers. They just quit and go home, or get defeated. Of course, some of them are happy being private members and don't want any more. They love the idea of being a House of Commons man. I remember one day I'd been raising a ruckus in caucus about how badly the Cabinet ministers were behaving and Senator Bill Benedickson came up to me in the lobby – I'd been really rough that day in caucus and I was talking to someone – and Bill put his arm around my shoulder and said, "Stick around Gene. Best damn club you ever belonged to." Many people felt that way.

While I was a backbencher I was on five committees and all that time I only had one secretary, no other staff. Not even an electric typewriter. Under Trudeau backbenchers had more money, more staff and bigger offices, so it's a paradox that they became more like mice than under Pearson, although it's true they do have less power when the government has a majority. If the currently proposed reforms of the House get passed they will improve the lot of backbenchers – at least temporarily – and make the ministers' lives much more miserable, because backbenchers will have some authority to cut off ministers' funds. I think it could be a good system. It wouldn't have bothered me that much when I was agriculture minister. I'd rather fight with backbenchers than bureaucrats any day.

Shortly before the election was called, I gave one of my rare speeches in the House. Of the speeches I made as a backbencher, it maybe got me the most publicity. The boys up in the Press Gallery loved it. They always used to enjoy it when I spoke because of my unusual way of saying things. I was always entertaining and I also had a reputation for making up words and using the English language – how shall we say? – creatively. They called my language Whelanese and my invented words Whelanisms, which I suppose was in part a compliment and in part to make fun of my lack of education. But most of the ordinary people I talked to, who saw me on television or heard me on the radio or giving a speech in person, said I was easier to understand than most politicians. Later I used to joke sometimes that I couldn't speak either official language.

Of course *Hansard* cleaned up all my words and made my speeches more grammatical, so if you go back now and read what I said in the House you can only get a flavour of it – just a taste. You had to be there. Anyway, on this particular occasion – just before the 1972 election – I rose to speak on a subject of great interest to me: the health of the Canadian people.

I'd seen some statistics comparing the average health of Canadians with the average health of people in one of the Scandinavian countries where the birth rate and the population were going down. And in the survey they'd found out that this drop was apparently due to the bad diet those people were eating – not enough roughage and that sort of thing. They were becoming impotent. So I said that this was clearly a serious problem because as population declines so does the output of a nation. Then I told the House that I'd done a little survey on my own and I'd found out that Canadians eat better and love more.

The press picked that up and Roschkov drew a beautiful cartoon in the *Windsor Star* of me as "King Gene the Eighth" with the caption "Eat Better, Love More." It kind of became my slogan. And in the 1972 election I had little buttons printed up that said, "Eat Better, Love More, Vote Whelan." They became a collectors' item.

So I ran in seventy-two and I won. But Trudeau had still never promised me anything.

7

Batting Average .500

I suppose you could say I became agriculture minister almost by default. In the 1972 election we barely hung onto the government with 109 seats to the Tories' 107 – Trudeau was right that he'd needed me to stay on and hold my seat. I guess with such unduly high expectations of him in 1968, it was inevitable that the honeymoon would end. The bloom was off the rose in his lapel. There was disillusionment that the Just Society he'd promised had not come to pass. Certainly I think Trudeau was still learning to be a good politician in his first term. I suppose something similar has been happening to Brian Mulroney.

In the election most of the party's agricultural spokesmen had gone down to defeat – Bud Olson had been defeated in Alberta – and I was practically the only farmer left in the caucus. So that left cranky old Gene Whelan as just about the only logical choice for the Cabinet; after all I'd been fighting on behalf of farmers for ten years. But I wasn't taking anything for granted – I'd been passed by too many times. For all I knew, the pipsqueaks around the Prime Minister would find some brilliant reason to appoint someone else – some city lawyer who didn't know the front end of a cow from the back. I didn't waste any time or any sleep hoping and worrying. Besides, I had other things on my mind. There'd been so much rain that fall that the dykes fronting on Lake Erie were breaking and there was bad flooding in Kent and Essex County around Point Pelee and Pelee Island, so I was busy trying to get the government to arrange some kind of relief for those constituents of mine who'd been hard hit.

On the evening of November 25 – with the floods still raging – I was at the Roma Club in Leamington attending the annual banquet of the local vegetable growers. But I could hardly eat my dinner because I kept being called to the phone, which was at the bar and not far from the head table. It was either farmers or members of the press who wanted to know what we were going to do about the flooding. After I don't know how many calls, I got up to answer the phone one more time and I said to the bartender, "This is the last call. I don't want to interrupt my dinner any more." Then I picked up the phone and it was Trudeau. He said, "Gene, I'd like you to be my Minister of Agriculture." I guess I wasn't quite ready to believe him because I said right back, "Are you sure?" And he laughed and said, "Yes." And then he said, "You won't have any problem with me, Gene, as long as you remain honest." He didn't always give me what I wanted as minister, but he always kept that promise.

In the Prologue, I've talked about my apprehensions at finally having the agriculture job and how it felt to be putting my name in the Oath Book along with so many famous names in Canadian history. But there's one more piece of the story – and that has to do with Lester Pearson. Early in 1972, before I'd made it into the Cabinet, he'd been interviewed by Patrick Watson. In the interview Pearson had said that if he had it to do all over again, at least 50 percent of his Cabinet would have been real Liberals. So I wrote him a short note. In it I said, "I was always suspicious that a great portion were not Liberals but I couldn't figure out what they were. I was also wondering, when you put that city lawyer Joe Greene in the Cabinet in 1965 as Minister of Agriculture, if the statement you made meant that you wished you had put that radical from Essex South in the Cabinet instead."

Mike died not long after the 1972 election, but before he did he wrote me a short letter of congratulation. I don't remember the exact words, but he said something like, "I'm so happy for you. I know it has long been your wish to be agriculture minister and it has finally become a reality. I'm sure you'll do a good job." It still bothered him that he hadn't made me Minister of Agriculture back in 1965. I remember Mary Macdonald saying to me that it was as if Mike had wanted to live long enough to congratulate me.

We may have been a minority government, but I was determined to make my mark while I could – many people were predicting that our government would fall early and that Stanfield would win the next election hands down. There were certain things I wanted to do and certain things I succeeded in doing. When I look back now, I suppose people could say, "Well, he didn't live up to expectations. He didn't do as much as he could have." But on balance I believe I accomplished a lot. You can never do everything you want to and it's one thing to be sitting on the backbenches making noise and another to be on the hot seat.

Agriculture is a very complex portfolio, much more so than most people imagine. I'd say that few bureaucrats (outside Agriculture Canada) and fewer ministers understood agriculture – and even some of the deputy ministers I was assigned knew little or nothing about the subject. They were bureaucrats pure and simple. Trudeau was actually quite willing to admit that he knew nothing about agriculture. One time in 1981-82 he commissioned a study by Martin O'Connell, his former principal secretary and former Minister of Labour who'd been defeated in 1979, but Martin gave up after six or seven months. He later told me that he said to the PM "Agriculture is so complex I don't know how Gene does as good a job as he does."

You see, there are so many competing interests, not only between the various primary producers but between the primary producers and the middlemen – the wholesalers and the food processors – and between the producers and the consumers who are always complaining about higher prices. In agriculture it has long been true that the primary producers are the ones who suffer while the middlemen do just fine. When people complain about high food prices, they usually think it's the fault of inefficient farmers, which is not the case. In 1972 Canadian farmers were only earning about $2.80 out of every $8.00 that Canadians spent on food – and often that barely covered their costs. To show how bad it had gotten, in the previous ten years total Canadian food expenditures by consumers had gone up by $4.2 billion, but net farm income by only $738 million – so it was obvious to me that the position of the farmer was getting worse. This was confirmed when I looked at the figures for the average farmer's income (at least those who made enough to pay taxes). That figure was $5,989, by far the lowest of any professional group. As I saw it, my foremost job as agriculture minister was to see that farmers got enough money to keep them farming – or agriculture would eventually disappear.

My main strategy for attacking this problem was marketing boards or, in broader economic terms, what is called management of supply or supply management. When I became agriculture minister there were already more than a hundred marketing boards in Canada – 108 to be exact, mostly provincial – which is something that everyone forgot in the fuss over the boards I tried to set up. The only federally operated marketing boards in 1972 were the Wheat Board (1935) and The Canadian Dairy Commission (1967), both established by separate Acts of Parliament.

I've always considered it a great irony that provinces with a long history of Conservative governments have also had a long history of marketing boards. Take Ontario. Under Bill Davis there were some twenty-five marketing boards covering more than forty crops and other agricultural commodities, and some of them were forty years old. All the crops I grew on my own farm were under one Ontario marketing board or another. There are marketing boards in every province and the first federal board, the Wheat Board, was brought in by the Bennett Tories. So it often amused me – and occasionally made me angry – when I was accused of being a terrible socialist or communist for trying to establish more marketing boards at the federal level. The way people talked and the way the press carried on in 1972 and later, you would have thought we were ruining the country.

Marketing boards vary in practice but the principle is fairly simple. It's a system whereby the producers – in this case farmers – pool their product and decide, based on a cost-price formula, when and how much to produce and how much to sell and at what price. One point I want to stress here – because it usually isn't understood – is that a marketing board is something that farmers have democratic control over. They run it themselves; it is not forced on them. A marketing board for perishables makes the most sense: wheat you can store in a bin for years, but you just try to do it with a pound of butter or meat. To produce a surplus of perishable products and assume the market is going to take care of it is just utter economic nonsense and wasteful as hell. So a marketing board is an efficient way of protecting domestic producers and assuring that you'll always have a supply for domestic consumption. Otherwise you're subject to the whims and fancies of the international market.

Consumers are protected because the price-setting formula the marketing boards use is always open to public scrutiny. And the marketing boards are monitored by overseeing boards that make sure they stick to the rules. If banks were as closely scrutinized, they wouldn't get into so much trouble. With the Wheat Board a farmer can produce as much as he wants, but he can only sell what the board allots to him, his quota. But perishable items are under a production quota; the farmer signs a contract in the spring to sell so much per acre. So the marketing board becomes the middleman, but this time the middlemen are the farmers themselves. The effect is to even out the ups and downs in the supply curve – so that prices don't fluctuate widely – by controlling or managing supply. The main thing is that a marketing board guarantees the producers a fair price for their product and doesn't pay for a poor product and doesn't pay farmers not to produce.

The agriculture minister's involvement with a new marketing board should pretty well end once the enabling legislation is passed. But that wasn't easy in 1972 when I put through the legislation for the federal egg marketing board. We had a minority government and the bureaucrats were opposed. But I knew I had the support of the NDP, which held the balance of power in the House, and also some Conservatives from rural ridings, so I took my case straight to the Prime Minister. I explained to him how the board would work, why it was needed, and he said, "Fine, Gene, go ahead." Of course it wasn't long before some people were whispering in his ear that he had to get rid of this terrible thing called an egg marketing board – but he stood behind me after I explained what we were doing. I think history will show that Trudeau stood behind his Cabinet ministers more than any other Prime Minister in Canada's history. If something went wrong, King and Pearson would chop their heads off. And Diefenbaker, his problem was that he tried to run a one-man show – a bit like Brian Mulroney.

The egg marketing board legislation passed, no problem, and I was feeling pretty good until eggs started to go bad. The problem was a result of the fact that nationally there was overproduction – before the egg board farmers threw lots of eggs in the manure pile – and the new board didn't yet have proper control over production. So they put the surplus eggs in warehouses, some of which were designed for apple storage, not for eggs. Now, in apple storage the first ones put in at the back are the last ones out – and there's often no back door, especially in the older storage buildings. To make things worse, the buildings they were using to store the eggs didn't have proper ventilation or proper refrigeration. You can imagine what condition the first eggs were in when they finally came out last. We had a whole pile of rotten eggs.

When the press found out, they had a regular picnic. There was a big to-do in the House, and in the newspapers there were cartoons, editorials, letters to the editor. The CBC and the newspapers made a big thing of the fact that so many million eggs had spoiled, making it sound like an astronomical number – instead of using boxes or cartons or dozens. The press blew it up out of all proportion. There were editorials calling for my resignation and calls in the House from the Opposition benches. It was one of the worst experiences I went through during my whole tenure as minister – even some of my colleagues in the Cabinet were against me.

But Trudeau held firm and I fought back. I explained that the number of eggs spoiled was actually quite small if you took it in context – only about one-half of 1 percent of a year's production, which under any circumstances isn't bad for a perishable product. I explained that I was not responsible for the storage facility but only for the legislation establishing the board. And on and on. Eventually the noise died down, the management worked out its problems, and my egg marketing board became a great success – although people still come up to me today and say, "Remember the eggs?" In fact I became the first agriculture minister in Canadian history not to have to subsidize the poultry industry. So in the long run eggs turned out to be one of the best four-letter words I've ever heard. But I certainly didn't think so at the time.

Apart from the establishment of more marketing boards that would ensure farmers' income, I had several other goals when I first became minister. I wanted to see the department expanded to include forestry and fisheries – all the primary producers of the land and the water. I wanted to gradually phase out federal subsidies to farmers, establishing marketing boards instead that would enable the farmers to receive their fair return from the marketplace. I wanted to turn the federal Farm Credit Corporation into a genuine farmers' bank that would forever end the dependence of farmers on bankers who don't understand or sympathize with their problems. I wanted to limit food imports that threatened Canadian farmers by working within the General Agreement on Tariffs and Trade (GATT), which is a multilateral trade agreement aimed at lowering tariffs – very different from bilateral free trade with the Americans. And I wanted the Wheat Board to become part of my department, which is where it had always belonged. I also argued over the years that many agriculture-related activities were being handled by other departments, such as Industry, Trade and Commerce. I wanted them all as much as possible to come under Agriculture so that the Minister of Agriculture would well and truly be running agriculture in Canada.

I'd dreamed about a farmers' bank since I'd first entered politics – a rural bank that understood rural agriculture. I don't think there's a bank today that understands farmers. As it was, we did the best we could through the Farm Credit Corporation – it was often our money that kept farmers afloat. But it would be so much better to have the farmers helping themselves – as with the marketing boards – than for the federal government always to have to come to the rescue.

When I became agriculture minister, the Farm Credit Corporation behaved quite a bit like a bank. They would brag about the fact that they'd never had a deficit and they hardly had any losses. That just proved to me one thing: that they weren't taking the kind of risks that they should have been. There were a lot of people being left out in the cold.

I wanted to make the Farm Credit Corporation into more than a bank. I wanted it to start a system of education, or agricultural extension – advising farmers on how to invest and how to farm. But we never got that far in my term of office because we always ran into difficulty with bureaucracy and with other ministers who didn't think we should be interfering in the private banking sector more than we were and because education is a provincial responsibility. But it's quite obvious, even in 1986, that the private banks haven't looked after the farmers properly.

However, I did manage to get the Corporation to lend more money. One of my accomplishments was to revive it to the point where it was the tenth largest lending institution in Canada – which made it one of the biggest banks in Canada. I used to laugh sometimes to think how after all I'd said about banks I'd become a banker myself, so to speak. My last year in office, 1983-84, we loaned $758 million to farmers. (In 1985 the Tories had it down to $258 million and falling.) I say farmers, but most of that money went directly to private banks which were owed money by insolvent farmers. In many instances these farm debts were incurred through bank loans that I considered just short of fraud.

Not getting a real farmers' bank was one of my greatest disappointments as agriculture minister. Other countries have very successful farmers' banks: in France the farmers' bank is one of the largest banking institutions in the country. But the Trudeau Cabinet never paid enough attention to the needs of rural Canada – including Quebec – and I could never talk them into giving me my farmers' bank.

In addition to eggs, I did succeed in establishing more federal marketing boards – for broiler chickens and for turkeys. (I tried and failed to get marketing boards for beef, pork, and potatoes.) And I did make some progress in phasing out subsidies and in increasing the role of the Farm Credit Corporation. And I'm extremely proud of what I did for the dairy industry in Canada – although the dairy farmers were pretty mad at me for a while. But in my first two years, the biggest battle I fought for farmers was with a lady named Beryl Plumptre who was in charge of something called the Food Prices Review Board that the government set up after the 1972 election because of our alarm about what was happening with inflation in the food sector. I think Beryl had had it in for me ever since those rotten eggs. She and others didn't understand marketing boards. She thought they meant higher prices and nothing else.

She used to attack me and she used to attack farmers. She didn't have much use for farmers, I knew that. Charles Munro, who was president of the Canadian Federation of Agriculture, told me that when he was on the Economic Council of Canada he had been at a meeting and they were going around introducing themselves and he introduced himself as Charles Munro from Embro, Ontario. And she said, "What do you do?" and he said, "I'm a farmer and I'm president of the Canadian Federation of Agriculture." And she said, "What is a farmer doing on the Economic Council of Canada?" She didn't think he had any business there. This was the kind of thinking that I had to deal with throughout my career. And Beryl had it bad.

She was one of the ones who thought my egg marketing board should be killed almost before it was hatched. And we became very popular with the press and with the cartoonists because pretty near every day we were in a controversy about the price of some food product. She'd make a statement and I'd make a statement counteracting it.

She went right across the country meeting the provincial agriculture ministers but she never once asked for a meeting with me. I met her only one time, in the elevator at the Chateau Laurier. Somebody in the elevator said with a devilish gleam in his eye, "Mrs. Plumptre, have you met Mr. Whelan?" And "Mr. Whelan, do you know Mrs. Plumptre?" We each said, yes, without looking at the other. And then she said, "Yes, I know him, but we've never met." That was the only meeting we had. I guess she thought I was too inferior.

For a long time Beryl was the best thing I had going for me. It was attack, attack, attack. I was putting out the facts – "just the facts ma'am," that's all. I remember making a speech at the opening of the Canadian National Exhibition in Toronto – a very emotional speech about eggs and Mrs. Plumptre. It was broadcast on CBC radio on the farm program. That was the speech where at one point I said, "I'd like to take Mrs. Plumptre into a laying house." And the crowd laughed. I didn't know what they were laughing about because where I come from a laying house is a place where chickens lay eggs. So I said it again, and they just hollered and laughed louder. The audience had a different interpretation. They were thinking, "What's that old rooster been doing?"

As my battle with Beryl illustrates, one of the things that made my job as agriculture minister a lot easier was the quality of my department. When I arrived in 1972 I was handed one of the finest outfits in the government. With very few exceptions I had good deputies and good assistant deputies and the civil servants right down the line were very dedicated to their jobs and to agriculture. Since Confederation, Agriculture had been the most decentralized department of government – and this was something I continued to encourage – with offices and research stations in every province. In 1972 I had about ten thousand permanent people working for me and when I left in 1984 that had risen by only twenty-six full-time positions, so you can understand why I'd get mad when people tried to cut my budget. You hear all this talk now about decentralization. Well we were doing it before anyone was talking about it.

Every department in the government has a permanent staff of civil servants. Then each minister brings with him his so-called political staff. These people often don't last too long because of the long hours and constant pressures. It's never easy to get the right balance. Keeping a minister's office running smoothly is like baking a cake or mixing feed: you have to have all the right ingredients and a good recipe.

The two most important political staff are the executive assistant and the policy advisor. The executive assistant handles liaison with the department and with the minister's offices. The policy advisor, as the name suggests, helps develop policy in co-ordination with the department bureaucrats. In my last years I had a total of eleven political staff, including four special assistants in Ottawa, two in my riding to stamp out political fires before they could cause trouble, and one in our Regina office to keep close to the West. (I was the only minister – except our rare minister from the West – who had a Western office.) Then there was my research assistant, and my private secretary. Finally, there's the staff in the parliamentary office, located on the Hill, at the heart and core of the minister's political life.

It would take too much time to mention here all the fine people who worked with me over the years at Agriculture. But, as the old saying goes, I couldn't have done it without them.

Where you can get into problems running a department is if your deputy and assistant deputies are not experienced and if the minister doesn't know his stuff. If the deputies haven't come up through the ranks, you're in trouble. That was the great thing about Syd Williams who was my deputy for the first five years. He was a great big fellow who looked like a hawk – and had a mind like a computer – but was generally a very gentle and likeable person. He'd joined the department when he was an eighteen-year-old university student. Once he got his agriculture degree he worked for the department until he retired, except for four-and-half years in the army during the war.

Syd's philosophy was the correct one for a civil servant. As far as he was concerned, the minister was always right. He had his views and I had mine. But if I won the discussion and said that's the way it's going to be, Syd would turn and look at the assistant deputies and say, "That's what we're going to do folks. You heard the minister and that's what we're going to do." When they tried to move Syd to another department he took early retirement at age sixty-three. He never worked in another department and said he never would. Agriculture had been his life.

I think moving him was a mistake. I think it should be the minister and not the Prime Minister who appoints the deputy. The system is designed so that the Prime Minister can exert control over the departments through the deputies he appoints. That's no way to run a government. In reality what happens is that the powerful deputies, the ones with seniority who've generally been there much longer than any minister, are the ones who really run the show. This is a particular problem when a new minister comes along who doesn't know his department and doesn't make the effort to take control. He or she ends up doing what the deputy and the other bureaucrats tell them. One of the things that helped me gain the support of my deputies was how successful I became at defending the department. If they gave me the ammunition I'd more often than not win the battle. They certainly found that out when I had to fight with Beryl Plumptre.

Other than Syd, the deputy who stands out is Gaétan Lussier. Gaetan was a former deputy minister of agriculture in Quebec whom we stole away after the PQ won in 1976. I knew he was a strong federalist and he knew agriculture. He was the youngest deputy in the federal civil service when he started working for me – although I didn't know it at the time. He'd been a whiz kid when he was young and he was a speed reader – he could read fourteen hundred words a minute. All my deputies, including Syd, were bilingual, which was a necessity for me given the state of my French.

Getting Lussier was the closest I came to actually hiring my number two man myself. After my second deputy had left, I went to Trudeau and told him I wanted Gaétan. Pierre said, "You know, Gene, I make the selection for deputies." And I said, "Well, I can let you know my preference." And he said, "That doesn't mean I'm going to go along with it." But he promised to check Gaétan out and I guess he liked what he saw.

One of my ongoing battles in the department was in the area of economics. You know, you always have people in a depart-

ment with certain economic ideas. And we had so many economists in the department that I used to refer to them as the
Dalmatian pups – the 101 Dalmatians. I don't think they liked
that much. But a good economist can bring in any kind of program you need. And I made it clear quite early that it was my
ideas and the government's ideas that we were setting out to
accomplish. If a policy paper came in that didn't reflect what I'd
requested I'd just send it back until they got it right. I think I
had them pretty well trained, but they never stopped trying to
sneak in their own ideas when I wasn't looking. I liked to joke
about them and with them, but they were the best economists
any department could have and they were loyal as could be.

One of my best friends over the years was the senior assistant
deputy minister of Agriculture, Dr. Gerry Trant. He was our
top economist and he and I used to have some terrible arguments, but he'd support me when my view prevailed. When we
were together in front of an audience I'd often introduce him
as "the man in my department who makes certain proposals on
the economic management of agriculture in Canada, but that
doesn't necessarily mean those are the proposals I'm putting
before you today." When I did that he'd just about have a fit.
But we did have a good rapport. We had many discussions
about Canada's agriculture and we could tell one another just
what we thought. He came with me to practically every World
Food Council meeting and my other international meetings. He
was a fine adviser.

Peace in your department is difficult to achieve – and we had
our wars, most often between the political staff and the departmental staff, who didn't always see eye to eye. Peace was equally
difficult in our relations with the provinces. That's why I'm
particularly proud of the success I had at bringing harmony to
federal-provincial relations in agriculture. As soon as I was
appointed minister, I wanted to meet with my peers and establish our common ground. Within the first month I travelled to
every provincial capital. I wanted to show the provincial ministers that I was no Ottawa big shot who was too good to come
to them. Of course, I knew many of them already, but whether I
knew them or not they welcomed me warmly. Soon afterwards

I invited them all to Ottawa. It was the beginning of what turned out to be mostly a very friendly and co-operative federal-provincial atmosphere. When Mulroney goes on about how there was no co-operation under the Liberals and that he's introducing this new era of consultation and so on, that's a load of gibberish. Whelan and Chrétien, to name two, were doing it long before he was on the scene.

When you look at all the fighting that so often does go on between the levels of government, I think what we in agriculture had was quite special. It was Bill Newman, I believe – at the time he had just become agriculture minister for Ontario – who commented after his first federal-provincial agriculture meeting that he couldn't believe a group of ministers could get along as well as we did. He'd just moved from being the Ontario environment minister and he said that all the environment ministers did when they met was argue. It made no difference to me whether the minister was Liberal or Conservative or whatever: we had to work together. In fact, I occasionally got criticized by my fellow Liberals in Ottawa – or in the province in question – for working so closely with a Conservative provincial minister. They said I was making him look too good.

Under the constitution – the British North America Act – agriculture was more a federal than a provincial responsibility, but it was a shared jurisdiction. Even today, there are more federal agriculture employees than provincial ones in most provinces. We had federal agriculture department employees in every province. Under the BNA Act it's very clear that agriculture is a dual responsibility – it's probably one of the clearest sections of the original act. Federally you can assume total control if the provinces are neglecting the health of the nation – meaning that they are letting the land go to hell through erosion and so on. The provinces own the resource – the land – but the federal government is the safeguard of the health of that resource.

So there are many areas in which Ottawa and the provinces work together. For instance, crop insurance in Western Canada. There we worked directly with the producers and paid 50 percent of the premiums on crop insurance. The farmers pay the other 50 percent and the provinces, who administer the program, take 100 percent of the credit. Ottawa does practically all the publicly funded agricultural research in Canada except in the richest provinces, and all the provinces want that to continue. Education, or agriculture extension, on the other hand, is clearly a provincial responsibility. Ottawa does the research and the provinces make it available to the farmers through agricultural extension. Food inspection is a joint responsibility. In the case of federal marketing boards the provinces have given up certain areas of authority to the federal government for the greater good. So you can see that a great deal of co-operation is required.

At the first meeting we had of all eleven agriculture ministers my provincial counterparts met by themselves for two days and on the third day along came poor little Gene Whelan. That was the tradition they'd had up to that time: they'd meet in advance and plan their strategy on how to team up on the federal minister. It still works that way in a lot of areas. Now I've played a lot of hockey and other games – I've played hardball and softball and lacrosse – but in every game I've known we always had even sides. So when I got to that meeting I told them straight off that I thought playing ten against one was a bit unfair and that this wasn't some great competitive sport anyhow. This was a working relationship that we had to develop for the betterment of Canada. From then on, on the whole, I had pretty good co-operation from the provincial ministers, even though much of the time they were pretty well all Tories.

Sometimes politics did get in the way – I guess it's unavoidable. During my first term, I proposed to the provinces a program that would provide 100 percent income assurance for farmers; it was designed to protect them during bad years. Even though it was a pretty good program they wouldn't go for it. So I went home feeling a bit dejected and they went home feeling fine and the next thing I noticed was that David Stupich, the B.C. agriculture minister, had introduced practically the same program in his province as if he'd thought it up all by his lonesome. That sort of thing happened more than once.

One of the worst for stealing federal programs and pretending he'd thought them up was Jean Garon, who was the Quebec minister after the PQ came to power in 1976. Garon is as clever as a fox. I know his type well – he's half Irish and half French (which isn't far from my own make-up), a dangerous combination. Garon was supposed to be anti-federalist like all the separatists, but he told me once, "You know, I have instructions from my premier to take all the money I can get from the federal system." He used to brag about the dairy program we'd developed in Ottawa as if it was his own idea. He'd listen to all our programs, then steal the parts he liked and put them into effect in Quebec and pretend he'd thought them up himself. He was like a fox, but I liked him a lot. We got along well.

One of the greatest frustrations I had in dealing with the provincial ministers was that I found they often didn't speak for their own governments – they couldn't rely on the support of their own premier and his Cabinet. I never brought a single proposal to a meeting without knowing that I had my government's backing, but they would often come with long lists of things they wanted for their provinces and no authorization to do so. I'd tell them to go back and get an okay from their own Cabinet and then I'd bring it forward at the next federal-provincial first ministers' conference. Very rarely could they get their provincial governments to support what they were doing.

And sometimes my own government backed down, after I had their support. A good example was when my department developed the Agri-Food Strategy for Canada which we presented to the provincial ministers in July 1981. It was a total plan for the progress of agriculture and food processing in Canada for the next twenty years. In it we emphasized developing new markets, improving the existing agricultural resource base, and implementing a research strategy with specific goals, including development of our untapped northern agricultural potential. We held nearly three hundred public meetings across Canada before we wrote the final policy and I fought for it in Cabinet and had it approved. But then I couldn't get funding for it. The bureaucrats double-crossed me and the Cabinet gave in. It was a hell of a good program. I made it part of my platform when I ran for the leadership and, if we had it now, agriculture would not be in the difficulty it is.

One of the best provincial ministers I worked with was

Malcolm "Mac" MacLeod from New Brunswick, who was in the job almost the whole time I was. He was a Tory, and he wasn't even a farmer (he'd run supermarkets), but he grasped the need for co-operation and for development. Because of that the agriculture industry in New Brunswick made great progress under MacLeod and Whelan. I used to catch hell from the provincial Liberals because I worked too close with Mac, particularly when I said one time that I thought he was probably the best Minister of Agriculture New Brunswick ever had.

One of the more unlikely provincial ministers was Jack Hawkins of Nova Scotia, who served when Gerald Regan was premier. He was a former English professor but he did a lot for agriculture in Nova Scotia. He worked hard and was easy to work with – and he ran the toughest meetings I've ever seen. He always had a stopwatch, and on the agenda for the meeting there'd be a time marked beside each item – a topic had three minutes, or two minutes, or a minute and a half. When your time was up it didn't matter whether you were in the middle of saying that the federal government was willing to give Nova Scotia $5 million for such and such, he'd shut you off and move to the next topic.

Sometimes the Liberals were harder to work with than the Conservatives – for instance the time we decided to build a veterinary college on Prince Edward Island. When we decided on the project (before the 1979 election) the premiers of P.E.I. and Nova Scotia were both Liberals, Alex Campbell and Gerry Regan respectively. We would be paying the lion's share of the cost and an independent commissioner appointed by the provinces had concluded that the best place to build the college was on P.E.I. Well, Gerry Regan wouldn't have any part of that. It had to be at Truro, Nova Scotia, or else. So he held it up. Five years later – after having to fight with Regan's Tory successor, John Buchanan, who took the same line – we finally did start to build the college on Prince Edward Island. But if it hadn't been for the delay caused by Nova Scotia the first graduates would be receiving their diplomas about now.

The other side of this story is how I got Ottawa to fund the college at all. By the time we'd agreed on the site, Ed Lumley,

the Minister of Regional Industrial Expansion, was the man
with the money. I waited until I had him where he couldn't
escape and where he was softened up for the knockout punch.
It was on a little Department of National Defence Falcon going
about four hundred miles an hour at an altitude of 25,000 feet
on our way to a meeting in P.E.I. When we got there, I was
able to announce to the farmers the news of Mr. Lumley's
generosity. Ed was a good one to work with.

On the provincial scene I dealt with good ones and bad ones,
but the worst I had to deal with was Dennis Timbrell from
Ontario. I'd worked well with his predecessors – Bill Stewart,
Bill Newman, and Lorne Henderson. They were all Tories, but
we became friends and we trusted each other. As with most
provincial ministers, I could talk to them on the telephone about
anything and know that the conversation was private unless
we both agreed it was going public. But with Dennis you never
knew what he was going to do after he'd hung up the phone.
It may have had something to do with the fact that he was
getting ready to run for the Ontario Tory leadership and was
using Agriculture as his stepping stone. I don't know. It wasn't
that he didn't have some good ideas; some of the proposals he
made were more radical than anything I ever brought in. But
he didn't carry them through, and I think many areas of the
province felt let down.

One time in the 1980s he crossed me up over extra funds for
the veterinary college at Guelph. I could never get from him
his government's approval for their share of the extra funds
that we both knew were needed. Then when the 1984 federal
election campaign was on, he maintained that he had received
approval from his Cabinet but that the federal government –
meaning Gene Whelan – had held things up. It simply wasn't
true. No other agriculture minister ever did that sort of thing
to me.

After joining the Cabinet in 1972, I soon learned the limits on
the power of a minister – however well he may know his department and however well he knows the government. The two
main obstacles I had to overcome were the bureaucracy and the

Cabinet system. Agriculture is not a glamorous portfolio like External Affairs and it doesn't wield the power of Finance or Treasury Board in the overall system of government. More times than I can count, I found myself fighting against what seemed to be impossible odds. Sometimes I won and sometimes I lost – even when I knew I was right and events proved my case. Overall I had a batting average of about .500 – which is terrific in baseball and not bad in goverment.

One battle I lost, was in the spring of 1976 when the world price for industrial dairy products – skim milk powder, butter, and cheese – collapsed. Over a period of six weeks it dropped to about two-thirds of its former value. The European Common Market had a huge milk surplus and so did the U.S., so both put their milk products on the market at distress prices and the world price fell rapidly. As a result, the regular foreign customers for Canadian milk products reneged on their contracts and dairy farmers from Nova Scotia to British Columbia asked the government for $44 million to keep them alive through the crisis.

Now I've never been a believer in subsidy for the sake of subsidy – in fact marketing boards do just the opposite: they free farmers from the need for subsidy. But I do believe in helping people in an emergency, particularly when common sense also makes political sense. At this point we were in the process of phasing out the annual dairy industry subsidy – we had it down to about $111 million that year. This would have been an emergency subsidy, a one-time thing, justified by the fact that there was an international crisis that our producers weren't responsible for.

I took my case to Treasury Board, which had to approve any expenditures not already approved as part of an annual department budget. The President of the Treasury Board at that time was Jean Chrétien, who'd replaced Bud Drury in 1974, and his assistant deputy was George Fleischmann, who's now head of the Grocery Products Manufacturers of Canada. I told them that the subsidy was needed to keep the industry alive and that if they refused me they would be giving a great gift to the separatist party in Quebec, since that province accounts for more than 50 percent of the industrial dairy products produced in Canada and, more important still, that 50 percent of Quebec farmers' income comes from dairy products. Of course no one knew at this point that Quebec Premier Robert Bourassa would call an election so soon afterwards, but we knew the separatists were coming on strong.

At Treasury Board, George Fleischmann advised against the subsidy. He said the dairy farmers would survive fine without it – of course, he'd never been a farmer himself (although his father had). And my friend Jean Chrétien went along with him. Maybe Jean didn't believe the separatists were as strong as they turned out to be, but he should have known better. So I took my case to Cabinet.

I remember as clear as day what I told them: "You do what you're doing and you will elect a separatist government in Quebec – all for the lack of $44 million dollars given to farmers right across Canada. To say 'no' now to Quebec dairy farmers would be political suicide." But the Cabinet wouldn't listen. The advisers to the Treasury Board and the advisers to Finance Minister Donald Macdonald ganged up on me and I was outgunned. The great Don Macdonalds and Marc Lalondes (Lalonde was Quebec leader then) and the others didn't pay attention – they didn't believe me. I remember Trudeau saying at the time, "Sorry, Gene, you lost another."

Naturally the Quebec dairy farmers became enraged. They felt I'd betrayed them and that the Liberal government they'd recently helped to elect had betrayed them. Here we were already phasing out the old subsidy and now we refused them help in their hour of need. They painted anti-Liberal slogans on their barns and ten thousand of them marched on Parliament Hill. I didn't want to face them, I can tell you.

The day they marched I went out to face this huge crowd of angry farmers, many of them old friends. As a minister I had to support my government publicly even though personally I didn't agree with what we were doing – that has always been my approach. I began to speak. I said, "Mes chers amis . . ." That was about as far as I got. They'd been waiting for me and they threw milk all over me while the photographers snapped away. The next day the picture of my whitewash was in every major newspaper in the country – and every small-town paper in Que-bec. Russell Mant, the photographer who took the picture that was in almost every paper, won four prizes for it as the best news-action photo of the year – so at least somebody benefitted.

Many of the farmers in the crowd – my friends and others who knew I was against the decision – broke down and cried when they saw what was done to me. They knew I was still on their side. Later, some of them asked me why I didn't get angry when the milk-throwing happened. And I said, "If I'd been a dairy farmer, I would have been throwing milk too." Shortly after the incident the dairy farmers from Alberta sent me $250 to buy a new suit and apologized on behalf of their fellow dairymen. (I couldn't accept the money, so I gave it to a charity.)

Later that day I was to take the Czechoslovakian Minister of Agriculture, Dr. Bohuslav Večeřa, to my home in Amherstburg for dinner. Right after the milk was thrown I just walked off the Hill by myself, got into my little Chevy Nova, which was the car I had as Minister of Agriculture (I could hardly fit into the thing), and drove by myself to the airport to board a Defence Department Falcon that took me to London, Ontario, where I was meeting the Czech minister. I'd slipped away so quietly that some reporters thought I'd been kidnapped by the dairy farmers and was being held for ransom.

When I met Dr. Večeřa's plane in London I apologized for my condition. I was wearing a suit that didn't show up the milk stain too bad, but I still looked something less than Canada's ambassador for agriculture. I wore that suit because I was expecting trouble (and I've kept it as a souvenir). That night after dinner we watched the news on television and there I was in all my milk-covered glory. Dr. Večeřa couldn't believe it. He said such a thing would never happen in Czechoslovakia. I knew what he meant: in his country the army would have been there, not the minister.

I couldn't believe it when Bourassa called an election for that fall, so soon after we'd done so much to hurt Liberal support in rural Quebec. That was exactly where the Parti Québécois needed to gain strength if it was going to win. Of course, to almost everyone's amazement, but not mine, Lévesque did win and he got his majority thanks to the rural Quebec vote. I still firmly believe that we elected René Lévesque with our dairy policy. Not long after the election, at my first meeting with Jean Garon, he jokingly offered me an honorary lifetime membership in the Parti Québécois for my part in helping them win the 1976 election. God, was I mad.

The greatest irony of this whole episode is that the very next year, 1977, we were forced to raise the dairy subsidy by $150 million – by then the great Don Macdonald and Marc Lalonde had realized what had to be done, but it was like locking the barn door after the horse was stolen. In the coming years we would spend many more millions than ever before on anti-separatist propaganda and programs for Quebec. It all made my measly $44 million look pretty insignificant. Trudeau later said to me, "Why didn't we pay more attention to you?" I could have told him, "Because you listen to your bureaucrats – who know nothing about politics – more than you listen to your own political ministers."

I may not have liked every decision we made as a government, but I was never afraid to defend my policies in any part of the country, including the West. I won't say I conquered the West, but I certainly believe that I won the respect of Western farmers. They knew where I stood, whether they agreed with me or not. I used to have certain set lines that I'd use. For instance I'd often say, "Everybody thinks that I created marketing boards. But the first marketing board in Canada was created in British Columbia in 1928 by the milk producers in the Fraser Valley. At that time I was only four years old. I wasn't creating marketing boards then, but I was a good market because I consumed quite a lot at that time."

I particularly remember going to a meeting in Hanna, Alberta, to talk to a group of beef farmers about my proposals for a beef marketing board. This was in 1983 at the height of the beef marketing board controversy and the meeting hall was packed and there were television crews there to cover the expected lynching – a room full of Alberta cattleman versus poor old Gene Whelan, Pierre Trudeau's Minister of Agriculture.

To make matters worse, I'd been sick in Saskatoon the night

before and then on the day of the meeting it turned foggy and since we were flying into Hanna in a small plane it was a near thing getting there. We were late and those ferocious cattlemen were sure that I wasn't going to show up at all – that I was too scared. We were with a tall, handsome fellow from our Alberta office, Jim Lockhart – I called him "The Rifleman." He was over six feet tall, but he knew these cattlemen better than he knew Gene Whelan and he was pretty nervous about the meeting. He didn't need to worry. As I always did in situations like this, I simply told the farmers what I thought, straight out. "Agree or disagree," I said, "this is what I'm fighting for and this is why." I gave them one of my fire and brimstone speeches on marketing boards and talked about Canada.

The people in the hall received me well and gave me a big ovation – as much for having the courage to come there and speak to them as anything else. And afterwards I got a number of letters from people who'd wanted to speak up in support of me but had been too scared to risk the ire of their neighbours. No matter how hostile the audience, I was never received badly at any of the meetings I went to as agriculture minister from one end of Canada to the other.

Sometimes when I gave these speeches my famous way with words would get me into trouble. The press would take something I'd said and blow it all out of proportion or simply quote it wrong. (I taped all my speeches, so I knew what I'd said even if the press couldn't always get it right.) I don't think reporters realize the damage they can do. Most of the time, though, when I got into trouble in this way I'd try to have some fun with it. I kind of enjoyed the way people would get so riled up over something I hadn't even said – or meant.

Take the time I was giving one of my patented speeches on marketing boards. This was in Saskatchewan in the spring of 1977. At one point in my speech I said that our present marketing system was antiquated, medieval and ancient, that it had hardly changed since Biblical times. I was making a comparison to the time when Christ threw the money changers out of the temple, and said that our way of doing business was "as outdated and redundant as the marketing systems used at the time of Christ." Well, the next day I was quoted in the newspapers as saying that our marketing system was "as outdated and redundant as the teachings of Christ." By the time I got back to Ottawa I had ministers from every religious denomination phoning me to complain; there was quite an uproar. But I told each and every one of them, "I know what I said, and I know the reporter knows what I said, regardless of what you or anyone thinks I said or I meant to say." And I said, "I know 'He' – meaning God – knows what I meant and I'll let him be the judge, not someone who was not there and only read the newspaper."

One of my constant aggravations as agriculture minister was the red meat industry – both the farmers and the meat packers – and it was the subject of beef that got me into some real hot water in Calgary in November 1976. Farmers can be quite bone-headed and quite sensitive, beef producers especially – they're the most bullheaded group of all.

The occasion was another cattlemen's meeting in Alberta. After my speech I was fencing with the reporters and I made a bit of a joking remark. I said, "You know, if you eat too much beef you become ferocious and sexy." Well the reporters who were there just laughed. I was joking, but I was serious too. The reporters who were covering the meeting ignored my speech and concentrated on my joke. All but one – the exception being a woman reporter from the *Toronto Star*-quoted me incorrectly as saying that if you eat beef you become ferocious. All the men left out the part about being sexy.

When the beef farmers across the country – especially in the West – read this comment from the Canadian agriculture minister, they did become ferocious, which of course proved my point. I got a flood of letters from angry cattlemen. If they'd been thinking instead of being ferocious they'd have realized that I was giving them a lot of publicity.

In the weeks and months after, whenever I met with cattlemen I'd always try to soothe them with a few quotations to put things in perspective. I'd mention the time Churchill was presented with a great big Canadian salmon during the war and said, "No, take him away. We carnivores must win the war." And I'd tell them what Jean-Jacques Rousseau said about French soldiers: "Give them beef and steel and they'll fight the devil himself." But I could never resist adding the line from George Bernard Shaw (who later became a vegetarian): "I'm eating too much beef and losing my sense of humour."

This whole episode made me remember the time I'd been travelling across the country with a group of Commonwealth parliamentarians and we visited Al Oeming's game farm in Edmonton. Al kept great big grizzly bears that he'd raised from little teeny one-pound cubs. A big male bear weighs as much as a ton, but Al would walk into the cave carrying a big five-gallon plastic jug of milk with a great big nipple that looked like a big baby bottle and that big old bear would sit there with his paws out waiting to grab it just like a baby. So I said to him, "Aren't you afraid to go in those pens?" And he said, no. But then he said something I never forgot: "If I fed them fresh meat one day, I'd never go in the cage again because they'd become ferocious and they'd kill me." (He fed them alfalfa hay, grains, milk, and waste bakery products.)

The result of my comment about ferocious beef eaters wasn't all bad. I got lots of publicity—I think I could have had my picture in the paper every week if I'd wanted to—and a lot of people in Ontario read exactly what I'd said because of that one woman reporter from Toronto who'd reported me accurately. For the next few weeks it was not uncommon for me to be walking on a street in Ottawa or in the Toronto airport and for a woman to come up to me and say, "Mr. Whelan, I'm eating a lot of beef." I was never the most pleasant-looking character to come up and talk to but a lot of people did. I guess they found me approachable. I sometimes think all this attention I got sometimes made the other Cabinet members jealous as hell.

I never could get the majority of the red meat producers on my side—in spite of all the things I tried to do for them. And now they're in the worst position of any group in Canadian agriculture because they were stubborn and wanted to remain backward. I sometimes describe them as being like lemmings who are running over the economic cliff to self-destruction. The sad thing is that beef farmers are some of the hardest working and most efficient farmers of all. But they are poor marketers, almost always letting someone else do it for them.

One thing I did for them was to put controls on the import of American beef and foreign beef which was flooding the market (American imports were taking over 50 percent of our slaughter market)–that was back in 1974. The controls were perfectly legal under our international agreements but we had such fights over that in Cabinet, until I finally won. The Americans retaliated with pork quotas and veal quotas even though they never even came close to reaching the beef quota I'd set–which was 100 percent of their previous five years average–they never went past 30 percent of the allowed amount. Sometime later, on a visit to Rome for a meeting of the Food and Agriculture Organization, I ran into their special ambassador, Ambassador Ed Martin, and I asked him, "What was wrong with what I did?"–I meant imposing the controls on beef imports. And he said, "There was nothing wrong with what you did, but we couldn't let you get away with it."

To my dismay we let the Americans get away with their retaliation. I wanted to appeal the American quotas to GATT–I'd won a similar appeal before, on eggs–but I couldn't persuade my timid Cabinet colleagues. On that occasion our government was chicken about beef. You'd have thought the world would fall down if we stood up to the Americans.

8

Going to the People

One philosophy I followed as agriculture minister often got me into a lot of trouble with the Opposition and with the press. They accused me of doing too much travelling, of spending the taxpayers' money on frivolous junkets all over the country to talk to farmers and school kids – ordinary people. They wailed and moaned, but I never stopped. And I still believe I was right. You can't run a department from your office, particularly not one as big and decentralized as Agriculture. And you can't run a government by sitting in Ottawa, and listening only to the bureaucrats. Within the stone walls and marble halls of Parliament you couldn't possibly know what was going on in Port Hardy, B.C., or Come By Chance, Newfoundland. You had to go and see for yourself and listen and consult the people. I still believe that very strongly.

I've heard there's this new theory of management that's now a big rage. It's called "managing by walking around." The proponents of this theory say that the best manager is almost never in his office; he's always walking around talking to the people who work for him and finding out what they're up to. Well, I was doing that long before anyone dressed it up into a theory. And I'd do it again if I were agriculture minister because it worked. During my tenure we had the reputation of having one of the best run departments in the government – one time we even got a special commendation from the Auditor General – and I believe it was this approach that enabled us to do it.

In fact, I used to boast that I held the title as the champion traveller among ministers. I've travelled hundreds of thousands of miles and had some close calls, but never a serious accident. I used to say that it was a combination of my leprechaun and my patron saint, old St. Martin de Porres, that kept me safe. The leprechaun was given to me one time by some people from Ireland at an international cattle breeders convention in Ottawa; they put a little stamp on the bottom that said he was a "fog lifter" and that I should carry him in the airplane whenever I travelled. Certainly I got through a lot of storms and bad weather and we hardly ever missed a trip.

I got St. Martin de Porres when I first went into politics. He was given to me by a friend who was a very strong believer. He came to me one time and he had these two little statues of St. Martin, a black Peruvian Catholic missionary noted for helping the hopeless and the poor. He gave me one of the statues and I've carried it with me ever since.

I needed him one time when I flew to Medicine Hat, Alberta, where I landed in order to drive to a rural-urban night at Maple Creek, Saskatchewan. Even though it was a clear day the wind was so strong that the pilot couldn't land the plane the first time – the wind was blowing us sideways. So the next time he came in faster – they call it dogging the plane, sort of slanting it with the one wing down – and was going about two hundred miles an hour when we landed. He hit the runway hard. I knew something had happened when we landed but I didn't know what and I didn't say a thing to my wife and the kids who were with me. When we got out, the captain told us he'd blown a tire. St. Martin was with me on that occasion.

I used to go to a lot of places most people had never heard of; if it had a runway long enough to land on, I'd be going there.

Many people don't realize that there are military landing strips right across the country – every hundred miles or so. They were built during the last war for cargo planes and also to train pilots. Some of them are two miles long – enough to land a great big transport. Many of them didn't even have lights by the time I was using them – the lights had either been removed or had deteriorated beyond use – so you had to land in daylight. When I was going to an out-of-the-way place – and I did that more than anybody else – I'd often use these military airfields and fly on military or Department of Transport aircraft. I must have found every one of those airstrips during the twelve years I was agriculture minister. I'm sure I used some of them more than the military. I got to know the landing strips so well that I used to correct the pilots as to the length and whether or not they could land at a particular one.

The pilots who used to fly me and my aides in small aircraft really seemed to enjoy the trips. As often as not the military pilots made my flying with them simply part of their usual routine – especially the helicopter pilots. They were going to be flying anyway, so they just flew the agriculture minister as well – they had to log a certain number of hours in the air regardless. I used to get criticized for using so many military aircraft, but the criticizers either didn't know much about Canada or they didn't know much about my schedule. There were no regular flights to most of the places I visited and by using military planes I could sometimes visit four or five different areas in the same two days. (When I left office in 1984 I got a commemorative plaque from my friends at the Department of National Defence. It said, "Whelan's Falcon badge, officially retired on the occasion of his transfer from 412 (T) Squadron, 19 July 1984." The colonel commanding 412 Transport Squadron, which is in charge of all executive planes, said in his speech when they gave me the plaque, "We've never done this before, and it's not likely we'll ever do it again. But then there's never been a Gene Whelan before, and there never will be again.")

Often there'd be several hundred people at my meetings – people from all parties, or no party at all. I've gone to big cities where we drew a lot fewer people than in some of those towns and villages. I think I can say that no other minister travelled more within Canada or knew Canada better than I did. And that made me not only a better Minister of Agriculture and a better politician, but also a better Canadian. Most of the meetings I went to were non-partisan, though there'd often be a breakfast or other event with the local Liberals. So I was in constant touch with the grassroots of the party and the grassroots of the country. I spent more time in the West than any other Liberal minister. I went to little places like Milk River, Alberta; or Wadena, Saskatchewan; or Ste. Rose du Lac, Manitoba.

As a minister I made no secret of when or where I travelled. None of us did. I always made sure that copies of the speeches I'd given were available to anyone who wanted them. And if I knew I'd be flying close to where one of the members lived — whether he was a Liberal, an NDP, or a Conservative — I'd usually offer him a ride. And many of them accepted. I never had trouble defending myself in the House and it never caused me to lose an election. But that didn't stop the Opposition and the press from getting vicious about all my travelling. The *Windsor Star* even attacked Liz on one occasion. They had a big picture of her in the paper one time and called her "High-flying Liz." It hurt her, and a lot of people resented it when they attacked my wife. Anybody that's human would be bothered. The press could be quite mean.

Tom Cossitt, the Tory member from Leeds, used to make a specialty of questioning all of the ministers about their travels. He loved to get indignant about the expense and so on; he knew it was good publicity. Most of the time he left me alone, but there was one occasion back in 1974 when Tom really thought he had me. It was the time I flew to Miami.

After I got back from the trip Cossitt sent me a written question which I'd replied to in writing, as is customary. In my reply I told him, "Yes, I did fly to Miami." Period. So the next day Tom got up in the House and made a statement. He said something like "It's disgraceful that this minister flew to Miami at the taxpayers' expense." I didn't respond; I just sat there with a big grin on my face and didn't say a thing — just like the time our new elementary school teacher Miss Donnelly told us how she was going to whip all us bushwacker kids into shape. Cossitt should have known by the way I was acting that he was getting himself into trouble.

The next day the story hit the headlines – "Whelan Flies Free to Miami" – but I still didn't do anything to defend myself. Afterwards when the reporters asked me about the trip, I simply confirmed that I had indeed flown to Miami and they rushed off to meet their deadlines. Tom must have thought I was just hoping the whole thing would blow over. But a couple of days later a reporter finally thought to come and check out the story with me. He asked me what I had to say about flying to Miami on a government plane and I said, "Well, the only thing I've got to say is that it was cold as hell in Miami the day I was there and when I left the next morning it was forty below zero." The reporter looked baffled, then said, "It was never that cold in Florida." "Whoever said anything about Florida?" I said. "I'm talking about Miami, Manitoba. I was there to give a speech at the annual Manitoba Corn Awards Banquet. Over four hundred people were there." In all the fuss no one had ever checked to see where Miami was and I chided the reporter for not reading a copy of my speech beforehand. To give Tom Cossitt credit, he laughed about the whole thing afterwards.

At least the incident let the rest of Canada know that we do have our own Miami – even if it has a population of only 401. Actually, that trip was a very good example of the kinds of meetings I'd go to all the time – dairy meetings, cattle meetings, corn meetings, farm meetings in general. But I've almost forgotten to mention that there was another twist to the trip to Miami.

The corn awards were sponsored by the Manitoba corn farmers, the Manitoba government, and by Seagram, the big distiller. They use corn to make rye: Seagram V.O. has a lot of corn in it and they have a big distillery at Gimli, Manitoba. On this occasion Seagram had invited me to come and give their award and was kind enough to offer to fly me out on their company plane. After thinking about it, I'd refused, even though it might have saved a bit of money.

Afterwards Joyce Fairburn, who'd started out in Trudeau's

office as a secretary but had become a sort of political and legislative assistant, asked me about how I'd been smart enough
to know not to go to Miami on the Seagram plane. (I thought
Joyce wasn't too bad as far as the pipsqueaks around the Prime
Minister went. She was fair and she was a pretty good administrator.) I told her I knew it wouldn't look good for a minister
to be taking a free ride from a distilleiy. I had followed my
natural instinct and they thought this was politically brilliant.
Unlike the great Marc Lalonde, who let Seagram fly him to
Israel one time and was severely criticized. Or Otto Lang, who
had tried to send his family nanny home to Scotland on a
government pass without paying her fare. That sort of thing
was just plain dumb, it seemed to me.

I was in the West enough that I became a sort of honorary
Westerner. Maybe the best evidence of this came in 1974 when I
was speaking in Wetaskiwin, Alberta, just south of Edmonton.
It was a cold winter night when we drove from Edmonton to
the Wetaskiwin legion hall – thirty or forty below – but inside it
was warm with lots of people feasting on big barons of roast
beef. It was an open forum – anybody could come to the meeting. You just paid $5.50 and you had all you could eat, plus
Gene Whelan for dessert.

After dinner I gave a short speech and then we opened it up
to questions. And I'll never forget what one man who stood up
said: "Welcome to the West, Mr. Whelan. If you want to come
out here and run, we'll elect you. You're the best thing that's
hit the West since John Diefenbaker." This was in the heart of
Tory Alberta. I wish I'd had the tape recorder on.

My green stetson is something that represents my closeness
to the West. Actually, the first stetson I was given was a gold
one I got in Kamloops, B.C., back when I was still parliamentary secretary to Jack Davis. I was representing Jack at a local
Chamber of Commerce meeting on my way back from Fisheries
business on the West Coast. I wore the stetson that evening in
Kamloops and I wore it lots after that – for the next several
years. I've always liked hats and I liked that hat quite a bit. My
second stetson, a beige one, was given to me by the Saskatche-

wan Wheat Pool when I helped them open up a new livestock sale yard at Moose Jaw.

I got the first green one in 1974 when I was invited to open the Swan River Agricultural Fair and Exhibition in Swan River, Manitoba. When I got to the fairground they put a green stetson on my head and told me all the officals at the fair would be wearing one – that was how they would be identified. So I asked them what it stood for and they told me "It stands for hope and charity, fertility and growth and all good things in life – and last but not least, the Irish." I've worn it ever since. I guess you could say it's become my trademark.

I like to think that the green stetson stands as a reminder that if the world were green there wouldn't be anybody starving. And believe me, there are more people starving, many more tragedies like Ethiopia in the making around the world, than people think.

I now have about forty stetsons, of almost every colour you can think of. Often when I would open a new building or be at a fair I would be presented with a new stetson. I guess I've got enough of them to last me quite a while. What with getting all these hats I came to know how to tell a good one from a not-so-good. You can tell how good a hat it is by the number of Xs stamped inside the rim. Usually I'd be given a five or six Xer – the Xs tell you how much rabbit and beaver fur there is in the felt – a nine Xer is about the best you can buy. If it has no Xs, watch out, because there's not much rabbit in that hat.

Probably the best hat I ever got was when I opened the new PFRA Aqueduct near Brooks, Alberta. I believe the new aqueduct is the largest earth-filled physical structure in the world and the old cement aqueduct is a marvel. It was built between 1912 and 1914 by the CPR to bring water from the mountains across the valley to the flatlands where the settlers were starting to farm. They used the water for what they call flood irrigation – flooding the fields in about six inches of water. The old aqueduct is reminiscent of Roman architecture – it's a maginificent feat of engineering and I think it should be made into an historic site. Too few Canadians realize what great things we've built, even though we're still developing as a country. I have fond memories to go with my stetsons. They remind me of all the places I've visited and the people I've met in my travels around the country.

I don't think Trudeau liked me wearing the green stetson very much. He used to say to me, "What do you wear that hat for?" in a tone of voice that meant, "I think that hat's dumb." But whenever I don't wear it in public, people come up to me and say, "Hey, where's your green hat?" So I guess it really made a difference. Despite what Trudeau said, I kept on wearing it all the time I was agriculture minister, but I don't wear it so much anymore. People still ask where it is.

When I wasn't on the road, I kept in contact with ordinary Canadians through their letters. Every Cabinet minister receives thousands of letters every year but very few of them – if any – read every one. That was something I'd vowed to do when I became a minister. I swore I wasn't going to lose touch with people, become too important to listen to their concerns. Obviously I didn't have time to write an individual reply to each of the letters myself – and if someone sent us a form letter we just sent them a form letter right back – but I read every single genuine letter myself, read the reply my staff had written, and if I didn't like it I sent it back until I did. I signed every single letter that went out over my name. A lot people assumed that someone else signed my mail – or that I had a signature machine – and maybe some ministers did that, but not me. One year we kept track of how many letters I signed and it came to over eighteen thousand. Lots of times I stayed up until two in the morning just signing.

You sure as hell can learn a lot about Canada by reading the letters that come in. That's one of the things that bothers me when I read these books by people like John Roberts and Don Johnston. It's as if they've never really been in touch with the country they were supposed to be running. It makes me wonder whether they read all the letters they got. I'll bet there are some ministers who don't even read most of the letters that go out over their name. I wonder what they do when somebody comes up to them in the street – as people often did with me – and say

"I really liked that letter you sent to me." I guess the ministers who don't read their letters say, "Oh, you did? That's great," all the time praying to God that the person won't ask them another question. When that happened to me, I'd almost always remember what the letter was about – which would impress the person immensely. They say that one letter represents what five hundred people are thinking. By that measure I must have had a better finger on the people's pulse than just about anyone – including Goldfarb.

Many of the letters I got, of course, were people complaining about marketing boards or rotten eggs or milk subsidies or some other policy of mine. But I also got quite a few that congratulated me. I paid attention to both kinds, but those complimentary ones really meant a lot. I certainly got more appreciation from people across the country than I ever did from my colleagues in the Cabinet or the Liberal Party.

Sometimes the letters I got were cute or just plain funny. Like the time a man from Windsor wrote to me asking me to do what I could to find him a wife. Here's what I wrote back: "Thank you for your letter of December 3rd in which you advise me that you are looking for a wife. I can understand your concern but I am sure you realize that this matter does not come under my jurisdiction either as Minister of Agriculture or as member of parliament for Essex Windsor. If I should happen to learn of someone I will certainly be pleased to let you know.

Another letter I particularly liked was sent to me from a fellow in Kelowna, B.C. He'd heard a news report about a cow in Saskatchewan giving birth to a calf with two heads. In the letter he wrote: "To nourish the animal, the farmer is said to be feeding it through its two separate mouths. Undoubtedly it must moo through its two separate vocal organs. I understand from a reliable source that the Liberal Party is considering the nomination of this strange beast as its official candidate to run in the next election. Would you confirm the authenticity of this story, please?"

After I'd chuckled at this obvious swipe at Trudeau's bilingual policy I composed my response: "In spite of your kind suggestion, I doubt whether the Liberal Party would accept it.

I must say that my many years of personal experience on the farm make me doubt that the parent that gave birth to this aberration was sufficiently Liberal to run for Leader. Therefore, I figure that the bull must have been a Conservative one. It is true, as you say, that two heads are better than one, but two bodies would have been far more productive and to the liking of consumers who are complaining about the prices of beef. The productive part of the animal is at the other end from the head."

I wish all my letters could have been as much fun. Some of the ones I got were so sad they made me cry. One came in 1980 from a farmer in Saskatchewan who couldn't pay his bills and the bank was foreclosing on his farm. This was a time when the crops were bad, cattle prices had been low for several years, and interest rates were high. When I read his letter it really hit me hard. So I called Linda Clifford, a former Saskatchewan MLA then running our Regina office (she later became my executive assistant), and I tried to read the letter to her over the phone. I could hardly get through it. I felt so helpless but there wasn't much I could do. I knew what I'd feel like if I lost my farm and had no other source of income.

I would have been able to do more for that man and for all the other farmers who owed money to the bank and ended up losing what they'd built if only I'd been able to build the farmer's bank I'd dreamed about.

You'd think that my worst problems would have been with the farmers in Quebec, but just the opposite was true – with the exception of that brief period after we refused the emergency dairy subsidy in 1976. Even though I couldn't speak French I was very popular among Quebec farmers. They trusted me because I did so much for them. And when I went to a meeting I'd always have a French interpreter with me or one of my top officials, who were almost all fluent in French. I'd say my few words in French and then one of my parliamentary secretaries or one of my bilingual department officials would take over.

I went everywhere in Quebec and I only caught hell a couple of times for not speaking the language. When that happened, my reply would be that because Ontario had never made itself a bilingual province I'd never had the chance to learn French even though I'd grown up in a community that was part French and was part French myself. I'd tell them about the local separate school only a couple of miles from my house at Rivière Canard back home in Anderdon Township that taught all its classes in French. Teaching French like that was illegal, of course, and I've always thought that Ontario should become an officially bilingual province. With a very few exceptions I was never treated badly in Quebec. Perhaps farmers anywhere can communicate without speaking the same language.

One of my fondest memories of Quebec is when I was at Trois Pistoles in the Gaspé Peninsula to open a new addition to a large co-operative dairy plant. Before we'd brought in our dairy policy that area was pretty much a wasteland – barns falling down and farms going to bush and scrub. By this time the farms had been fixed up and it had become a kind of showplace. They were selling their milk to places like North Africa and their products were coming off the line labelled in Spanish, English and Arabic – all sorts of languages except French.

Archbishop Gilles Ouellet was at the meeting and I came with my deputy Gaétan Lussier and with Gilles Choquette, who was head of the Canadian Dairy Commission and had formerly been my executive assistant. The head of the dairy plant was a strong supporter of mine, even though he hardly spoke a word of English, and there was a big crowd of people on hand for the opening. I was standing there studying the people and Archbishop Ouellet noticed this so he asked me what I observed. And I said, "I see a fairly happy crowd of people – well dressed farmers, nice cars – and on the way here prosperous-looking farms." And he said, "Eugene, you can take credit for most of that. Ten, twelve years ago they never would have come to a meeting like this because they would have been too embarrassed. These are proud people and they would have been embarrassed then because they were so poor."

Rich or poor, I got to know farmers in every part of the country. And if they were in trouble, we did what we could to help. One time in 1976 I visited a group of cattlemen in Osoyoos in southern British Columbia right near the American border. Many of their cattle were dying of blue tongue disease, which is spread by small ticks. This blue tongue disease was an example of free trade since those little flies were coming across the border and no customs officer or anybody else was stopping them.

There's only one way to get rid of blue tongue and that's to get rid of the cows that have it. So we'd sent in one of our best department veterinarians, Dr. Ivan Reed, to supervise this and oversee the compensation payments to the farmers whose cows had to be killed. (The meat could be sold at the regular price but you couldn't export the cattle or the semen, which was important income when you had a pure-bred herd.) And I remember saying to him, "Now you be fair with those farmers because you're eradicating a pure-bred herd that they've spent their whole life developing – their own genetic strain."

Our department vets were great diplomats – they had to be – and Dr. Reed was one of the best. But when I went to Osoyoos to see how the farmers were doing and how our vet had done I was expecting them to be real mad at the federal government and at me. Instead the farmers were just as nice as could be. And after the meeting a few of them snuck up to me and jokingly said, "How do I get blue tongue in my herd?" That's how well the unlucky ones had been treated. (It also had something to do with the fact that the market for pure-bred cattle had collapsed so many of them were having trouble selling their beef at a decent price.)

This was in the south, but a lot of people don't realize how far north in British Columbia (and in other parts of Canada) there is farming. Some of the best cattle raising country is up north near places like Williams Lake and Smithers – they have big far-flung ranches up there. Smithers is where the current president of the the Canadian Federation of Agriculture comes from – Don Knoerr.

The Hereford calves they raise in those high pastures in northern B.C. are special and very pretty, too. The alpine grass is especially high in protein so the calves grow fast and, because it's so high above sea level and gets so cold, they grow an especially thick coat to keep them warm. They have nice flat

To SANTA
LOVE
Justin

Margaret Trudeau took this picture of Justin with me as Santa Claus at the annual parliamentary Christmas party. I'm probably saying to him, "Have you been a good boy?"

Here I'm with a bunch of "kids" at the Pacific National Exhibition in Vancouver.

I had lots of help turning the sod for the new school of veterinary medicine on P.E.I. LEFT to RIGHT: Philip Matheson, chairman of the board, Donald Downe, who headed the advisory committee, me, Premier Jim Lee, Mac Macleod of New Brunswick, Joe Goudie of P.E.I.
Gene Pierce

I brought U.S. Secretary of Agriculture John Block into the House of Commons to show him the seat of Canadian democracy. Unlike our ministers, he hadn't been elected and he never had to face a Question Period.

In 1983, my tenth annual meeting
with the provincial agriculture
ministers was in the same spot
as the first one back in 1973 –
Brudenell, P.E.I.

Canada does so much trade with
Texas that every year there's a
special Canada Day at the Dallas
State Fair. But I was probably
their first Canadian guest of
honour who wore a green stetson.

Bob Bergland was Secretary of
Agriculture under Jimmy Carter.
Nice guy, but he sometimes had
trouble making a decision.
Canapress Photo Service

I guess I made the Americans
pretty mad when I put import
restrictions on their beef. But
then, a little bull goes a long way.

Our trade agreement with Mexico in 1981 was a good deal for both sides. Trade Minister Ed Lumley is standing behind us and the man on the left is Trade Minister Jorge de la Vega.

During our 1981 China trip some of us visited the Great Wall. Left to right: Dr. Gordon Burton, John Smiley, Dr. Douglas Hedley, Peter Epp (kneeling), me, Henry Vandermeulen, Ambassador Arthur Menzies.

With the help of my translator Jean Duval, Chinese Vice-Premier Wan-Li was able to understand Whelanese.

I'm probably telling Israeli Prime Minister
Menachem Begin how much I like his country's
export agency, Agrexco. Soon after my 1979 visit
I tried to set up a similar one in Canada called
Canagrex. (Agriculture Minister Ariel Sharon
is on the left.)

When I was in Cuba in 1983, Fidel Castro paid
me a late evening visit to talk about prize cattle
and poor plumbing.

I had a lot of fun showing Mikhail Gorbachev our country. He was amazed at the variety and prices of the food in our supermarkets. The picture with the sausage was taken at the Schneider's meat-packing plant in Kitchener and the one in front of our house is with Liz and Alexander Yakovlev, then Soviet Ambassador. I wonder if Mikhail still wears the stetson I gave him.

This is the Ethiopian village we adopted just outside of Addis Ababa.

During my 1980 visit to Tanzania I showed President Julius Nyerere around our Canadian-run wheat farm. The Versatile tractor behind us was made in Winnipeg.

In 1983, I visited this dam in Eritrea with Ethiopian Agriculture Minister Tekola Dejene (left) and Saihou Sabally, former Agriculture Minister of Gambia and a Vice-President of the World Food Council.

Francisco Merino Rabago, a former Minister of Agriculture of Mexico, handed over the presidency of the World Food Council to me in 1983.

I'm looking awfully serious in this picture of me as President of the World Food Council. I had reason to be, since by then the famine in Africa was already a terrible tragedy.

Javier Perez de Cuellar, Secretary General of the United Nations, agreed with me that more had to be done to aid the victims of the African drought.

In March 1984 I asked Pope John Paul II to help
me in my crusade against hunger.

François Mitterand gave a nice-sounding speech
at the World Food Council's annual meeting
in 1985, but that was about it.
Associated Press

Not many members of the parliamentary classes of 1962 and '63 were MPs twenty years later. Most of them are in this picture. BACK ROW, LEFT to RIGHT: Jean-Luc Pepin, Jean Chrétien, Rosaire Gendron, Ian Watson, Alexandre Cyr, Lloyd Francis; FRONT ROW: Bryce Mackasey, John Munro, Allan MacEachen, Herb Gray, me, Gérald Laniel.
J.M. Carisse Photo

In 1982 my staff threw a surprise party to celebrate my 20 years as an MP. One of the guests was Red Kelly (my roommate back in 1963).

Trudeau showed up at the party celebrating my first ten years as a minister. I always knew I'd get him down on the farm one day.

Gaétan Boucher, the champion
speed skater, presented me with
a gold award on behalf of the
Dairy Bureau of Canada for my
promotion of the Canadian
dairy industry.

In 1983 John Mooney, Jr., on
behalf of Racetracks of Canada,
presented me with the award
named after his father for
"outstanding contribution to
the racing industry."

Major-General Richard Rohmer
presented me with my Honorary
Doctor of Laws at the University
of Windsor in 1983.

It really felt good to be honoured on my home turf when I received the Windsor/Detroit Freedom Festival Award in 1986.
Katherine Roth

Lt.Col. Bill Buckham presented me with this plaque in 1984 from the folks at 412 Squadron of the Department of National Defence because I'd travelled with them more than any other minister.

In April 1984, when I threw my hat in the leadership ring, Cathy (left), Terry (right) and Sue were at my side. What better support could I have asked for?
Canapress Photo Service

This is the picture we chose for our campaign brochure.
Its caption might have read: "A man out standing
in his field."
Ken Burnett

I was awful tired when I gave my speech but, like the chicken who went halfway across the road, I laid it on the line.

On the first evening of the convention the delegates gave me a warm welcome when I arrived for the tribute to Pierre Trudeau. Canada misses him.
Canapress Photo Service

We all needed to unwind on the eve of the convention balloting after the speeches took place.

This is the formal picture they took of me after I was appointed Ambassador to the World Food and Agriculture Organization in Rome. Nice picture, but it's all I've got to show for it.
John Evans Photo Ltd.

Many people commented afterward that Pierre
seemed touched by my convention speech.
(That's Tom Axworthy sitting on one side of him,
and his sister Suzette on the other. Behind him
are the co-chairmen of the convention, Iona
Campagnolo and Rémi Boujold.)

This cartoon appeared when the
Tories appointed Roy McMurtry
High Commissioner to the United
Kingdom – not long after Little
Joe Clark had fired me as F A O
Ambassador.
Globe and Mail/ Ed Franklin

My twenty-fifth wedding anniversary in 1985 was a good chance to think back over the many good things that had happened to me during my career in politics. LEFT to RIGHT: Terry, Liz, me, Cathy, and Sue.

backs with curly, curly hair which is lovely to the touch. These calves are so desirable that every year they're bought by farmers as far away as Nova Scotia and shipped all the way down East, which is more travelling than most Canadians do in their own country in a lifetime. I used to say that these calves were the greatest tourists in Canada – which I didn't think made much economic sense.

Unlike those beef calves, when I travelled to the East Coast I lived long enough to tell the tale and to return again. I've spent time in all three of the Maritime provinces and in Newfoundland, but I think my favourite one is the smallest, Prince Edward Island – although you never want to get involved in one of their fights. Islanders are funny people. They think it's all right to brawl amongst themselves, but don't you get involved. They're very friendly otherwise. (The same is true of the Pelee Islanders in my own riding.) I think it would be a mistake if they build the causeway to P.E.I. It will destroy the special quality of the place.

In particular I remember the time when young Alex Campbell, the Liberal premier, and I were travelling around P.E.I. with another Liberal I called Digger O'Dell – his real name was Sinclair Cutcliffe; I called him Digger because he was an undertaker. Anyhow, Alex was driving his own car and we ran out of gas. So we walked to the closest farmhouse. Turned out two old bachelors lived there – it was a well-kept place – and we told them our problem and they gave us five gallons of tractor gas and a flat fifty of cigarettes because Alex had also run out of cigarettes. They wouldn't take money for the gas because it was tractor gas and they gave Alex the cigarettes free, too. When I got back to Ottawa I sent them an autographed copy of a book on Canada and the two old gents sent me a note saying I'd just got myself two more Liberal votes. They hadn't expected any thanks for what they'd done. They were just being neighbourly.

On that same trip East I went with Alex to a political meeting on the Island. That time he had seven people in his car: I guess he wanted to save on gas. That Campbell was a real Scotsman; he was as tight as the bark on a tree. He was also very protective of everything that went on in his province and when I was there he'd coach me carefully on what I was to say. I used to remind him that his whole province was about the size of my one riding of Essex-Windsor.

Not only did I try to take the agriculture department out of Ottawa and into every part of the country; I also did what I could to show off Canadian agriculture to the world. It was my way of promoting our products and our agricultural technology. I fought for and finally got Canadian wines used in all our foreign embassies. And whenever we ate in a Canadian restaurant that didn't serve Canadian wine I'd hand them a little card that said: "We enjoyed our meal very much, but a wider selection of the better Canadian wines would have enhanced our dining pleasure." (I still keep up this practice.)

Like almost everything you do in politics, even my support of the wine industry got me in trouble with some of the voters. Paul Bosc of Château des Charmes, Don Ziraldo of Inniskillin, Ed Arnold of Brights, Andrew Peller of Andrés, and the many other fine Canadian winemakers who were active while I was agriculture minister had few complaints about my views on wine drinking. (In my own riding there are now two wineries – Colio and Pelee Island Winery.) But I got quite a few letters from people who accused me of encouraging alcoholism. In 1974 I got such a letter from a woman in Sudbury. She wrote: "I, for one, deeply resent the advice that you offered so glibly, that we as a nation drink more wine. It ought to be obvious to everyone that further consumption by the population of any alcoholic beverages can be detrimental."

I wrote her a nice letter back, pointing out the advantages of wine over other stronger liquor and added, "When consumed properly, with the meal, it aids digestion, calms nerves and enhances the taste and enjoyment of the meal. Wine is an agricultural product, made from the juice of grapes. It has been used for centuries and is mentioned throughout the Bible as a pure food. As with any food, however, there is the possibility of overindulging. This I do not condone."

I considered it an important part of my job to promote Canadian agriculture and agriculture products and in order to do this I wasn't afraid of publicity. For example, on one occasion I risked the wrath of ferocious apple growers in order to promote Canadian apples. I had heard of a scientific study that showed that if a woman ate an apple in thirty seconds she had an urge to make love. So I went on the radio and told about this study we had for apples and how they affected women more than men. Soon after, a man I knew came up to me on the street in Saskatoon and said, "You damn fool, my wife has the kitchen full of apples." I said, "That's the idea, we're trying to sell 'em." Then I added, "Knowing you, she better have it full of men, too." He laughed.

Something else I did to promote Canadian agriculture and Canadian food was to invite all the foreign ambassadors and trade officers to come to the Ottawa Experimental Farm every fall to show them what Canada was doing in the field of agricultural research and offer them a little hospitality. It was nothing fancy, just some good Canadian wine and food under a big tent. Loads of people showed up and the atmosphere was very friendly. People brought their families and made it an outing. I'm told the diplomatic corps still talks about these gatherings.

I would also often host foreign visitors at the Experimental Farm and the Agricultural Research Station, everyone from presidents and prime ministers to royalty. Mikhail Gorbachev was one of my guests there, as was Princess Anne. Before Anne was to arrive I had been warned to watch out for her–some of the people at External Affairs told me she was not a nice person and that she'd be bitchy and hard to get along with. So I was all ready for an unpleasant time with Her Royal Highness.

She turned out to be one of the nicest people I've had to deal with. We got along marvellous. Right away we had a rapport because she was wearing this big green straw hat and I had on my green stetson. The caption under our picture the next day in the Ottawa *Citizen* read, "And where did you get *your* green hat?" It was obvious to me after talking to her for no more than five minutes that she was better versed on the showcase herd I was showing off than I was. So I turned her over to Brian Harrington, a herdsman who worked at the farm, saying, "Your Royal Highness, I don't know all the pedigrees of these cattle, their genetic background, like Brian does, so I'll let him tell you."

Brian is a short fellow, only about five-feet-four, but I can tell you he grew to about six feet right away. And he did a tremendous job and got along great with her. She's a no-nonsense down-to-earth person, which I like – very easy to talk to and very knowledgeable about agriculture.

We looked at the beef herd and the dairy herd and she asked all sorts of smart questions. She knew all the characteristics of the Herefords and the shorthorns and the Aberdeen Angus. In one of the pens there was a big black Aberdeen Angus bull and he was in a black mood. He was pawing the ground and pacing up and down and bellowing. Princess Anne took one look at him and said, "I know what's wrong with him. He's been taken away from the cows. He's dissatisfied." She was quite right; he'd been with the cows until the day before, but there weren't any left that needed servicing.

I've met Anne's parents as well, though under much more formal circumstances, at an official reception at the Chateau Laurier during an official visit. I knew I'd be meeting the Queen and Prince Philip that day so I thought I'd put something different on my lapel – I usually wore a little Canadian maple-leaf-flag pin – because I knew the old Duke was very inquisitive and would be sure to make some comment about it. I put on a little pin that said "Mile Post Zero." It was a souvenir from mile zero of the Alaska Highway, which starts at Dawson Creek in the Yukon.

Sure enough, when I got to the Duke he asked me what it was. And I told him. And he asked me, "What were you doing there?" – he knew I was agriculture minister. I said, "We have farmers up there." And he said, "Impossible. That far north?" I assured him there were and offered to take him up there one day.

I don't think Prince Philip believed me. At least he never took me up on my offer. But we have had experimental farms and research stations as far north in the Yukon as mile 1019 of the Alaska Highway and at Fort Simpson in the Northwest Territories. In Alberta we still have a farm up at Fort Vermilion, near Fort McMurray where the main crop is heavy crude oil. We grow short-season barley and Canola and oats. The growing season is short but in the summer you get as much as twenty hours of sunlight every day. So even though there are only sixty frost-free days you can still grow a crop. There are some big farms up there. J. I. Case, the farm machinery company, owns a farm of several thousand acres in northern B.C. near Fort St. John.

Research stations and experimental farms – like those I wanted Prince Philip to visit – are the backbone of Agriculture Canada's research effort. Agricultural research was always one of my priorities as minister and I gave as much money to research as I possibly could. My philosophy was just the same as that old General Electric ad that said, "Research is our most important product!" When I came on the scene in 1972, the research budget was just over $50 million; when I left in 1984 it was almost $250 million, the largest of any branch or department of government except the National Research Council. Without research Canadian agriculture would never have become the world leader it is today. And without its continuation, we will soon fall behind other countries in the world.

Few people realize just how important research has been in the development of Canadian agriculture. When the West was opening up, the federal government built agricultural research stations and experimental farms as the settlers moved in. We helped our farmers adjust to the different growing conditions on the Prairies and developed crops that would flourish in the colder climate. In Canada we now produce 55 percent of our food further north than any other country in the world. People come to us from all over the world, including China and the Soviet Union, the two biggest countries on earth, to see how we're doing it.

One of the earliest successes of Canadian agricultural research was the development just after the turn of the century of Marquis hard red spring wheat (a cross between hard red Calcutta and red fife), which matured earlier than previous varieties, had an excellent yield and was outstanding for milling and baking. That wheat became the standard of quality for spring wheat throughout the world and without it our Canadian Prairies would not have become the great breadbasket they are today. There have been many other successes. A recent one is the development of triticale, a hybrid of wheat and rye that is the world's first man-made crop species. A lot of people around the world claim credit for triticale but the main work on it was done by three researchers, two of whom started out working on it with Agriculture Canada, Dr. Frank Zilinski at the Cereal Division in Ottawa, Dr. Glen Anderson at the Rust Research Laboratory in Winnipeg, and Dr. Leonard Shebeski at the University of Manitoba.

As I've said, much of early Canadian agricultural research was to develop crops that could flourish in our cold climate and short growing season. As well as spring wheat, we've come up with new varieties of winter wheat and a new strain of the old-fashioned rapeseed, to which we gave the name Canola. Canola is known as the "Cinderella" crop of Western Canada because it can be seeded late in the spring and still produce a good crop, yet its oil is equal in quality to that of the soy bean. Nearly 60 percent of the vegetable oil consumed by Canadians now comes from Canola.

Every year in Canada we release an average of fifty new plant varieties – many of these new strains developed by Agriculture Canada are available on the open market. The research station at Harrow, back home in Essex County, recently released a new strain of winter wheat called Harus that will increase Ontario wheat production by 10 percent. The scientists at Harrrow, with co-operation from plant breeders in Ottawa and in Morden, Manitoba, have come up with the first short-season soy bean and early strains of corn. Now Canadian farmers in many parts of the country can grow mature shell corn and soy beans where fifteen years ago this was possible only in the most temperate parts of Ontario. Imagine the economic impact of these kinds of improvements happening over and over again.

One of the things we developed at the Winnipeg Research Station is called a plant growth chamber. This is a large room that creates its own world with its own weather. You can have hailstorms, frost, drought, floods – whatever you want. So you can test new plant strains under a whole variety of conditions over a very short time. That means we can make them available to farmers much sooner. It used to take twenty years from making the first cross to introducing a new variety. Now it can be done in eleven or twelve. And the development of these growth cabinets has put Canada ahead of the rest of the world in their design and construction. A Winnipeg firm now exports $6 million worth annually.

The researchers are always looking for ways to make Canada more productive. For instance, no computer program could have predicted our success in growing feed grain around Dawson Creek. More recently we've been looking at Newfoundland, where there's tremendous potential for growing forage – immature grasses that are high in protein and can be harvested in the damp season. Newfoundland could become self-sufficient in certain kinds of feed that it now must import.

Our research now covers just about every area of agriculture you can imagine. Our genetic research continues as we aim to develop drought-resistant and disease-resistant grasses and cereal grains. At the experimental farm and research station in Regina we're investigating ways to use insects and bacteria to replace herbicides and pesticides as part of the larger study of how to become less dependent on chemicals in agriculture. Thanks to research and good inspection and control, Canada has the most disease-free livestock herds in the world. Agriculture Canada researchers were able to breed strains of poultry resistant to Marek's disease, a virus that had up till then been only partly combatted by a vaccine. As recently as 1965 Marek's disease caused annual losses in Canada alone of $20 million. Now we lose nothing.

At the research station in Fredericton, New Brunswick, and at several other stations, we have a window into a cow's three stomachs that allows the researchers to learn more about the way in which it digests food. (It's not a pleasant thing to see, but it doesn't hurt the animals at all.) No scientist has been able to develop anything that compares with a cow's ability to turn raw roughage into high-protein milk or meat.

Researchers are looking for ways to produce cheaper beef by producing hybrids between our British breeds and imported European breeds. Cows from the best crosses stand on the range longer, produce more calves, and the calves grow faster than the pure British breeds. At the research station at Lennoxville, Quebec, we're also breeding sexier sheep. In an attempt to extend the breeding season, they crossed Australian Dorsets with Canadian Leicester and Suffolk breeds. This produced a line called DLS which had a breeding season longer than any of the three parent breeds. To make them sexier still, the Lennoxville scientists imported some Finnish rams which were crossbred with the DLS ewes, who promptly produced fifty-five more lambs per hundred litters than before. Not bad.

One of our more amazing success stories was actually in food-processing. Engineers in Ottawa designed and built a blancher-cooker which they thought would use less energy in the form of steam and turn out a better product than standard blanching methods. To try it out commercially, the equipment they developed was sent to our food-processing laboratory at the research station in Kentville, Nova Scotia, where it was tested in a commercial plant under normal operating conditions. It not only reduced the cooking time by more than half, but retained more goodness and gave off less waste water. So the process was patented and the equipment is now manufactured by a Nova Scotia firm which has already made sales in the U.S., Europe, and New Zealand – and won several awards.

Finally, our agricultural researchers make extensive use of outer space. We use satellites to tell us what's going on on the ground. The satellites take pictures of the farms and tell us how the soil is doing and how the crops are doing on the land. The pictures can tell us what crops are planted and where there are problems with soil erosion or salinization. The people at the Chicago grain futures market watch the satellite pictures all the time to see what the crops are like. They can tell if the crops are heavy or light – even the protein content of a grain harvest. You can tell by the colour of the crops if they lack nitrogen and so on. And satellite pictures told us well in advance of the headlines what was happening with the famine in Africa.

Our agricultural research is also an important part of our foreign aid effort – something that became of increasing interest to me after 1980. Canadian farmers and scientists are among the best in the world when it comes to growing crops under dry-land conditions. As a result, many developing countries often ask Canada to help them learn how to grow food when they have low rainfall and not enough water for irrigation. Even developed countries such as Russia send their ministers and scientists to Canada to find out how we make our arid areas produce so much food. While I was minister I signed an agreement with the Soviet Union to exchange research and researchers. Now Canadian scientists work in Russia and their researchers come here. And we've helped India learn to increase food production on its rain-fed lands, Brazilian wheat breeders produce a better wheat for South American conditions, Pakistan improve its rapeseed varieties, and Chile grow better sunflower seeds.

The Harosoy bean that was developed at the Harrow Research Station was distributed all over the world. It's well adapted to a hot climate because in Essex County you get summer temperatures over a hundred degrees and humid, and it withstands the fungus diseases that are common in the tropics, so it thrives in southern China and in South America. The Harosoy bean probably did more to provide protein for poor countries than almost anything else we did. We also share our technological know-how – such as those growth chambers I mentioned.

It's impossible to calculate the full rate of return on agricultural research – although in some cases we can come up with impressive numbers. For every dollar we have invested in developing Canola, the return to farmers and processors is between $300 and $400 every year – and some of that comes back to the government in taxes. The same kind of calculation could be made for wheat, oats, barley, alfalfa seed, sheep, beef, and hundreds of other research projects. There's even a recent study that estimates the return from our research at between forty and five hundred times, depending on the item.

If we let research fall away, soon we won't be able to keep pace with other countries. In the tough world of international trade you have to stay one step ahead of your competitors, and agricultural research is the key to increasing agricultural efficiency and competitiveness. For instance, right now Western agriculture uses a huge amount of energy (for fertilizer, for hothouses, for processing, for transportation). Every time we increase the energy efficiency of our agriculture we're making ourselves more competitive on the world market. The provincial ministers I worked with all understood the importance of research. If you look at the minutes of the federal-provincial agricultural meetings I attended over the years you'll see that time and again the provinces were asking us for more research and wanted it to remain a federal responsibility.

I'm very worried that the new government doesn't understand this. They're already talking about cutting the amount of money spent on agricultural research and there are even rumours that they want to take research away from agriculture and put it under the National Research Council – an idea that was rejected as a dumb one back in 1938. They probably figure it will be even easier to cut then.

And now the Tories have come out with the Nielsen task force report on agriculture, which just burns my ass. The report seems to have been written by a bunch of economists and businessmen who know little or nothing about agriculture. I'll bet if you asked Darcy McKeough and the others on the committee that wrote the report how many federal marketing boards there are in Canada they wouldn't be able to tell you. There are only five, but in the report they don't hesitate to recommend that no new ones should be established and they talk about getting rid of the ones there are.

It's kind of funny that Darcy McKeough is now the man supposed to have all the answers. When he was Treasurer of Ontario he borrowed billions of dollars to build all those coal, oil and nuclear electricity plants and the province is still paying the interest on those loans – millions and millions of dollars. As a result of this overbuilding they shut down some perfectly good generating plants – and never started up some units that were built at great expense. I often say that the people who live in Ontario should curse Darcy McKeough and Bill Davis for their incompetence every time they turn on the electric switch. But old Darcy is going to tell us how to run agriculture.

When I was minister, many farmers didn't appreciate what I was doing for them. But now that I'm gone, they tell me over and over by letter and when I meet with them that they didn't know when they had it good. The Tories boast that they've passed more agriculture legislation in their short time in office than Whelan did in all those years. Well, my only reply to them is that paper doesn't feed cows and it doesn't feed people. The dairy industry certainly appreciates how much I did for them. We made the dairy industry in Canada probably the most productive and economically the most stable of any dairy industry in the world. A lot of dairy farmers voted against us in the last election – I can't exactly say that I blame them – but now they wish we were back.

When I look back on my twelve years as Minister of Agriculture I have some mixed feelings – I would have liked to have done more – but all in all I'm damn proud of what I accomplished. There were the new marketing systems for farmers – eggs, chickens, and turkeys. The farmers who went along with those systems are still doing pretty well economically. They're not the ones that are going broke that you read about in the paper. And we improved farm stabilization and crop insurance and gave the Farm Credit Corporation more muscle and I kept research on the front burner. And we did what we could to open up new export markets to Canadian farmers. One of the last things I fought for and won was the establishment of a centralized exporting agency for Canadian agriculture – Canagrex. Unfortunately, the new government has killed it.

I take great satisfaction when I drive through parts of the country where there are prosperous and well kept farms that weren't so prosperous or so pretty twenty years ago. I'm very proud of the general improvement of the overall farm infrastructure in Canada. Regardless of what people say, more young people entered agriculture in Canada while I was minister than in the previous twenty years. The average age of farmers actually went from fifty-four years of age down to about forty-eight-and-half.

I'm also proud of the good working relationship I had, not only with our neighbour to the south, but with the rest of the agricultural world. I helped build Canada's prominence as a great agricultural nation internationally and I gave agriculture a greater profile at home. And we did all the things we did without spending that much money, only about 1.2 percent of total federal expenditures.

All in all, I thought we ran a pretty good ship. If I could have done as much internationally, I'd be a much happier man.

9

Pipsqueaks and Politicians

Contrary to what many people think, Trudeau ran his Cabinet with a very loose hand. He seldom cut off the discussion, even when you could tell he was getting a little upset by the repetitive presentations that were being made and how long the talk was going on. I used to wonder how he put up with some of the things that went on – and I certainly wasn't the most innocent one, either. When I saw he was getting impatient I'd often cut my remarks to a simple "I agree" or "I disagree" and pass to the next person. Trudeau ran the Cabinet by consensus. I was never in the Pearson Cabinet, but I gather from those who were – people like Jean Chrétien and Paul Martin – that he was in many ways tougher and more impatient than Trudeau when the discussions got too long. Trudeau loved to argue and he loved to win an argument, but he was willing to let others talk. How he put up with us I sometimes wondered. I always laughed when people described him as a dictator.

The atmosphere in the Cabinet room was usually pretty friendly. In 1972, Dan MacDonald from P.E.I. was the Minister

of Veterans Affairs and, like me, Dan is partly deaf. Hugh
Faulkner was a minister then and he used to sit between us –
which was a risky place to be. Whenever someone was speaking
a bit softly I'd hit Hugh on one side and Dan with his artificial
arm would hit him on the other and ask him, "What did he say?"
Hugh used to joke that sitting between us two so-and-sos he
was black and blue all the time.

Dan didn't say much in Cabinet, but when he did he generally
got his way. Trudeau had tremendous admiration for him – and
he made his points rather forcefully. MacDonald had only one
good arm and when he wanted to speak he'd say, "Mr. Prime
Minister," and he'd bang his hand on the table, "I'd like to be
recognized." When this happened the whole room would be quiet
as a mouse. He'd been Minister of Agriculture in Prince Edward
Island before he came to Ottawa and he was one of my strongest
backers at the Cabinet table.

My main fights in Cabinet were usually with the finance minister or with the Minister of Consumer and Corporate Affairs. I
dealt with quite a few consumer ministers: Herb Gray, Bryce
Mackasey, Tony Abbott, Warren Allmand, André Ouellet, and
Judy Erola. The portfolio was a bit of a revolving door, while I
stayed put. Herb Gray was appointed to the job in 1972 when I
entered the Cabinet and lasted until 1974. We had some terrible
disagreements, despite our long friendship. It was a very trying
time for me because I thought his department bureaucrats were
being most unfair and this was while I was still learning the
ropes. But I held firm because they were trying to zero in on the
group of people that could protect themselves the least – farmers.
There aren't enough farmers and they aren't organized like
unions. They don't have the same clout as other groups in society. At one time I even advocated that farmers should form something like a trade union, just so that their voices would be heard.

The fight was always pretty much the same. The Consumer
and Corporate Affairs bureaucrats and the minister would argue
against anything that raised prices for food; they wanted control
in the name of the almighty consumer. They were very much
against marketing boards. They couldn't see that marketing
boards guaranteed that food prices could not rise irresponsibly

– the price always had to be related to the cost of production – because they were under stricter control. (We proved our case afterwards when commodities that were outside marketing boards had worse inflation than the products that were under marketing boards.) And I would argue that my agricultural programs were protecting the consumer much better in the long run because prices would go up more gradually and in a more orderly fashion and because I was protecting the food supply. I'd point out that North Americans only spend a small portion of their disposable income on food compared to Europeans. And so on. I'm sure John Wise, the new agriculture minister, is having the same arguments in the Tory Cabinet today.

I fought with all of them, but André Ouellet (who had the job after the 1980 election) was probably the easiest consumer minister I had to deal with because he was from Quebec. He had to behave or else the Quebec farmers, who were supporters of my policies, would get after him. The Quebec farmers are probably the strongest organized farm group of all. So, unlike all the others, Ouellet didn't always go along blindly with the consumers without considering the larger picture. But on the whole, it was Consumer and Corporate Affairs that was the hardest for me to deal with. They were a small department and the bureaucrats wanted the department to be bigger and have more power – so that was part of the problem.

I wasn't only concerned with defending Agriculture, of course. I was on the Defence and External Affairs committees almost from the beginning, the latter in large part because of my interest in food aid and foreign aid in general. I became quite a strong advocate of a sort of world police force that you could send in with some authority to put down unrest and help them organize countries into viable democratic entities. But I wouldn't have set this up as part of the UN, which is an inefficient old thrashing machine when what you need is the most modern combine you can buy. Of course, one day someone would have to come along and shake up the world police force because all these organizations become bureaucratic and obsolete over time.

I was also very active in the economic and social areas of Cabinet. For example, I can remember when we were discussing

the development of the Alberta tar sands and all the great economists were against it – this was in my first term. It was going to
cost us something over seven dollars a barrel and the world
price was much lower. So we backed off and it wasn't very many
years later that we went into the tar sands at forty some dollars
a barrel. I was one of those who felt very strongly that we should
have gone ahead earlier.

I also took a strong interest in reform of unemployment insurance (I'd served on that committee as a backbencher) and I was
a big supporter of the Minister of Health and Welfare, even
though I did think the department spent too much of the government budget. I used to have fun with Monique Bégin (who took
the post after 1980) because I spent 1.4 percent of the federal
budget and she spent more than 30 percent, but she could never
get as much publicity as I could.

One of the things that always bothered me about Cabinet
meetings was how much paper you were supposed to shuffle. You
went to each Cabinet meeting with two fat briefing books covering the items to be discussed. There was no way any minister
could go through all that material and also look after his own
department. What many of them did was read the briefing books
right there in the Cabinet room while the others were talking. If
you were a quick reader you could read enough on the spot to
make a great intelligent contribution, as if you'd studied the
matter deeply. This seemed silly to me and I thought most
Cabinet meetings were pretty much a waste of time.

Agriculture is considered less important than many other
portfolios and many of the ministers didn't like to deal with
Agriculture because they knew nothing about it. So when it
came to my presentation there would sometimes be only a corporal's guard left in the room. Trudeau himself seldom left a
Cabinet meeting before the end; and if he considered an item
important, he'd be sure everyone stayed. (The Deputy Prime
Minister or a senior Cabinet minister would chair in his absence.)
Many times the agenda was too heavy and my item would be
delayed to the following week. It didn't just happen to me, of
course; other departments also got shunted aside. Maybe I was

too soft about this, particularly later on when I was a senior minister.

There's no question that there were deals made between ministers: "I'll support you on this if you'll support me on that" – that sort of thing. And everyone was competing for the support of Finance. I don't remember ever getting involved in making deals, but I did have my friends and allies. In 1972 my natural allies were Paul Martin and Herb Gray. Paul was Government Leader in the Senate and so was automatically in the Cabinet. All three of us were from Windsor and we used to be called the Gang of Three. Because Herb was then the great friend of the consumer, we fought on some things but we cooperated on anything that affected our area. For instance, in 1972 and 1973 there were serious floods in our ridings and we had three voices and three votes in Cabinet arguing for emergency relief. We got it, too.

One of the few good things about Cabinet meetings was that there were very few bureaucrats present. But the bureaucrats had already done their work, whispering into the minister's ear and influencing what would be talked about during the meetings of the Cabinet committees. Some ministers relied solely on briefings by their bureaucrats.

One thing I learned right away was that Trudeau never overruled his finance minister. That was equally true for John Turner, Don Macdonald, Jean Chrétien, Allan MacEachen, and Marc Lalonde. If the finance minister disagreed with my position, that was it, unless there was sufficient support for me from other ministers that Finance could be won over. But this happened very rarely since nobody wanted to cross the finance minister – he was too powerful and could kill you in Cabinet. Time and again I'd lose, no matter how right I was, because Finance was opposed. And Trudeau would usually turn to me and say that familiar line: "Sorry, Gene, you lost another one." Sometimes I'd get so mad I'd just slam my books together, stand up and walk out.

From 1972 to 1975, when John Turner resigned as finance minister, I would sometimes sit next to him at meetings. That's when I discovered his secret. He was a good reader. He always had his briefing book prepared for him by his deputy – until 1974 that was Simon Reisman, who took early retirement and became a consultant. The book was easy to read because it contained very short summary statements on every subject and it was nicely indexed with little subject tabs sticking out. I guess you could say it was a version of the famous Turner cue cards. When he was asked a question or it was time for him to make a comment, he just found the right tab and read from the book. Hell, I could have been that kind of finance minister.

After Turner announced he had resigned, I called him several times to find out his reasons. But he never called me back. There were a lot of stories going around and I wanted to find out for myself. Most people think it came down to his being frustrated by the fact that Pierre showed no signs of wanting to retire. He wanted to be Prime Minister and he knew he wasn't going to be for a long time. But there was certainly more to it than that. A few months before Turner quit I remember him saying to me, "Gene, I gotta make some money. My friends are all earning two hundred grand a year and I don't intend to be an economic eunuch. I'm getting out of here." He certainly did what he said he would.

Most Ministers of Finance, Turner included, thought they were too good to come to Cabinet committee meetings – where the real work of Cabinet was done. They'd send their deputy if we were lucky, or an assistant deputy. So I'd go to committee and fight like hell and win my case there and then be overruled by Turner or one of his successors in full Cabinet. That's one of the things that really made me mad. If we'd won in committee, it should have been approved automatically in the Cabinet. I won about 75 percent of my battles in committee but once Finance was finished, my percentage was down to the 50 percent I mentioned earlier.

By the time Marc Lalonde was Minister of Finance I'd learned to work the system better. I think Lalonde came to more of my Cabinet committee meetings than any finance minister I'd known. That was at least partly because I used to get after him pretty vicious. I'd warn him that if I got something through Cabinet committee when he wasn't there I'd go straight to Trudeau and tell him his finance minister was absent and that I didn't want it turned down at Cabinet. Lalonde got the message.

It was in Cabinet committee where you saw the real action – that was where the ministers and their deputies would really tell one another off: we had some great fights. And it was in committee between 1972 and 1974 that I had a chance to take the measure of Simon Reisman, now our free trade ambassador, who was, in my opinion, a very overrated person. In those days my deputy Syd Williams could out-argue old Simon any day. I can remember him one time telling Simon, "You're full of that brown stuff, not up to here, but right up to here. You don't know what the hell you're talking about." They talked to each other like that, but they were good friends, too.

Next to Finance, the most important committee of all was Treasury Board. As Minister of Agriculture I used to appear there at least once a month to get approval for any spending that hadn't been approved as part of the department's annual budget. Those meetings were tough and there would sometimes be some pretty rough language. There was always a big crowd of bureaucrats when I came to present my case. For a long time I thought they all hated me and were there to gang up on me because I used to put up a hell of fight. But not long ago I ran into a fellow who'd been with Treasury Board for some years and I said to him, "You must have hated my guts for all the mean meetings we used have." He said, "On the contrary, we thought you were great." So I asked him why so many of his colleagues came. "When they knew you'd be there," he said, "they wanted to come because you were the best prepared minister who came before the board."

I can thank my deputies and my department for that. Agriculture Canada when I was there did by far the best job of preparing their minister for a debate. It also helped that I was stubborn and persistent. I remember a bureaucrat on the board telling me about a particular occasion when he wanted to turn me down. And my deputy – who at that time was Gaétan Lussier

–turned to him and said, "You can turn this one down if you want, but he'll appeal your decision and be right back again with another request." So I got what I wanted.

When I first arrived in Cabinet, the President of the Treasury Board was Bud Drury from Montreal, one of the veterans of the Pearson years. He didn't always give me what I wanted but we got along well. We had a sort of friendly feud going. I'd come in there all fired up and we used to have lots of fun. In the last war he was Canada's youngest general; so any time I was losing a battle I'd start to call him Sergeant Drury just to irritate him. He was very businesslike, and I liked him very much.

I had my criticisms of the Cabinet system under Trudeau but I thought one of the biggest problems with the way we ran the government was the failure of caucus to make the ministers really listen. Part of this was Trudeau's style of running caucus meetings. He tolerated much less unruly and rambunctious behaviour than had Pearson. But I also think it had a lot to do with the changing nature of the MPs themselves. They were getting better educated and becoming less effective than in earlier days. Many wanted to be ministers right away and they looked at someone like me – someone without much formal education – and got all disillusioned because they equated intelligence and ability with education. They'd think, "How come he's sitting there when I'm so smart and he's so dumb?" Another thing is, many of them wanted to be technocrats rather than politicians – hair-splitters instead of log-splitters. And they were lazier too, on average: they wanted their staff to do all the work.

If you measured MPs today by the quality of their letter-heads and the initials they have after their names they'd probably seem the finest we've ever had. But when you look at what goes on in Parliament and in caucus they sometimes begin to look like highly educated buffoons. I never got over the way they treated Mme Sauvé when she had just become the Speaker. You may remember they were screaming and shaking their fists like a bunch of mad people. No bunch of ignoramuses could have behaved worse in my opinion. Maybe television is partly to blame.

I liked Jeanne Sauvé very much. In my opinion she was one

of the best politicians of all. If she lost a fight in Cabinet she might be annoyed, but she'd never hold a grudge. She'd be back the next day as if nothing had happened. Hers was a very classy act. And I think she made a fine Speaker, too. I think the members of the club known as Parliament were unduly hard on her because she was a woman.

I also had a lot of respect for Iona Campagnolo – it's not easy being a woman in politics – but she wasn't as sweet-tempered as Jeanne. When Iona was mad you could practically see the sparks fly from her eyes. If she didn't get her way she used to really lose her temper in Cabinet and stay angry for a couple of days afterwards. But she didn't try to wreak revenge either. She's a hard worker and a strong Canadian and that's why I supported her when she ran for the presidency of the Liberal Party.

Time and again when I first entered the Cabinet someone would get up in caucus and take issue with a minister on some subject without having gone through the proper procedure of attempting to deal with the minister directly beforehand. When this happened to me I'd get up and say, "If my memory serves me correct, the honourable member never even mentioned this to me and now he's raising it in caucus." When this happened, Trudeau would usually say, "Well, you two get together and if you can't settle it between yourselves, then come back next week." But it should never have happened in the first place when backbenchers were dealing with a conscientious minister – they should have followed the proper procedure.

All these things led to the caucus under Trudeau having less clout so that ministers were allowed to get away without paying enough attention to what the grassroots were saying. If the caucus didn't bring it up, the ministers couldn't hear it. As I've already said, Trudeau's ministers listened too much to the bureaucrats. I believe strongly that the minister's job is to carry out the policy of the party and not the policy of the bureaucracy – the bureaucrats should not be fighting contrary to what their political masters have decided. But that's exactly how some of them behaved. And despite all the high-priced political staff around Mulroney's ministers, that's how they're behaving today. More so than ever.

The period 1972-74 was a very difficult one. We had a minority
government and we were often held to ransom by the NDP. As a
minister you had to work very closely with the Opposition. I
found this easier than many of my colleagues. A lot of the
Opposition members representing farmers already knew where
I stood and were fundamentally in support of what I was doing,
so they were reluctant to attack me. The Social Credit and the
New Democrats and the Tories all had quite a few members
from rural parts of Canada who could usually persuade their
party to support me. Actually the people who hated minority
government the most were the bureaucrats and the top party
people because it didn't give them the authority they wanted.
They had to really pay attention to the politicians – including
the Opposition.

It wasn't until I became agriculture minister that I really got to
know John Diefenbaker. I'd seen him in action and occasionally
joked with him during my years as a backbencher and I'd
admired his oratory, if not always his politics. He was a real
House of Commons man who took great pride in knowing every
member's name and his constituency, something he kept up
pretty well to the end. But once I became Minister of Agriculture
I got to know him better. He used to write me letters and even
earlier we'd started to exchange notes during debates in the
House. In 1972 and for a few years after he was still in fighting
form – even though he hadn't been leader since 1967. When Dief
was going to speak, the House was generally packed. No one
wanted to miss it because they knew he'd put on a good show.
It must have bothered Bob Stanfield, who could never be accused
of being a great speaker and was always struggling to control
his caucus. And Dief wasn't above making the occasional sly
jab in the direction of the leader who'd dethroned him. Later he
was even worse with Joe Clark.

Dief had been a successful trial lawyer and each time he spoke
in the House he was very much like a lawyer making his final
summation to the jury. You could always tell when he was about
to deliver his punchline because he would actually turn around
and look at his own members. Sometimes he'd make a complete

little circle – he did it deliberately to let his own members know that the punchline was coming. It got so we'd all be ready for it – which meant that even when his line wasn't too good we were still all prepared to laugh and applaud – and almost always did. Even though I didn't always like his politics, I liked him a lot.

I think Dief kind of admired me as an underdog who'd been stubborn, fought long and hard, and finally won. After all, he'd become leader at a time when just about everyone had written him off after two previous defeats – and he'd been defeated more than once before he finally managed to get elected to Parliament in the first place. He and I felt the same way about Bay Street and all it represents. In many ways he was more a populist – a man of the people – than he was a Conservative. He was very big on the rights of the common man, brought in his Bill of Rights and so on. He was always taking the side of those he felt were discriminated against (including himself), people who'd suffered wrong. For instance, a lot of people give Lester Pearson the credit for aiding Cuba right after its revolution, but it was that Tory Diefenbaker who refused to stop trading with Cuba during the U.S. embargo in 1960 – he'd even had a big fight with Kennedy over it. The old guy must be rolling over in his grave watching the way Mulroney is cuddling up to the Yanks. I think Dief liked the way I acted – often fighting with my own party when I believed I was right. I sometimes think he was especially nice to me because he knew I was real Liberal and not a pretend Liberal like some of the ones they had there then and some they have there now.

After he'd lost the leadership, he'd acquired the habit of writing letters or telephoning members of parliament to let them know what he thought – members on both sides of the House. He always read *Hansard* religiously, so even if he wasn't present when you spoke he made sure he knew what you'd said. When I became Minister of Agriculture, if he liked something I'd said he'd write me a little bit of a note and I'd write him back. Then we discovered that my mother had the same birthday as his – September 18 – so he used to send a card to my mother and she would send one to him. My mom certainly got a kick out it, even though she was a Liberal from way back. Every September when I'd first see him he'd say, "It's about time to send those cards."

We were also both partly deaf, although he was much more self-conscious about it than I was – we never spoke about it. One time I met the daughter of an ear doctor who'd examined Dief; she told me he had made the doctor swear he would never tell anybody Dief had a hearing problem. I took the opposite tack. Sometimes at meetings I'd nonchalantly put in my hearing aid or take it out.

A woman came up to me once after a public meeting and said, "Mr. Whelan, I thought you were great." I replied, "You liked what I said?" And she said, "No, I liked what you did." I said, "What did I do?" And she told me, "When it came time for the questions, you said, "Whoa, wait a minute, I've got to put on my little electronic gadget so I can hear your questions." She worked with hearing impaired people and told me that most are so self-conscious they never would have done what I did. I just thought it was the natural thing to do.

One Monday morning, not long after I'd been made minister, I was in my office and my secretary, Mrs. Harry, came in and said, "Mr. Diefenbaker's on the phone." I remember saying back to Janis, "So what?" And she said, "Well, it's the first time he's ever called you and I think you should take his call." I usually did what she said – she ran our office with an iron hand – but I wasn't too eager to follow her advice on this occasion because the previous day, Sunday, I'd appeared on CTV's *Question Period*. And I'd forgot myself a little bit during the show and referred to certain people who were ripping off consumers as "bastards" – I'd used a swear word on television, which I always tried not to do. (My three daughters weren't very old at the time and that night they all gave me hell for swearing on TV.) So on this occasion, I thought right away, "Mr. Diefenbaker is giving me a call because I swore on television. He won't approve of that." He may have been past his prime, but his thunder was still pretty terrible to hear.

So when I picked up the phone I said, "Yes, Mr. Diefenbaker, what can I do for you?" And he said, "Well, Mr. Minister" – usually he called me Gene – "I watched you on television yesterday." And I said, "Yes, Mr. Diefenbaker," all the time thinking, "Boy, here it comes." Then he said, "Mr. Minister, Mr. Minister" —he always repeated himself like that—"I think you should know my views." And I thought, "For sure, it's coming now." I could just imagine him swivelling in his seat getting ready to deliver the punchline. Then after a short pause he finally said, "Mr. Minister, I thought you were superb. I thought you held those four fellows"—the four reporters on the program—"at bay almost as well as I would have." That was as humble as he could be. And that's all the conversation was. He simply wanted me to know his views.

On a few occasions I felt the full force of his rhetoric in the House. We had two or three exchanges in Question Period. But he was never vicious with me as he was with some members with whom he shared no mutual respect. More often we'd have fun with each other in the House—if the debate was boring we'd send nasty notes back and forth.

I remember one time I got into the elevator to the parliamentary restaurant with Diefenbaker and several other members, one of whom was Richard Cashin from Newfoundland. Dief, as usual, held the floor. First he looked at me and he said, "Well, Essex County. Southern Ontario. There's nothing so bountiful and so productive as Southern Ontario and Essex County." Then he did the same thing with several others in the elevator, priding himself on knowing every member's name and his constituency, until he came to Cashin. So he started: "Newfoundland. Newfoundland." He was trying hard to find something nice to say about the bounty of Newfoundland. So in the long pause I jumped in and said, "Best damn moose pasture in the country." (Many years earlier the federal government had transferred some moose out there.) Well Dief took a fit of laughing and looked at Rick Cashin slyly and and kept repeating, "Moose pasture, Newfoundland, ah ha." Cashin got mad as hell, but there was nothing he could do about it. The moose did quite well there, too.

Dief never missed a chance at a good joke and he could also laugh at himself. He told a bunch of us once about the time—when he was still Prime Minister—that he'd gone to

Mexico to give an important speech. He'd practised his speech for a month because he wanted to give it in the language of the country. So he went and gave the speech and afterwards he was really proud he'd managed to get through it all in a foreign tongue. So he said to his host, "How did you like my speech? How did I do?" And his host said he'd done pretty well, but told him, "You know, you spoke beautifully in Portuguese, but we speak Spanish here in Mexico." Dief must have been mad as hell at the time but he laughed about it later with us. It must have sounded pretty awful, because he had as much trouble as I did with languages other than English. We both spoke French about equally bad.

Since the provincial election of 1959 I'd spent most of my political energies fighting Tories in Ottawa. But in September 1973 there was a movement to get me back into provincial politics. A lot of people thought I should run for the provincial leadership and I must admit it was tempting. We were in a minority position in Ottawa and there was a good chance we'd lose the next election to Bob Stanfield. Besides I kind of liked the idea of taking on Bill Davis. I'd known him since long before he became premier and I was sure he was beatable.

The first time I met him was at a mayors and reeves convention in Thunder Bay in June 1962 (in fact I was called away from it to go to Ottawa for my very first caucus meeting as a Liberal member of parliament). Davis was then the new Minister of Education in John Robarts' government. I have to say that I wasn't all that impressed when we were introduced. All he could say was "Hello." That was it. I never dreamt then he'd be Premier of Ontario. He was not a very colourful politician. And I think his skill was exaggerated. He was more lucky than he was smart.

People from all parts of the province were urging me to run, but I particularly cherish the telex I received from Don Smith. Don was then president of the London West Liberal Association, but he's now president of the provincial party, and it occurred to me that he might enjoy seeing his words in print. He wrote, "Dear Mr. Whelan, I feel very strong that if the province of

Ontario does not have a man of your calibre leading it, the Liberal Party throughout the country will suffer. The province needs a man of your stature as Premier. You could count on the support of our executive if you decide to run for the leadership."

I gave serious thought to running for Ontario leader, but in 1973 I was just getting to know my department and just beginning to really enjoy my new job. There were a lot of things I wanted to do for Canadian agriculture. So I decided not to run. I didn't have another shot at beating the Tories until 1974.

The election of 1974 was the one we weren't supposed to survive. On May 8 we lost a vote of confidence in the House, Parliament was dissolved, and an election was called for the eighth of July. Everyone expected Stanfield to win since he'd come so close in 1972. But there were a few things the pundits hadn't banked on. The Tories foolishly proposed a ninety-day wage-price freeze followed by wage and price controls, which gave us a clear target to shoot at, and Keith Davey was back running a campaign, his first since 1965. Keith knew better than anyone how to get everyone working.

The Rainmaker promised me the Wheat Board if we won – that meant I would finally have control of Canadian agriculture. And the agriculture policies we were proposing, including a national marketing board for broiler chickens, were ones I really believed in. Keith Davey promised me both the Wheat Board and that I'd have those policies implemented. In an election campaign, you have to be like a race horse – you have to really want to run. When Keith made me those promises, that was like putting a carrot in front of a horse, and by God I ran like the wind in 1974. I've never worked so hard in my life, but I never seemed to get tired.

This was the first campaign for which the party used Martin Goldfarb as pollster. Marty was in on all the strategy, but at the time his involvement was a secret. I was one of the few ministers who was invited to Toronto at the beginning of the campaign to meet this group of smart people – Goldfarb, Jerry Grafstein and a few others – the wise young men, I called them. At the meeting I told them, "Don't let the Tories attack you; what we have to do is fight the bastards. Challenge them and confront them; tell the people what we've done for Canada and what we believe Canada is all about. We've got a great country to sell and the Liberals had more to do with building this great country than anybody else. The people are proud of this country, so that's what we've got to tell them and tell them hard."

When Goldfarb took his poll he came out with pretty much the same answer. Unlike some politicians I didn't need a Goldfarb to tell me what the people were thinking. I just listened to the people and read my mail. He also found out that I was a good person to sell the message he thought the people wanted to hear. That was how I became Goldfarb's guinea pig.

If you can imagine me giving the same speech ten times a day, that's what I did. It's pretty difficult, you know. I was like a trained computer. Every speech I gave had the same three or four points in it. I'd change the opening a bit to suit the place I was in – to make a joke or a comment about a local person I knew or the local Liberal candidate. Otherwise I was programmed like a robot. And every night we'd get new instructions from Goldfarb. I had a guy with me, Don Gracie, and he would stay up late at night to send tapes of my speeches to Ottawa so the campaign could use them with the press.

Of course, it helped that Stanfield had given us something to shoot at – wage and price controls. My favourite line when I was talking about that was, "Would you ever buy a pig in a poke? Would you buy a tractor that's under tarpaulin? If I were you, I wouldn't buy this one. Why don't they uncover this great plan they have for us? What are they hiding?" But most of my speeches would be about Canada and what the Liberal Party had done for Canadians and what a great country Canada is. If you heard those speeches now, you'd think I stole some of my lines from my friend Jean Chrétien. But it was more the other way around. This was before Jean got a name for going around singing the praises of Canada. I always used to kid him that he got the idea from me and that a lot of my best lines from 1974 seemed to end up in his speeches. He never denied it.

During the entire campaign I think I was in my own constituency of Essex-Windsor only six days. I spent most of my time travelling by helicopter throughout rural Ontario, sometimes giving eleven or twelve speeches a day. I did a swing out

West and made a brief visit to the English-speaking parts of Quebec and the Maritimes, but the vast majority of the campaign I spent in Ontario – which was the key to winning the election. This was Davey's and Goldfarb's strategy and Gene Whelan was their secret weapon. I drove my staff so hard that they must have thought I was a miserable so-and-so. We often left Toronto airport at six-thirty or seven in the morning and we never returned to headquarters earlier than midnight. Sometimes I rode that helicopter fourteen hours a day – me and five others. Fortunately the gods smiled on us that spring – the weather was good and the crowds kept getting bigger and more friendly.

The interesting thing was that our successes were hardly reported at that time. I'd have breakfast with two or three hundred people and lunch with another few hundred and supper with a few hundred more – and quite a few in between – and sometimes we were getting crowds as high as three thousand people to our meetings. There were nearly three thousand at a pork barbeque in the arena at Milverton up in Perth County and Bill Jarvis, the Tory MP, told me afterwards that he thought for sure we had him. We didn't get that seat, but 1974 was the closest we ever came.

My experience demonstrates one of the problems with the way elections are covered – the media men and women all follow the leaders like sheep, leaving most of the rest of the campaign unreported. It took quite a while for the press to catch on because we were going to little places, places where the big media don't often go. But in the last couple of weeks a reporter for *Time* magazine in Toronto followed me around for a while and wrote a story that predicted the Liberals were going to win the election based on the response I was getting – mostly in Ontario. But his editors didn't believe him. They said, "What was Whelan feeding you? What kind of booze?" They thought he'd lost his mind – so they didn't run the story. It was only after the election that there was a story in *Time* that gave me a lot of credit for helping Trudeau get back his majority; the article had a picture of me with a baseball cap on – this was before I was given my green stetson – getting into a helicopter.

I was so fired up during the campaign that I almost didn't need to sleep. The people travelling with me would always take time during our helicopter hops to snooze, but I couldn't sleep with this beautiful Ontario landscape below. It was springtime and fine weather and everything was green and growing. I got to really admire Canada – especially Ontario – in that election campaign of '74 because I saw it all from a thousand feet up in the air: fields and barns and forests and lakes; cities and towns and villages; tennis courts, playing fields, swimming pools, gardens and lawns. That spring the country seemed just like you'd dream it should be. I remember flying at night with my aides asleep, looking out at the darkened landscape and the stars and praying to old St. Martin de Porres. St. Martin was with us all the time.

I got cranky sometimes, what with all the long hours, and I later asked the campaign staff if I was rough to work with compared to the others. And they said, "Hell, you were the easiest to get along with." Afterwards some people said that it was two people more than any who really won the election. One was Gene Whelan and the other was Margaret Trudeau. Margaret campaigned with Pierre that year and the people loved her.

The press may have been slow to pick up the trend, but some people could see it coming. The Ontario Tories caught on in the final week of the campaign, but by then it was too late. They tried to stop me, though – they got the Big Blue Machine to take away my helicopter. The provincial government made up this phoney excuse that more choppers were needed to fight forest fires in northern Ontario. But the only fire they were fighting was the political fire we were lighting among the voters.

It didn't save the election but it may have saved them a seat or two. I remember Eric Cunningham who was running in Hamilton-Wentworth lost by only seventy-four votes. We'd missed his riding in those last three days because we couldn't cover as much ground in a small plane as in a helicopter. The meeting had been scheduled and they were all ready, but I didn't make it. He always blamed me for keeping him from winning his federal seat.

By the end of it all I was just bone tired, but you don't feel it so much when you've won. I can remember sitting in the House on the opening day of Parliament and I was so tired. Allan MacEachen was sitting beside me all pleased with himself that he was still on the Government side and he said to me, "In my wildest dreams I never dreamed we would be on this side of the House even in a minority position, let alone a majority." By God I couldn't hold my tongue. Mighty Allan had hardly been off Cape Breton during the whole election and I'd spent six whole days in my own riding; I'd risked my own political life for the sake of people like him. So I looked at him and I said, "Al, if we'd all sat on our ass like you, we wouldn't be sitting here, we'd be over there," and I pointed at the Opposition benches. He didn't speak to me for six months after that.

When MacEachen worked, he was a very fine member and a very fine minister. He was a brilliant mind and all that, but in the 1974 election he was as lazy as a pet coon.

Maybe I made a mistake in 1974. I'd worked so hard and then the party let me down. The Wheat Board remained a separate portfolio and was left with Otto Lang from Saskatchewan who was the justice minister – a funny combination that, wheat and law. So Keith Davey never did deliver on that promise. Maybe I was naive to believe that he would or he could. But he had come through on every commitment he had made to me before. In fact, I think that was the only time he let me down. I really believe to this day that Keith thought he could fulfil his commitment to me. I don't think he was one who went around and made a lot of rash promises.

I didn't get the Wheat Board and then the bureaucrats in Finance and on Treasury Board fought me at every turn on the agricultural policies I'd run on – but in the end I got quite a few of them through the Cabinet. Still, some of those who'd believed in me and voted for me thought I'd broken faith with them. And, from their point of view, I guess I had. That was one of the real heartbreakers in my political career – to fight so hard for things I believed in and to win, only to be turned down by the bureaucrats and by the staff in the Prime Minister's Office – the ones I like to call pipsqueaks. Ten years later when I was running for the leadership I thought about how many people I'd helped back in 1974 (not to mention '72 and '79 and '80). One of the things that hurt me in 1984 was that so few of them were willing to support me.

A lot of people told me I should have made my move after we won in 1974, fought harder for what I wanted. They figured I should have used my clout while I had it. But I was never one to push beyond a certain point and I don't think it would have done any good with Trudeau if I had – he resented it when you became belligerent. He didn't like loud voices, and I'd raised mine often enough.

In 1976, I finally did get my marketing board for broiler chickens – Coutts and Pitfield had held it up for two years. Two years. We had a terrible battle over it. I'd had to fight all over again for what had been promised to me and should have been mine automatically. I still remember the note that Jim Coutts sent me after I'd won. It said, "Now you've got your f——ing marketing board, I hope you're satisfied." Instead of that note two years down the road, I should have got one right after we formed the government in 1974 saying, "You deserve it, it's automatically yours." I will say one thing for Coutts, though, even if I didn't agree with him much and thought he had far too much power. He never ignored me; whenever I called him or asked for some kind of response, he always got back to me.

I never had much use for the people around Trudeau and I told him so more than once. One time Michael Pitfield had some kind of disagreement with Paul Babey, who was the chairman of the National Farm Products Marketing Board, and he forced me to remove Paul and put him with the Farm Credit Corporation as vice-chairman. I liked Paul and he was doing a good job so I found this a very hard thing to do. I always resented the pipsqueaks in the PMO. Pipsqueaks are always covering their own ass and exceeding their authority. But I'd taken my oath of loyalty and my oath of secrecy and I never made my disagreements public. I fought like hell and when I lost I stayed loyal.

Trudeau made a point of thanking me for my role in winning the 1974 election and I said to him, "Don't just thank me, thank old St. Martin, too, because he helped a lot." And Trudeau said, "What do you mean?" And I said, "When we were flying in that helicopter, a lot of the time I didn't have nothing to do, so I'd just say a Hail Mary or pray to St. Martin de Porres." He just looked at me funny and sort of laughed. I don't know whether he believed me or not.

Bob Stanfield really missed his chance in 1974, and he knew it. I'll never forget when he was making his speech during the debate on the Speech from the Throne after the 1974 election and I was sitting there smiling at something he had said. Bob noticed me grinning away and he said, "Look at the Minister of Agriculture, Mr. Speaker. He's sitting over there smiling and he doesn't smile very often. Mr. Speaker, he thinks he won the election singlehanded. But, Mr. Speaker, I want you to know that I helped him."

Bob Stanfield's problem was that he was too much of a gentleman. He always put Canada ahead of his own political well-being. (The present Prime Minister certainly doesn't have this problem.) The very fact that he let Pearson survive after he lost a money vote in the House early in 1968 – this was after Pearson had resigned but before the leadership convention had been held – shows what kind of a man he was. We'd have had a terrible mess if he hadn't let us off the hook in 1968. And he was fairly responsible all the time in the House. He wouldn't do something just to be nasty – it wasn't in his nature – and a lot of Tories resented that.

I never had a close relationship with him but we used to talk from time to time. I respected him. He was a very decent man and I think it was quite a common feeling that he was too decent for politics. He didn't give the image of a great brilliant scholar, the way he talked and the way he looked, but he was a smart man and a very human man. But then he wasn't a real Tory; he was probably more Liberal than John Turner. His connections were not that strong with Bay Street and those places. That's one of the reasons they didn't come out and support him. It's why they didn't support Little Joe either. And Diefenbaker, they always used to say that he got lost in a snowstorm on the way to his nomination meeting and ended up at the wrong one–he'd been going to the Liberals, but he ended up getting nominated by the Conservatives.

After 1974 was the period when Margaret and Pierre began to have their problems, something that was of great interest to the press. We were all concerned, of course, but nothing much was said about it in the Cabinet. I hardly knew Margaret at all. I saw her rarely–for instance at the parliamentary Christmas party every year. I used to play Santa Claus, so every year I bounced Justin and Sacha and Michel on my knee. And chatted with her a bit. To me she was a pleasant, pretty young woman. She always treated me nice.

I don't think she realized how hard her husband would have to work. I remember her talking about those damn brown bags her husband brought home all the time–the books of letters for him to sign and the briefing papers for him to read. I don't think she really understood what it would be like to marry a Prime Minister. When things got rough I used to defend her. I used to refer to that old Biblical quote: "Let he who has not sinned cast the first stone." That would usually shut people up. I guess you could say that we were all surprised when Pierre married this young woman, and we were surprised and sad when their marriage fell apart.

One of the biggest political surprises of the 1974-79 period was the election of Joe Clark as leader of the Conservative Party. I'd known Joe since before he was a member of parliament– when he worked on the Hill at Conservative Party headquarters. In those days he was just a gangly young guy running around doing errands. No one would have suspected he'd ever become Prime Minister. I sometimes wonder if he believed it himself. But he was certainly ambitious and anyone who knew his wife Maureen McTeer–who worked for him when he was elected as an MP–knew that she was ambitious, too.

Sean O'Sullivan, who'd been a young MP when I was first elected and who'd worked with Maureen as a young Conservative said to me once, "Maureen is a very determined person." We were on a street in Rome at the time (he was in seminary there studying to be a priest) and he pointed to the wall along the street and said, "See that wall? There's a door here and there's a gate down there but if Maureen wanted something on the other side of that wall she'd go right through the middle." I'm sure she had a lot to do with Joe running for the leadership and a lot to do with managing the success of it, too.

I never knew Maureen very well, but I think she's a very smart person. I don't agree with all her philosophies and I'm sure she doesn't agree with all mine. But there was one time when I got the impression she rather approved of what I'd been saying. That was after Brian Mulroney had won the leadership and I made a speech where I said, "Brian shot down Little Joe like a dog in his tracks the way he took the leadership." I saw Maureen in Ottawa soon after and she said, "I see you have been making speeches again." And she had a big smile on her face. That's all. She never said anything else.

When Joe surprised himself and won the leadership I figured he was our best asset. Joe never managed to create the image of leader and he doesn't even today when he tries to be forceful as Minister of External Affairs. Joe isn't that kind of a person.

But when Trudeau finally called the 1979 election I didn't have the feeling that we could win, even with Clark running against us. We'd waited too long and we hadn't kept enough of our promises. I knew all the promises I'd made to farmers in 1974, and knew the ones I'd been unable to deliver. And it was true for other ministers in other departments. Probably the biggest thing the voters remembered was how we'd fought against wage and price controls in seventy-four and then brought them in ourselves soon after. I don't believe we were double-crossing the voters. We'd campaigned against a pig in a poke, not a carefully explained program.

We definitely waited too long before calling the election in 1979. There were quite a few of us, myself included, who wanted to go sooner, but the others were afraid of losing. They figured it would look bad if we went before our four years were up. And the longer we waited the worse it became. We were tired and maybe we even gave the impression that we were tired of governing – which certainly was not the case. But there wasn't much infighting leading up to 1979. Not like there would be in 1984.

I campaigned in 1979, but not as much as in 1974, not by a

long shot. I spent much more time in my riding where I had a strong challenge from the NDP. I could tell how we were doing because of the way the crowds were acting. They were polite enough, but they weren't responsive. It was a rough election and I could tell we were not getting through. And the press had it in for us. We should never have waited until 1979; we should have gone in 1978 or even 1977 when our popularity was greater. But Trudeau's advisers thought differently, so we waited and we lost.

I had a much tougher time winning in 1979 – we had to really work hard because many of our supporters were disgruntled and quite a few sat out the election – and I managed to win by only about eighteen hundred votes over Steven Langdon of the NDP, but I'd won by almost ten thousand in 1974.

The 1979 election was John Diefenbaker's last. He died soon after, before Joe Clark called the House into session, and some of us said at the time that Dief had died on purpose because he didn't want to be in the House with Little Joe as Prime Minister. His private secretary was quoted not long after in the *Toronto Star* as saying the same thing, so there may be something to it.

I certainly didn't believe that old Dief ever wanted Joe Clark to become Prime Minister, and I said as much in public. I made the remark during a speech in Red Deer, Alberta, before the election was called but after Clark had been leader for a while. I was speaking to a group of students at the local high school and I was replying to a question. I was very careful how I put my response. I think the words were, "I believe that Mr. Diefenbaker doesn't want Mr. Clark ever to become Prime Minister." The reporter wrote it exactly as I said, so I've got no complaint there. Of course, somebody sent Dief a clipping and he sent me a cold little note. He'd been calling me Gene for years and he wrote, "Dear Mr. Minister." That was his way of telling me, "I'm mad at you, boy." In the letter he called my statement in Red Deer "an unadulterated falsehood" – that's politicians' talk for "You're a damn liar."

So I wrote him back and I referred to the Bill of Rights that he'd been so proud of bringing in. I reminded him that his Bill of Rights guaranteed the right of anyone to believe anything they wanted. And then I said, "I *believe* I was right in what I said and that's my right to believe it." And I closed with the line, "And I *believe* we can still be friends." When I saw him in the House of Commons a week or so later, all he said to me was, "You're a terrible fellow, a terrible fellow." And he shook his head and laughed. I think this was the last time Diefenbaker and I crossed swords.

Early in 1981, the winter after Clark's defeat, I was speaking to a group of Liberals in Yorkton, Saskatchewan, and was talking about Diefenbaker. He was always a good topic when talking to a Western crowd, whatever their political stripe, because they knew he knew the West and had understood it. I told them that just after the election I'd been walking on the campus of the University of Saskatchewan in Saskatoon where Dief is buried, overlooking the Saskatchewan River. It was a clear, frosty, moonlit night and as quiet as the hereafter. And I told them that I could swear I heard old Dief laughing. There was no mistaking it. I was walking by his grave and I could hear that laugh.

Like everyone else, I was sure Pierre Trudeau was going to quit after the 1979 election. We were a pretty demoralized bunch after our defeat – it was the first time we'd been out of office since 1963. Some people said at the time that we'd have done better if Trudeau had stayed retired and either Turner or Macdonald had won a leadership convention. I don't buy it. I believe we did as well as we did only because Pierre was back on the hustings. Of course the defeat wasn't as bad as in 1958 or as it would be in 1984 – we did have 114 seats to the Tories' 136 – but we'd all gotten used to being in power and now it looked as though we'd be in the wilderness for quite a long time. The situation put me in mind of 1962 when I'd first arrived in Ottawa and we were still in Opposition to the Diefenbaker government. I've mentioned how vicious the old guard was – people like Paul Martin and Jack Pickersgill – but in 1962 they'd already been in the Opposition for five years. We were still getting used to the idea.

I certainly never dreamt I'd be Minister of Agriculture again, not in my wildest dreams. Even though I had joked about the possibility with my department staff at our farewell just after the 1979 defeat: I told them, "We're just experiencing technical difficulties, but stay tuned and don't adjust your set. We'll be right back." As it turned out, I was right, but I never dreamt that we'd defeat Clark so quickly, on his first budget, or that we'd win a winter election. And I was sure Pierre was going to quit when he said he was going to quit.

Still, I think all the talk about Allan MacEachen engineering Trudeau's comeback is some of the most overrated talk I've ever heard. Knowing Trudeau as I did I would think he made up his own mind, and that was it. Of course some of the members tried to talk him into staying on and running again, and some of them just stayed away and said nothing. I was asked what I thought and I said, "Well, if he wants to come back I'll run with him; I'll be on his team. I'll work with him to win the election." Then I went home. All this talk about intrigue is mostly to keep the journalists happy. I don't believe half of it.

I went home and spent some time with my family. After the 1979 election I really thought about quitting, especially if Trudeau didn't run again. Although when it looked as if Pierre would be gone for good, I did have a telephone chat with Don Macdonald whom I thought would have been our best choice for a new leader. But during the conversation he intimated to me that he had no desire to run at that time and I never pushed him any further. I talked with Liz and Terry and Susie and Cathy about whether I should run again. They said it was up to me. But it made it a lot easier when Trudeau came back.

You may remember that Joe Clark was scared to recall Parliament. He waited almost six months, from May 22 until October 9, longer than anyone who'd been elected since Confederation. Maybe he had a premonition of what was going to happen to him. Even on the hustings in 1979 Joe seemed almost scared of the idea of being Prime Minister. He was like someone who'd grabbed a bear by the tail – he had the bear but he didn't know how to hold onto it, though he knew it was too dangerous to let go. When he did let go – when he got a bit overconfident even though he didn't have a majority – the bear turned around and bit him.

When Clark finally did recall Parliament, I was named the Liberal agriculture critic and almost immediately I got into trouble for being too nice to my friend John Wise, the new minister, who was from Elgin County in Ontario. I personally think that such talk is a load of manure. I've never liked to be mean in the House of Commons; I can't see any point in it except getting a few headlines – and that's something I've never had trouble doing. You can deal directly with the minister and ask tough questions in the House without being nasty just for the sake of it. And I didn't think John was doing too badly, considering he didn't know his department yet.

Joe Clark never really had a chance to prove himself as Prime Minister, but I had the impression that, as Senator Croll would have said, he wasn't enough of a son-of-a-bitch to do the job. He made the mistake of trying to run the government as if he had a majority, instead of as if he could be defeated at any time. Even when we had our majorities in the 1970s the Whip would make sure that not too many of us were out of the country at any one time. But not Joe Clark. Of course, he thought he was going to win the election – which showed just how much political sense they had.

When you think about it, Trudeau's decision to run again was really the only choice he had. The party was in an impossible position to run an election without him – whereas his old team was still in place. And, once the campaign got underway, I had the impression that Trudeau was actually starting to enjoy himself again. I certainly had a lot of fun in 1980. It was as if we had nothing to lose and winning would be just a big bonus. It was a February election but it was one of the nicest, mildest winters we'd had in years. That's when I knew that God was a Liberal because he didn't give us any blizzards or bad snowstorms.

It was also more fun because of the way my three daughters gave my campaign a boost. Terry was then president of the student body at General Amherst High School and she and her sisters really got involved – Sue worked hard and so did Cathy, as young as she was at that time. They used to organize and go out in teams with their school friends – anywhere from twenty to sixty young people in an evening, canvassing the different areas. They did one darn good job and made a wonderful impression – they and the many other young people who worked on the 1980 campaign.

When it was all over, we had our majority back and I had Agriculture back. We'd surprised our little selves, just like in 1974. As it turned out, this would be Trudeau's most important term – patriating the constitution and seeing the beginning of the end of separatism in Quebec.

Right after the election the main thing on Trudeau's mind was the referendum fight in Quebec. Even though I was an English-speaking minister I did my bit in the campaign, mainly by sending a letter to every dairy farmer in Quebec. It had a picture of me and Liz and our three daughters on the letter – which was in French and English – telling them the advantages of staying in Canada and pointing out what the Canadian Dairy Commission had done for them. Many of the Quebec members told me that was one of the most effective things we did. The people in Quebec really liked the fact that I'd put my family on the letter.

I knew there were lots of strong Canadians in Quebec. Many of the farm people I'd gotten to know certainly were staunch federalists. And Quebeckers are just as patriotic about Canada as any other Canadians. They also understood the value of the federal system. They knew that it had protected their language and their culture and their religion. If they'd been part of the United States they would have been swallowed up. And we stressed that sort of thing in all our speeches.

What most people will probably remember about Trudeau's last term from 1980-84 was bringing home the constitution. What many don't remember – or simply didn't know – was the part that many ministers played in selling the federal government's position to the people during the national constitution debate. Jean Chrétien was the spearhead of this campaign – and he'll always have a place in the history books for what he did to bring the provinces and the federal government together in a compromise that saved the day. But before that happened I and many others travelled to many parts of the country explaining our policy and talking about our vision of Canada.

As one of the few Liberals other than Jean Chrétien who dared set foot in Western Canada, I spent most of my time out West. Jean used to joke it was only safe for two Liberals to go West and that was Chrétien and Whelan. I was out there as many as two or three days a week for almost a year, visiting the towns and villages and the cities as I'd always done. But this time, instead of talking about agriculture I was telling them about my passionate belief in this country and the importance of bringing the constitution home in order to make our country really ours. Jean took a similar line and I think that's when he really became known and liked out West.

I did more speaking than anybody else in the Cabinet excepting Chrétien – not just out West but in the Maritimes and in Ontario too. People used to warn me before certain meetings that I was going to be ripped limb from limb, but that never happened. Just the opposite. Sometimes they were hostile when I walked in but when I left it was very rare that I didn't get a pretty good ovation. I used to be gone some part of pretty near every week and I'd speak as many as three or four times a day.

I really believed what I was saying, so it wasn't that hard. I talked about Canada and how it had been put together back in 1867. I explained about how we'd created our country without bloodshed, something a lot of other nations only dreamed of doing – putting two founding cultures, French and English, together without a war. Then I used to say, "But agriculture played a big part in getting the agreement. Macdonald liked his Scotch and Cartier drank rye, although Cartier drank his rye with water and Macdonald drank his neat. And both are made out of agriculture products. They just sat around a fireplace and drank and talked and said to their officials the next morning, 'You heard what we said and we want to see it on paper.'"

When I was out there speaking on the constitution I was attempting to destroy the myth that there are big differences between East and West. It's been a major theme of my political life – that there are no fundamental differences between people that can't be solved by talking around the fire – like Macdonald and Cartier. I'd remind my audiences that when Confederation was formed people didn't think it would last ten years.

Every week in Cabinet Trudeau used to ask for reports on how things were going, what sort of reception I was getting. Sometimes we'd have a special little session on the constitution. That was the Jean and Gene Show. It used to make some of the others mad that Chrétien and Whelan were so much in demand.

One of my stories Trudeau liked best was about Biase di Pasquale, one of my constituents (and the best sign man in my campaigns). Biase is a very strong Liberal, a factory worker and a farmer. One day during the constitution debates Biase called me up on the phone and said, "Gino. Could I ask you a question?" (My Italian friends always call me Gino.) I said, "Sure Biase, go ahead." Then he said (in his Italian accent), "Gino, I don't know too much about the constitution. I don't understand all the talk that's going on, but some of the things the people say about our country, Canada, are bad, bad, bad, and I'm not sure what they mean." I said, "Biase, if I told you that I understood everything that's being said about the constitution I'd be lying, so don't feel bad. A lot of people are saying things about it that aren't right and some are saying things that are right, and a lot of things that shouldn't be said are being said and a lot of things that should be said aren't being said." Then Biase said, "Gino, you care if I describe Canada in my own way?" And I said, "No, go ahead, I'd like to hear you." And Biase said, "The world, she's one great big roast beef. And Canada, she's the best slice of that roast beef."

Old Biase put it better than any politician or any professor of political science. I used to tell this story a lot in my speeches — all over Canada — so that I could lead up to the punchline about the best slice of all. After I'd used it in a speech in Parliament, Chrétien and a lot of others who saw it on television called me Gino.

Biase grows figs in his backyard in Amherstburg, and he got me one time to carry a basket of figs to Ottawa for his Prime Minister. He had wrapped them up in a nice little foil basket which I carried right from the plane into Trudeau's office. When his staff asked me suspiciously what I had I said, "These are figs I picked myself; they aren't going to blow him up." They were always suspicious of food people sent, that there might be something wrong with it. So Joyce Fairburn said, "If you say they're safe, Gene, I'll give them to him and tell him you brought them." Trudeau took them home and ate them and later said to Joyce, "Find out from Gene the name of the man who sent the figs." Apparently the note Biase put with the figs had gotten lost. Trudeau wrote him a letter that Biase has framed in his house today. It said, "I had your figs with prosciutto ham and melon and I never ate better figs in my life."

Trudeau had a sixth sense about thanking people. If someone knitted him a sweater and gave it to him on some trip (it was not uncommon for people to want to give him a personal gift), he always made a point of writing a letter of thanks. Sometimes, weeks later, he'd come into the office and say, "I'd like to see a copy of the letter we wrote to Mrs. So-and-So thanking her for the sweater she gave me in Nanaimo." And every time he asked that sort of question, they wouldn't be able to find the letter. When he asked, right away his staff knew that somehow the letter hadn't been sent. Somehow he'd remember. And he used to read a lot more of his letters than people thought he did, too.

After the constitution was home, Trudeau seemed to lose interest in running the country and the ministers with leadership ambitions started to jockey for position, just waiting for the moment that Pierre would step down. The atmosphere in the Cabinet room became most unpleasant.

Actually those last four years in Ottawa were more difficult from the start because of the changes in the system Clark made during his nine months in power. I've already mentioned that in 1980 Trudeau decided to keep the spending envelope system Clark had introduced; this was at the same time that we were trying to reduce the overall expenditures of the government. As a result of the spending envelope system it was every man and every woman for themselves. Cabinet minister was pitted against Cabinet minister, just to get enough money to run the department. Bitter fights took place and some of that bitterness continued outside the Cabinet room. This competition became downright vicious. There was only so much money to go around and ministers were fighting each other constantly for their piece of this little pie called the envelope. Bill Davis tried it in Ontario and then had to throw it away because it caused so many problems.

Don Johnston was at the centre of all the squabbles during Trudeau's last term because he was the Minister of State for Economic and Regional Development (MSERD) with responsibility for overseeing the spending envelopes. His initials spelled MSERD but I always used to say it was *absurd* the way he and the others were behaving. The idea of spending envelopes sounds good in theory, but you can't operate that way in a democratic government that has to deal with sudden changes in the market such as a collapse in price. All Johnston did was follow the advice of his bureaucrats. I think he enjoyed all this power, too.

In his book, *Up the Hill*, Johnston complains about not being consulted before the Petrofina purchase by Petro-Canada and not being consulted before Trudeau appointed the Macdonald Commission on the economy. But I always thought the problem with Don Johnston was that he thought he could be minister of anything when he'd had no background experience except coming from a big law firm in Montreal. If I'd been in his place I would have recommended to the Prime Minister that we get rid of those god damned envelopes (it was one of the first things Turner did – I have to give him credit for that). Don was one of those who'd been appointed to Cabinet without very much experience on the backbenches. Which I thought was wrong.

As far as I was concerned, Don Johnston was a very nice person – you couldn't hate the guy; we used to talk a lot and he played a mean piano – I just didn't like the way he did his job.

The other bad thing that Joe Clark left behind was an even more uppity bureaucracy. He'd only been there nine months and he'd managed to institute a system that meant more paperwork and less getting done. When I arrived back at Agriculture I discovered that every letter that we wrote had to go through an average of seven people before it ever got to my desk. And if I said no, this letter's no good, the thing had to go back down through seven people and start again. The change was made in the name of more efficiency in the department, but it actually covered up an attempt by the top bureaucrats to run the department without the minister. They took advantage of Clark's new and inexperienced government to grab more power, and this was true throughout the government.

If I'd had the chance, I would have instituted a massive reform of the Cabinet system. I would have started by making ministers completely responsible for their departments. I'd have given them a budget and told them to spend it wisely – as long as they stuck to party policy – and if they made too many mistakes, I'd fire them. Ministers should not be spending half their time in committees arguing and in Cabinet listening to the same old arguments when they could be running their departments. That's no way to run a railroad. I would just say to my ministers, "You've got a budget and you've got a program – go run your department. But you better adhere to the general wishes and wants of the party and the caucus or you'll be out like a light."

If you threw away the current Cabinet and committee system, there would be a much smaller government, a lot less paper, and a lot fewer paper pushers. Right now it's always a competition between departments (and bureaucrats) to see who can be more important – who can be bigger – when the competition should be to see who can run their department the most efficiently and to do the best job for the least money. I laugh when I read about the current government's efforts to cut down the size of government. At Agriculture we were always doing more with less – my first deputy, Syd Williams, was a master at creating programs with virtually no money.

I also think that this thing about Cabinet secrecy is all wrong. Every minister must swear an oath that everything that goes on in Cabinet is confidential. All the Cabinet documents are secret – you aren't allowed to photostat them and that sort of thing. I've often thought that it would be a good idea to televise Cabinet meetings, open them right up to public scrutiny. This obsession with secrecy had a lot to do with my losing many fights. I would have won even more if the public had been watching. The secrecy was as much as anything to protect the bureaucrats' asses. It isn't the politicians that are scared of openness in government, it's the bureaucrats. Many of the papers that were put forward by the various departments would never have been put forward if Cabinet meetings had been public. We had to shred them all afterwards. I wish I'd photostatted a whole bunch of them and kept them.

No, I didn't like the system but I learned to work with it well enough. And, unlike some ministers, I kept my oath of secrecy – when I make a promise I keep it if it's humanly possible. There were many times when I would have liked to have gone public after losing a battle in Cabinet, but I never did. And I remember Trudeau telling me one time, "You're one of my most loyal Cabinet ministers. When you lose a fight in Cabinet, you never take it to the streets."

The closest I ever came to resigning from the Cabinet was around 1982 when interest rates were so high and farmers and small businesses right across the country were going bankrupt. I saw these people being destroyed and I thought it was wrong. I had studied what other countries such as Austria and Japan were doing – setting their own interest rates – and believed we should do the same. I got so frustrated that I actually took a sort of swipe at MacEachen in public (he was finance minister during this period) – although my remarks were misconstrued. Right after, Trudeau took me aside and said, "You can say anything you like about the banks, but leave MacEachen out of it. He's one of us." I shut up after that, but maybe I should have quit. It's certainly the closest I ever came.

As the 1980 mandate wound down, it began to look pretty clear that Trudeau would resign. I could tell by the way he talked to me, the way he talked in Cabinet and the way he was letting other people do things. The odd time he'd drop a hint – something like, "If you want a good job, you'd better come get it." And he'd tease the ones who were after his position. He didn't seem to have a desire to govern during the last year he was there – the last six months anyhow.

For about six months before he resigned it was obvious that a lot of them were already on the move – John Munro and John Roberts and some of the others. They'd been writing letters to potential supporters. I knew some people who'd received letters from them. And they were bending over backwards to get support from other Cabinet ministers. They were making special deals and so on. That's something I never would do. And suddenly they were paying all sorts of attention to certain backbenchers who wanted this project or that project funded in their riding.

The mood in the House of Commons was mean, meaner than I'd seen it since the Diefenbaker minority of 1962. Brian Mulroney was the new Tory leader and he was as hungry as a wolf in winter to get over on our side. And we had the press after us, making every little thing so big and bad. They were baiting the likely leadership contenders, trying to get them to show their hands. I'd had thoughts about going for the leadership but I was making no moves until Pierre made his. Besides, I was occupied with my increasing activism on the world stage – and the growing famine in Africa.

10

Gorbachev and the World

During my last four years as Minister of Agriculture I was more than ever involved in world affairs. Of course, I had been meeting foreign visitors to Canada and visiting other countries since 1972. In my twelve years in the job I got to know personally many of the world's agriculture ministers, some of whom went on to more prominent posts – Jacques Chirac, for example, who is now Prime Minister of France, and Mikhail Gorbachev who now runs the Soviet Union. In the course of my career as Canada's chief ambassador for agriculture, I met my share of heads of state – from popes to presidents to potentates – many of whom showed a surprising interest in agriculture and a surprising knowledge of the subject, President Marcos of the Philippines being a case in point. During these thousands of miles of travelling to all sorts of places I'd never imagined I'd visit, I would sometimes stop for a minute to consider what an amazing thing it was for the farm boy from Anderdon Township to be shaking the hand of this or that famous person. Looking back, I can see what a good beginning I got. The world I grew up in was neither as backward nor as isolated as you might imagine and, in a way, it was a miniature version of the United Nations.

I realized how lucky I was to have come so far, but I hope and believe I've remained pretty much the same person I was when I was reeve of the township. I've never treated any of the important people I've met much different from some farmer or labourer or small businessman in my own constituency. I didn't put on airs and I usually found that this approach worked, however different a person's culture and background. Under the surface, I've never found people much different anywhere in the world – "clothes on the baby and bread on the table" aren't just the concerns of North Americans or Europeans. Even the so-called intellectuals – and this was true of Trudeau – are ordinary people underneath. Sometimes my down-home approach must have terrified the diplomats with their great love of protocol. But on more than one occasion I broke the ice where diplomatic formality only made it thicker.

One of my first foreign trips as minister was to Brazil in 1974. Brazil is a major importer of Canadian wheat as well as a strong competitor in other commodities. I went there to promote agricultural trade while emphasizing common areas for co-operation, such as research in cereal varieties and livestock breeding. In my early years at Agriculture I made a number of trips to Central and South America. The economies of these countries were growing rapidly and so were their populations – and their agriculture and food sectors could not keep up. As a result they wanted Canadian agri-food technology – the sorts of things I mentioned earlier when talking about Canadian research. And they represented growing potential markets for Canadian products. I agreed to share our technology with these countries on the understanding that they would look to Canada for more of their import requirements. I think it was a match that satisfied both sides.

Before I went to Brazil I made it clear that I didn't like formality and when I arrived I discovered that the Brazilians had issued orders to everybody I was going to meet not to wear suits   and ties – which made sense anyway in such a warm country–because they wanted me to feel comfortable. That's true diplomacy for you.

I spent nine days in Brazil and I never stopped travelling – mostly by small plane and sometimes on the national airline, Varig. It's a huge country and we saw quite a bit of it–five states in all. I had three plainclothes guards with me for the entire trip–bodyguards–the first time I'd ever seen anything like it. (Ten years later I had similar protection when I was in Colombia.) Every morning when I woke up in the hotel, there they were outside my door. The people and their disguises changed, but there were always three of them, pretending to be doctors or lawyers or plumbers. Whether they carried a toolbox or a briefcase what they really had in there was a vicious little machine-gun and under their coats they all wore a shoulder holster with a revolver inside. One of them told me his machine gun could cut you in two in about four seconds–it made holes about an inch in diameter.

One day I asked one of the guards why they were protecting me like this and he said, "Because we have had no terrorism in this country for seven years and we're determined it will stay that way." I laughed and said, "Canada wouldn't pay a wooden nickel to get me back if somebody kidnapped me." And he laughed back and said, "We don't care about that at all. We just don't want any terrorism to take place." This didn't make me feel a whole lot better.

My guide and constant companion was a young assistant to the Brazilian agriculture minister. Unlike his boss, he was from a poor family, and we talked quite freely about the problems of his country. I told him what I thought and we found we agreed on a lot of things–the problem of poverty, the lack of education, the need for land reform. After we'd been together a while he said, "You know, I talk much more easily to you than I do to my own minister. You and I can talk about anything." And I said, "That's because I can't fire you." I was teasing him, but he was serious. "No, it's because you understand our problems better than my minister; he doesn't even want to talk about them." He predicted there would be a revolution in Brazil. I think he put it that, "We're sitting on top of a dynamite keg."

The keg hasn't blown yet, but unless they solve more of their problems than they have – and I don't know how in hell they're going to overcome them – it will, sooner or later.

In Brazil, farmer meant landowner. I still remember his boss, Alysson Paulinelli, saying to some of the Brazilians I met, "When you see a Canadian farmer, shake hands with him because his hands are hard and rough from working." They couldn't get over the fact that in Canada a farmer actually did his own work. Their attitude was much more like the wife of that first farmer my brother and I worked for in Alberta during the harvest of 1942 – they were people of leisure. The peasants did their work for them. The peasants had to work for practically nothing.

Despite the awful contrast between its rich and poor people, Brazil is a beautiful country. Like Canada, it has some natural wonders and we took a side trip to see one of the most spectacular of these – the Iguazú Falls on the Paraná River in the state of Paraná – near the border with Paraguay. They had built a big hydro-electric dam downriver from the falls and had cleared the land right up to the river edge for farms so that they were having a terrible time with erosion and were worried about what this would do to the hydro dam. This sort of thing is a huge problem in the tropical areas of the world; when they clear away the rainforest the soil soon degrades and washes away because it is mostly humus; soon there's a desert where there was once all this rich tropical life. And once the trees are gone, the weather changes – there's less oxygen and less rain. It's a terrible tragedy and an example of bad development. But this sort of thing doesn't only happen in developing countries. We in Canada are also guilty of not always looking after our environment and we lose more land to erosion and bad farming practices than through urbanization and industrialization.

Anyhow, because of all this erosion the Iguazú Falls were muddy, but they were still spectacular – incredibly high. We toured the falls in a little helicopter that was nothing but a frame with a four-cylinder engine which barked and howled behind me while I sat with a seatbelt and a little plastic bubble over us. Some people wouldn't ride it, but it gave you the best view of the falls. The local people tell you a story when you get there that really sums up how impressive they are. It's about the time Eleanor Roosevelt was taken to visit Iguazú – this was before development when the falls were all by themselves in the middle of the wilderness – and she took one look at that great cataract with its crystal clear water and do you know what she said? "Poor Niagara."

The Brazilians were good to us but I wouldn't want to live in their country. I wouldn't be able to stand the difference between rich and poor. We get all worked up about the famine in Ethiopia but Brazil has had its own famine, which a lot of people don't know. In the last five years two million people died of starvation in the northeastern part where they'd gone for years without rain. There are more tragedies like this in the world than people think.

With the exception of Costa Rica and Cuba, all the countries I visited in Latin America were much the same in the terrible inequality, the class society. This is true of Peru, Venezuela, Colombia, and even Mexico. In Colombia in 1983 I could see that the landowners still had nice soft hands and the poor people still worked the fields for next to nothing. The only difference from Brazil in 1973 was that these landowners had to have hired guards to protect them and their families from the banditos and the guerrillas. At one of the receptions I went to, one of the wives was wearing a diamond big enough to buy my whole farm in Canada and then some.

In some ways, Cuba was the most impressive of all the Latin American countries I visited. I was invited many times, but didn't make it there until 1983. My wife had been there before the revolution and she remembered just how bad it had been – troops with machine guns at every corner, ragged kids and beggars filling the streets. Liz was astonished at the change and I was impressed with how different Cuba is from most of the rest of Latin America. Wherever we went we saw healthy, well-dressed kids. The gap between rich and poor has pretty well disappeared. You have to give Fidel Castro a lot of credit for this. He's accomplished great things in his country, although he still has a way to go – as I inadvertently communicated to him during my visit.

Our first day there I went to take a shower in my guest house and all I could get was a trickle of scalding hot water. So I was not in a good mood when I met the Minister of Foreign Trade, Ricardo Cabrisas. We talked tourism and we talked trade (about $350 million annually with a big deficit in Canada's favour). And Ricardo said, "One of the ways we could improve our trade would be to get more tourists to come here and spend money." And I said, "Well, I want to tell you one thing. Canadian tourists won't come here if the bathrooms don't work." And he said, "What do you mean?" And I explained my problem with the shower.

The next evening we were supposed to see Castro, but something kept delaying him. He ended up arriving at our guest house at eleven that evening – I gather he often turns up at night. We mainly talked about cattle – he knew the pedigree of every prize cow Cuba had ever bought from Canada and I couldn't help from thinking that I'd love to hear him having this conversation with Pierre Trudeau, who knew absolutely nothing about bulls and heifers.

Finally Castro said, "How are they treating you?" I said, "Fine." And he said, "But I understand the shower doesn't work." I hadn't figured that such a trivial complaint would go right to the top, to the president of the country, and I immediately began to worry about the repercussions for the people responsible for guest house maintenance. But I couldn't get over Castro knowing about the broken shower.

Of all the Latin American countries, I got to know Mexico the best – I must have been there at least ten times over the years, first as Minister of Agriculture and then as President of the World Food Council. Canada does a lot of agricultural trade with Mexico – milk powder, Canola seed, cereal grains, and breeding stock – and we have usually had pretty good relations with Mexico because we share one problem in common – it's called the United States of America.

At a meeting of the Mexican-Canadian Chamber of Commerce in Mexico City in 1983, I gave one of the most emotional speeches I've ever made. It was right after my conversation with that retired Canadian businessman I spoke about back in chapter six, the one who thought the poor Mexicans were just blissfully happy—he really got me fired up. My speech was about the outrage I felt at the poverty of Mexico and the rest of Latin America. I talked about what it meant to live poor and I asked the audience how we could call ourselves civilized people as long as this type of poverty existed. I really hit them hard, saying, "Don't you think these people have a brain? Don't you think they have eyes that can see you as you drive by in your big limousines or as they watch you on TV? Don't you think that they'd like just a little bit of what you've got? Don't you think they've got any feelings? Don't you think they're part of human society?" I was much wilder than I can describe—much more emotional.

Both Canadians and Mexicans in the audience were crying during my speech. They reacted to it that way because I was telling the truth. The next day, what I'd said was on the front page of every paper in Mexico City. The Canadian ambassador, Russell McKinney, assured me he was happy with what I said, but I don't think the Mexican businessmen were too pleased. The truth hurts. And now it's worse because of the drop in oil prices. But that's because Mexico thought it could get rich on oil, instead of building its economy from the ground up, putting in the infrastructure and the diversity of industries that would make it more stable.

An example of what can be done in a country that starts out with much less in terms of natural resources than most South American countries is what they've done in Israel. Through research, they have developed agriculture out of a wasteland. They have developed a new form of irrigation—what they call trickle irrigation—that is now used in various parts of the world. It uses one-third the amount of water required for sprinkler irrigation. They've grown trees on what was waste land and turned it into beautiful forest. They've developed new varieties of crops to grow in their arid climate, and even tomatoes that are nearly square, which makes them easier to pack in cartons. They produce strawberries over eight months of the year, and orchids and roses—thousands and thousands of acres of roses—all for export to earn foreign exchange. They also have turkey and chicken farms, and advanced poultry-processing plants. They export meat to Europe, which just amazed me. In the Negev Desert I saw them growing fruit trees using brackish water from the desert – water that was hot when it came out of the ground. They used the same water to keep the greenhouses heated during cold weather and at night, and pumped the water in plastic pipes under the seed bed to get the plants started.

My first and only trip to Israel was in January 1979 for nine days during the Christmas recess. At the time the Israeli Minister of Agriculture was Ariel Sharon, who went on to become famous – or infamous – for things other than agriculture. One of the purposes of the visit was to sign an agreement to exchange research data and scientists. Every trip I took had certain official purposes – to co-chair joint agricultural committee meetings with my foreign counterparts, to discuss bilateral agricultural-trade irritants and issues, and to sign other agreements aimed at making it easier for Canadian industry and federal and provincial governments to do business with the country in question. And always there was the unofficial purpose of increasing knowledge and improving communication between our countries. I often picked up ideas that would be helpful in Canada. For instance, it was on the trip to Israel that I became convinced that a central export agency for agricultural products was a good idea.

I met Ariel Sharon on a visit to a *moshav*, or co-operative farm, in this case a dairy co-operative. I knew his reputation in advance – that he'd fought with distinction in the Israeli war of independence and been a successful general in the Six Day War with Egypt in 1967. I also knew that many people thought – rightly as it turned out – that his ambition was to become defence minister. Given these things, I thought I'd play a little joke to find out what sort of person he really was. Before I'd left Canada my staff had made me a little tank commander's hat like the Israeli and Canadian and American officers wear – it had four gold stars and gold braid on it. That day at the *moshav* I was wearing my beige stetson, but I was holding this little military hat behind my back. The minute I saw Sharon – he was dressed in khaki pants and shirt and heavy army boots, looking like he was ready to hop in his tank and go off to battle – I whipped off the stetson and whipped on the army hat. Right away he smiled a great big smile. By the way he'd responded I knew he was my sort of person; that he could take a joke and laugh at himself.

Before we left for Israel I'd been told Sharon would have time to spend only an hour or so with us. But we got along so well that he spent four days with us and even had us to his house for dinner – he has a large ranch in the Negev, much bigger than most Israeli farms, which are generally limited to thirty acres. I was told a group of American friends had bought it for him. It was a very productive farm, however, not a country retreat. He had a couple of riding horses but the rest was agriculture. This visit to his home was the only time I saw him not wearing military fatigues.

He was pleasant enough, but I could tell right away that he could be tough too. He seemed a determined person, but he didn't seem the type who would order or condone a massacre, as he was later accused of doing when the Israelis invaded Lebanon. And he could talk about anything, including agriculture. I think the Israelis are much more conscious than most developed countries of the importance of agriculture because of what they've done in so short a time – going from being a net importer to a net exporter of food. Our conversation ranged over all sorts of topics: agricultural production, trade, research, politics. We got along amazingly well. Nothing in our conversation indicated to me that he was a warmonger, but that doesn't mean he couldn't be a real tough soldier.

It was the Israeli government corporation called Agrexco – a centralized agency (shipping, warehousing and selling) for exporting agricultural products – that convinced me something similar would work in Canada. All the farmers shipped their produce to a warehouse right next to Tel Aviv airport where it was stored in big cooling rooms. The products of individual producers were tagged and kept separate so you still could sell your roses, or whatever, to a specific customer in another country.

I thought it was a beautiful system, and Canagrex, which I introduced in 1983, is essentially the same thing. Within its first nine months, the corporation had signed or had in the works quite a few contracts with foreign importers, largely to the benefit of small Canadian exporters – exactly the people we designed it for. But when the Conservatives got elected in 1984 one of the first things they did was to shoot Canagrex down while it was still on the runway, before it had a chance to fly. Michael Wilson axed it even though the present agriculture minister, John Wise, supported it.

China is one developing country that has made great progress in feeding and educating its people. You'd have to say that these are the greatest successes of the Chinese revolution so far. I think it was Winston Churchill who once called China a sleeping giant. Well, the giant is already wide awake and, as I found out when I visited there in August and September of 1980, the Chinese already export some food and will soon be exporting more. Once they have developed the necessary agricultural infrastructure, there will be no stopping them.

I believe that Canada missed and is still missing an opportunity to take full advantage of its special relationship with China. We officially recognized China in 1970, beating the Americans to recognition, and we had already sold them wheat. But the Americans soon outdid us in developing business with the Chinese. Both of the Chinese ambassadors I knew in Ottawa told me they thought we had not been aggressive enough in developing our trade. They said we didn't try hard enough.

While we were in Peking we met with the Vice-Premier Wan-Li in the Great Hall of the People. Everyone talks about how formal the Chinese are and how if you don't follow the proper etiquette you'll offend them. But I decided that I was no good at pretending to be different, so I wore my green stetson to this meeting and treated the Vice-Premier just like an ordinary person.

We were scheduled to meet with him for fifteen minutes, just a formal courtesy call before we went off to tour the country. When the fifteen minutes were up somebody handed me a note – I saw he was watching me, so I said, "The note says our time is up." He put his hand on my shoulder and said, "My son, we can take all the time we want." We spent an hour and a half together.

He was in his sixties, and over six feet tall – which is very unusual for a Chinese. Before I met him I'd been briefed on his background and knew, for instance, that he'd had both his legs broken by the Red Guards during Mao's Cultural Revolution.

He talked a bit to me about that period and how difficult it had been. The thing that seemed to impress him, and many of the other Chinese I met, was that I was a farmer – that Canada had a genuine peasant as their Minister of Agriculture. They also liked the fact that I'd worked as a tool-and-die maker.

Afterwards, Ambassador Arthur Menzies told me that my trip to China had broken the ice for those that followed. The ones who came after didn't have to worry so much about protocol and formality, thanks to the man in the green hat.

Everywhere we went, of course, there were formal dinners with many toasts. The danger at these things is that you end up drinking too many toasts and sliding under the table. So I used to follow the Danny Rosati method for not getting drunk, which Danny taught me when we were together on the Anderdon Township Council. In those days he used to make some pretty good wine using empty whiskey barrels from the old Calvert's distillery in Amherstburg which is now owned by Seagram. He used to say that the secret to drinking wine – or any alcohol – is lots of dried bread, cheese and salami. The cheese and bread soaks it up and the salami keeps your stomach lined. The bread is the most important thing, as I found out in China.

I'd followed his advice in Yugoslavia on my first trip there in 1963. And it came in especially handy in the same country in 1975 when I got into a wine-drinking contest with Vice-President Bec. He proposed a toast and I took just a sip and put the glass back down and he said, "No, no, if you don't drink the glass dry, some lady will cry someplace." At this point, my wife was the one who was ready to cry because she knows I don't drink too much. So we got to drinking toasts and after each one we threw our glasses into the fireplace – this is another Yugoslav custom. Later my wife told me that after fourteen toasts I was completely missing the fireplace; she figured I'd die for sure. But I was eating the way Danny Rosati had taught me – and by then I'd already practised my technique in China and in Russia. The next morning I was the first one up and knocking on the doors of the other members of our delegation.

At our first formal dinner in Peking, with the agriculture minister Huo Shilian, I was introduced to this drink called Mao

Tai. I believe it's made from sorghum. It's a traditional drink always served at banquets, very strong, with a funny, musty flavour. I was told, "When you drink it you'll be warm from the top of your head to the tip of your toes, but the next day your head won't feel bad." Zhao Fan, the Vice-Minister for State Farms and Land Reclamation, who was at the dinner, had also been to Yugoslavia, and he told me, "I drank those Yugoslavs under the table." So I challenged him to a drinking match, telling him no Yugoslav can outdrink a Canadian.

During the contest I had to use the modified Rosati method, because there was bread on the table but no cheese or salami. But it worked. I matched Zhao Fan glass for glass and the next day at the Great Wall of China and I was one of the few who climbed the steps all the way to the top of one of the towers. Zhao Fan only went halfway up and I met him when I was coming down – he was sitting on a step resting. When I met him, he said, "Oh, I've been to the top before." We both laughed. He knew I'd won.

China is a funny combination of the very old and the brand new and this is certainly true of the country's agriculture. For instance, they refused to show us any meat-packing plants – even though we'd brought with us Jean Bienvenue, a meat processor from Quebec, and Carol Teichrob, a turkey producer and the president of a poultry-processing plant in Saskatchewan. The only reason we could figure for this refusal was that they didn't want us to see how backward they were. (I know they've made some improvements since, and perhaps they wouldn't be so shy now.) We went to dairy farms with beautiful Holstein cows from Canada, but they were still milking them by hand: they told us they'd been waiting for several months for a milking machine. They were nice-looking cattle and they seemed to be well cared for.

The Chinese wanted to show us their best side, but I think only once did they put on a real charade for us. That was when we went to visit what they told us was a horse-breeding farm. The minute I saw the stalls I knew this was no horse-breeding farm because the stalls were too clean – they did not have that used look. I figured they'd brought the horses in for the day just to impress us. They were big, chubby work horses that could have been descended from Russian stock. That afternoon on the road after we had left the farm, I noticed a man riding a stallion leading two or three of these horses. I told our Chinese driver to stop the car so I could get a better look, because the man and the horses looked awfully familiar. Then I said to the official who was riding with us, "Those are the same horses we saw at your research station. I even recognize the man riding the horse – he was there too." The official argued with me that I was wrong, but my eyes told me otherwise.

Although much of Chinese agriculture is technologically very backward, some things they do might be useful in other parts of the Third World. For instance, they have these little two-wheel tractors, millions of them. People laugh at them, but they're an all-purpose vehicle. They use the engines to pump water, grind grain, and sharpen tools; they even use them as tractors – to pull things. Similar machines are used in some other Asian countries. People laugh at them but I think small tractors like these could be used in Africa and other places instead of oxen that eat every damn thing in sight. The problem, of course, is fuel, but I always say that if these places have enough fuel to fight wars they can surely fuel a few tractors.

China was the first place I ever saw ducks being force-fed. This was at a big farm where they had thousands of Peking ducks – big white ducks. The ducks were actually lining up to get fed. The man feeding them had a machine with a plastic spout or tube and when the duck was ready he'd give a little press with a lever and the feeding machine shot a mixture of this soft wet mash down the duck's throat. After they'd had one shot, the ducks would go quacking away, as happy as could be. That's what this man did all day long. He just fed ducks.

One of the greatest problems with Chinese agriculture at the time I was there was the poor post-harvest storage and processing. The Chinese openly admitted that they were wasting about 50 percent of their food because they had no place to store it or process it. In the years since, they've already expanded and improved their storage.

We were in China almost eighteen days and got along marvellously with the people. At a silk commune we visited I teased the workers about their pay, telling them that the workers in the city silk factories were making more money than farm workers and that they were making silk for western bourgeois people. Besides, I told them, food was more important than silk – that sort of thing. And when I gave a speech at the Dr. Bethune Medical College in Changchun City, Jilan Province, I really went after them on the subject of women. I said, "You're supposed to have equal rights here and yet no place I've travelled in your country have I seen a single woman in charge of anything." There were about three hundred doctors in the audience – mostly men and a few women. Afterwards one of them came up to me, an older woman doctor, and said, "When you talked about the rights of women, you sounded just like Chairman Mao." Apparently Mao talked about it a lot, but the Chinese women still don't have their rights. So I introduced my wife and Carol Teichrob to her as my vice-presidents. We had a lot of fun.

The funny thing was that after I made this speech about women's rights, we suddenly started to find women in charge of the places we were visiting – even a pump-making factory in Shanghai. But I got the strong impression that they'd been appointed the day before and would probably be demoted the next.

The government officials we met were trained to be formal, but we found that none of them really like formality that much. Underneath they're plain, ordinary, honest people. If they like you and trust you, I think you can do pretty near anything. For years afterwards when other ministers went to China, the Chinese would say, "We can't remember his name, but he had a green hat on when he was here and he was just great." When I was there, they told me what my name means in Chinese; it's very complimentary. It means great white orchid. I guess I was known as great white orchid with big green hat.

One thing that was reinforced by my trip to China was my belief that Canada is too timid at selling itself to other countries. I saw a perfect example of this on my visit to Indonesia, which was right after my 1980 trip to China. While there, I was taken on a tour of a research centre that was supposed to be for goats and sheep – it had been built by the Australians and was being run by an Australian researcher. He showed me the work they were doing and I found it quite impressive. Then we passed by these three box stalls and I noticed that the animals in the box stalls were not goats; they were three beautiful Holstein bulls. We'd walked by the stalls rather fast, so I said to my guide, "What's this?" And he said, "Oh those are red and white Holstein bulls." And I said, "I may be colour blind but I can see that – and I know a bull from a cow." And he laughed and said, "Those are gifts to the President of Indonesia from the West German government.

This made me think how Canadians sometimes consider themselves too pure to get out and compete with the rest of the world. While I was agriculture minister the government would never have allowed me to give such a gift. And who knows what business Canada might have gained as a result – and what goodwill? To the West Germans such a gift was also a part of the cost of developing their trade.

After the Mexican earthquake in 1985 Canada gave Mexico a big gift of skim milk powder – more than they received from any other country. In this case it was okay for us to give something because of the terrible tragedy – a gift called emergency aid was pure enough for our noble Canadian consciences. The funny thing is that the Mexicans turned around and bought 47,000 tonnes of skim milk powder from Canada, which just about took care of our surplus at that time. Indonesia may not have had an earthquake but it was at least as needy as Mexico. Those West German bulls may have improved the breeding stock of Indonesian dairy cattle and made their entire dairy industry more productive. The more prosperous a country is, the better that is for Canadian trade.

Of course not all agricultural interchange works so well or so fast as the Mexican gift. After we were re-elected in 1974 we made a sale of condensed milk to Algeria and shipped it from Vancouver, of all places, but that's where the milk was. It was put on a boat in Vancouver and it went down the Pacific coast, through the Panama Canal, across the Atlantic, and through the Strait of Gibraltar to Algeria. The trouble was, they'd put all these little cans of condensed milk on the bottom of the load and then put other heavy cargo on top. So, as you can imagine, some of the tin cans got squeezed and some of the milk began to leak when they unloaded them onto the docks in Algeria.

The Algerians wouldn't accept our condensed milk; they told us to take it back. My reply was, "It wasn't our fault that someone loaded the ship wrong; it's the shipper's fault. And furthermore, those cans have been sitting on that dock where the rats can get at them – and you've got some bad rats in Algeria that might have infected that milk with bubonic plague – so I'm not letting that milk back into Canada." The Algerians wouldn't listen to our officials. They loaded the milk back on the boat and I think it went back and forth across the ocean two-and-a-half times before they finally gave up. We were suspicious about that last half time; we figured they'd just dumped the cans in the ocean, because we never did hear what happened to them.

By contrast with China, the Philippines is a country that hasn't begun to live up to its potential. Perhaps the new government will change that. Of the Asian Pacific countries I've visited, I've been to the Philippines the most – three times in all – and in 1980 I had a meeting with President Marcos at Malacañang Palace. I didn't spend much time with him, so I have only a fleeting impression of the man but afterwards I said to Arturo Tanco, his Minister of Agriculture, "Arturo, the president knows more about agriculture than you do." And he said, "Marcos knows much more than people think he does, that's all." On none of my visits to the Philippines did I get the impression that his wife Imelda was the real power (and I knew Arturo didn't like her at all). And having met them both, I can say I was much more impressed with him than with her.

On my last trip to Manila in 1985, as President of the World Food Council, I met Mrs. Marcos for the second and last time (the first time had been at an annual meeting of the World Food Council). On this occasion I made a point of mentioning to her that I had been a good friend of Arturo, who had recently died of cancer. She said, "I know," and nothing more. That meant she knew I knew what he thought about her. The occasion was a fancy official function she was putting on for the International Rice Research Institute near Manila, which is funded by donations from the developed world and conducts research into improved varieties of rice. Although Canada used to be the second largest donor I wasn't even invited to her party, but one of the guys who used to work for Tanco saw me and offered me a ride up in his car.

It was a noontime extravaganza in this posh place up on a hill that had been built just for big events such as this; it even had a helicopter landing pad. I noticed that even the highest officials of the Institute were afraid of Mrs. Marcos. They shook when they were near this powerful woman – and these were international people, not Filipinos she could have put in jail on some whim – they didn't want to say anything that would offend her. But she didn't bother me.

The rural people in the Philippines are generally very poor. They don't live much different from the way they did a hundred years ago or more. I took a trip out to the rice paddies once with a bunch of young Filipino agriculture experts – technicians and economists. When we got to the paddies, they all just sat on the bus. So as I was going to get off I asked them, "Aren't you getting off the bus?" And they said, "No, these people are too dirty." So I shot back, "So you're too good to associate with these people, but you eat their rice." After that a couple of them got off with me, but the rest of them sat there the whole time.

I took off my shoes and socks and went into the rice field in my bare feet where I planted rice and talked to the farmers. While I was there I saw the most incredible sight. Along came this man on a motorcycle wearing a three-piece suit. He got off his little motorbike and set up a table under a tree and that was the local bank. He was from the Bank of Nova Scotia. When I found out he was charging 14 percent interest at a time when the interest rates in Canada were 6 or 7 percent, I thought it was just terrible. But the farmers I talked to said, no. They thought he was just great, that he was one of the best things that ever came to their country, since before he came they used to pay over 50 percent interest. One thing you can be sure of, that banker was making money, or he wouldn't have been there in the first place.

The Filipino rice farmers are a good example of how foreign

aid can go wrong. Agricultural aid people from the International Rice Research Institute had taught them how to produce five crops of rice in the same time-span that they used to grow two and a half. They introduced short-season hybrids and that sort of thing. So the Philippines went from a deficit position in rice to a surplus position and the middlemen made a fortune – the rice millers and the rice traders. But the peasants – the farmers – worked harder, produced more, and made less. They told me, "You showed us how to produce more rice but you never showed us how to make more money." They were mad and they had every right to be. One of the worst things you can do in a developing country is to encourage them to increase production of a certain product without guaranteeing them a decent return.

The new government has a hell of a big job on its hands. I wish the new agriculture minister and Mrs. Aquino well. Their country has great potential and the Filipino people are generally intelligent and hard-working. Give the Philippines a chance and it could become another Japan.

Naturally, not all of my travelling was to the developing world. Canada exports a higher percentage of its agricultural production than almost any country in the world and we do a lot of trade with Europe and with Australia and New Zealand. But the most important international relationship in Canadian agriculture is the one we have with the United States, our biggest trading partner. Elsewhere in this book I've complained about U.S. trading policies, which sometimes have hurt Canada. And it's true that Canadians always have to stand up for their rights on the North American continent. It's also true that the Americans are our best friends and I certainly had no trouble making friends with the three U.S. Secretaries of Agriculture I got to know over the years. All their names began with B – Earl Butz, Bob Bergland, and John Block.

In 1972 Butz had already been there a while. Richard Nixon had made him agriculture secretary just before the 1972 election, and Gerald Ford kept him on after Nixon was forced to resign. He wasn't a farmer. He was an economics professor who'd taught agricultural economics at the University of Purdue.

Before my first visit to the U.S. capital in December of 1972 I remember saying to Syd Williams, my deputy minister, "I'm kinda scared about going to Washington." And he said, "There's no reason to be. You'll see when you get there that there's not a worry you should have." He meant that the staff I had with me were all experienced pros, whereas none of Butz's people were that experienced. So we actually were at an advantage. That's because of the number of political appointments there are in the U.S. every time a new party wins an election. It's not a good system.

Butz and I had a good relationship. Our meetings were generally to settle disagreements between the Canadian bureaucrats and the American ones. He was very quick to make decisions and if we came to an agreement, he'd say, "Gene and I have agreed to do this and that's what we're going to do." We worked well together. He loved to tell jokes. Every time we went down to Washington he'd have a couple of jokes for us and if you were any good you had a couple for him.

Jimmy Carter's agriculture secretary was Bob Bergland, a farmer from Minnesota who knew Canada better than the others. He even used to go to hockey games in Winnipeg and listen to the CBC. His problem was maybe a bit similar to that of his boss. Bob often had trouble making decisions. He was a nice enough man, but a bit timid. That time when the farmers went to Washington and were parading and brought goats and turned them loose on the White House lawn, he moved out of his office because he was scared of the threats he was getting. This was after I had the milk thrown at me, so I knew what it was like to have the farmers against you.

Once, after Bergland and I talked about agricultural exports and how we had to have more agents in foreign countries, he went home from the meeting and within a month he'd hired six hundred extra agents to sell American agricultural products all over the world. Our Treasury Board wouldn't approve even ten.

John Block, who resigned from Reagan's Cabinet in early 1986, was the former Secretary of Agriculture for the state of Illinois. He was a farmer, so we had a natural respect for each other right away and we could settle most anything with a phone call. It didn't seem to make much difference that he was a Republican. He also liked to have fun. At international meetings he would always bring his guitar and sing folk songs and cowboy songs after the work was done. (We worked closely together at the World Food Council.)

I did think he got involved in some things that seemed awfully small to me. One time he called me long distance to complain that we were not letting Oregon pears into B.C. This was during an election campaign and the congressmen out there were giving him hell. I had to laugh because it had nothing to do with Canada. I said, "John we didn't change our regulations, those are your regulations." Those pears had a certain amount of pesticide above the maximum level permitted by his own regulations.

Really I got along with all three of the "BB" boys, as I like to call them. We had the kind of rapport where we could talk on the phone and joke – this went for all three of them – and solve our problems without too much fuss. The American officials sometimes treated us a little bit like we Canadians were unimportant but never the Secretaries themselves. But of the three, Earl Butz was the one I liked the most, even if he was an economist.

Of the important people I've met around the world, I've found very few whom I couldn't talk to as an equal – this includes Mikhail Gorbachev and Pope John Paul II. But François Mitterand of France is one of the few I'd describe as arrogant, pure and simple. This certainly wasn't generally true of the French Ministers of Agriculture I met over the years. Jacques Chirac, for example, treated me well when I was still a new boy on the world scene in 1973. He was tough and straight and he certainly didn't have any great love for the United States and I'm sure he'll give old Mitterand a rough time in his new role as French Prime Minister.

I didn't meet Mitterand himself until 1985 when I was presiding over the annual meeting of the World Food Council. He was there to open the event and gave a great and stirring speech about the tragedy of African famine which had recently become a fashionable topic. While he was speaking I thought to myself, isn't it odd that many of the worst-off countries in Africa are former French colonies–Burkina Faso, Chad, Niger, Mali, Rwanda, Burundi. The French left them without anything and use them to this day as sources of raw materials.

And when I met Mitterand–which was only for a few moments –I wasn't too impressed with the man, or those around him. He was cold and aloof, the epitome of arrogance. When he said hello, you felt as though he were saying, "You're inferior to me and don't you forget it." Of course, if you study his background you'll find that, although he may have been a socialist, he was never a working man; he was from the bourgeoisie, as were many of his ministers. And I couldn't get over all the young people around him and the airs they put on as well. The young minister Henri Nallet who was elected to succeed me as President of the WFC, you would have sworn he was president of the world, not just the World Food Council which only had thirty-six member Ministers of Agriculture and a staff of thirty-three people. You would have thought he had thirty-three thousand people working for him.

Edith Cresson, who was Mitterand's Minister of Agriculture in 1985, was from an upper-class background–her husband was a big executive with Citroën, the car manufacturer–and I doubt she'd ever been near a farm. I asked her, "What do you think you have in common with the working people, the ordinary rank and file?" She laughed and said, "Oh, Eugene, anyone can make common cause with the workers." And I said, "You mean for power, you can make yourself almost anything." She just laughed and didn't say more.

Power didn't make Mikhail Gorbachev arrogant–perhaps he's changed since he moved from running Soviet agriculture to running the whole country. I was originally supposed to meet him during a six-week trip to the Soviet Union in 1978, but Grandpa Pollinger, who'd been sick only about two or three weeks, died just before the trip was scheduled and I had to cancel the whole thing.

The 1978 trip had been arranged by Alexander Yakovlev, who was then Russian ambassador to Canada. (Gorbachev recently made him chief of Soviet propaganda, so he's become a powerful man in the new regime.) He'd been in Ottawa for years and we'd become quite good friends. I used to enjoy debating with him about our system versus the Soviet system. I'd tell him the reason Russia never met its five-year production plans was because the farmers didn't have enough incentive to produce. I think he actually agreed with me much of the time, but of course he couldn't say so. Most Russians are easy to talk to and Yakovlev was one of the easiest. I liked him a lot.

One of the reasons Alexander was so keen on my going was that Mikhail Gorbachev was his former pupil, and he wanted me to meet him. I guess Yakovlev would be about my age – he'd been sixteen when he fought in the siege of Leningrad during the Second World War. His body is covered with scars and he has one metal leg, which means that he walks with a limp. I met many Russians over there with similar experiences. It helps explain how they feel about war and peace. I used to love to pull Yakovlev's leg – metal or not. At one time a distiller in St. Catharines was making an apple brandy called Northern Spy. When he gave me two bottles of his finest, I couldn't wait to present one to the Soviet ambassador. When he saw the name on the label, he just howled and laughed.

Anyway, when I informed the embassy that I was cancelling the trip, Alexander called me up at home to try to persuade me to change my mind. "I've arranged the best trip in the world for you; you can't let me down. Nobody's had a trip like this to the Soviet Union." What he said was true – it was a wonderful six-week trip that he'd planned; every place I'd requested to go, they'd said yes – but I still said no. I know he was disappointed, but we continued to be friends. I got the impression that he thought I knew they were going to invade Afghanistan and that that was the real reason I cancelled. If I'd gone I would have been in the Soviet Union right at the time of the invasion. To this day I believe he believes that our secret service warned me to stay home.

Because of the invasion, which temporarily messed up relations between the Soviet Union and Canada, I didn't end up going there until 1981 – and then for only eight days instead of the original six weeks. Alexander was then still in Ottawa and he organized my trip. I was the first Canadian politician to visit the Soviet Union since 1977. So I finally made old Yakovlev happy. And wherever I went they used to introduce me as "the bravest Canadian of all" because I was the first minister to go there after the invasion.

As usual on my major foreign trips, Liz came with me. It was normal for wives to be invited and some countries – like Japan – absolutely insisted that ministers' wives come too. But on these trips I found my wife to be a great asset (it was also a chance for us to spend some time together). We don't talk enough about Liz in the book – she'd say that's because I'm too busy talking about myself, as usual – but she has been a great political asset from the day I married her.

I've already mentioned how she managed to look after three little girls and also handle much of the riding business after I was first elected. In my early days in the Cabinet she travelled a lot with me around Canada and she made friends wherever she went. Liz has more than the average knowledge of life. She'd worked in various kinds of jobs – from legal stenographer to factory worker to picking potatoes by hand – grown up on a farm and been born in a country on the other side of the ocean; she could talk to just about anyone and they'd know she knew what she was talking about. She still speaks fluently the German she learned as a child and can understand some Serb and Slovak. At a state farm near Leningrad in the Soviet Union the scientists said to my wife, "This is the first time in weeks we've had sun. And we have to dig potatoes. We want you to stay until we finish digging potatoes because you'll keep our good weather here." They knew she was one of them.

I used to enjoy teasing people in the Soviet Union about God. They have a saying they use a lot, *spasibo*. It means, thank you, but some people from the Ukraine translate it as "God be with you." Whenever Soviet farmers asked how we in Canada produce so much with so few people, I'd say, "Well, we work hard but then we have help from Him," and I'd point at the heavens. All they did was laugh. And I noticed that even though the Soviet Union is the atheist workers' state, they don't work on Sunday. Everything stops.

In the Soviet Union, as in all Slavic countries, they expect you to do a lot of drinking. But by this time I'd perfected the Danny Rosati method. The Russians were surprised that I was willing to challenge them and that I'd learnt the trick they use to stop any cheating: you pour the glass upside down over your thumbnail and lick off any drop that is left.

Wherever I went in the Soviet Union – state farms, formal dinners, research facilities – they always drank a toast to peace. And whenever I spoke and said something about how Canadians wanted peace, the audience would always cheer. It was as though everyone was trying to impress us with the fact that the Soviet people are not a bunch of warmongers. I'm convinced that they really don't want war and realize they're spending too much on military might, and I got the same strong impression from Gorbachev when I met him.

The main event of the eight-day trip was my meeting with Gorbachev, who was then Minister of Agriculture and a member of the Politburo. Since the Soviet Union is so big, and since agriculture is so important, Gorbachev had a number of sub-ministers working for him. I'd entertained one of them in Canada, a man named Valentin Mesyats, the minister responsible for food production. I'd taken him to see the McIntyre ranch in southern Alberta which is now owned and run by Ralph Thrall – 56,000 acres I think it is, with thousands of head of cattle in some of the prettiest country you'll ever see, just like a movie setting – rolling hills and little lakes and lowing cows and an old ranchhouse down a winding road. Just a beautiful place. When I took Mesyats there I could tell from the look in his eyes that he was utterly amazed – that he was thinking, "This isn't real." He was like a kid, absorbing everything. When I got to the Soviet Union, I could see why. They have nothing like it there, at least nothing that I saw.

They try to run their farms like factories in the city, and they just don't work that well. That's partly because the workers there don't care as much. I used to remind the Soviets that our farmers run their own farms. The state farms in Russia aren't very productive, but the little private plots are. The people who are growing food for themselves produce much more than their share of the total – in some cases more than half. Gorbachev realized this and while he ran Soviet agriculture he expanded the private agricultural sector.

Before I met Gorbachev I'd been briefed on him and knew he was smart and an up-and-comer. The Western press don't like to admit now that he was once in charge of agriculture, because farmers aren't supposed to have enough brains to run a country. Our embassy in Moscow had told us about his background, for instance that he wasn't a pure Russian but of mixed stock from Stavropol near the Black Sea, which made his success all the more remarkable. I knew he'd grown up in a rural area and had worked on a state farm as a combine operator as a young man. This was a man who'd driven a tractor and tilled the soil; he wasn't just a bureaucrat who'd never gotten dirt between his toes or under his nails. So I knew already we'd have a lot in common.

Our ambassador in Moscow, Geoffrey Pearson, warned me that he'd be surprised if our meeting lasted more than fifteen or twenty minutes. That was the standard. But diplomats were always telling me things like that and they were always turning out to be wrong. When we arrived at the Kremlin, we were brought into a small room with a little table that had four chairs on each side. I had a couple of aides with me and, as always, my own interpreter.

When he walked into the room, the first thing he said was, "You look tired." And I said, "You would be too if you'd travelled halfway around the world and you'd been drinking with Russians for several days." Then I said, "But I haven't found a Russian yet who could drink me under the table." At this he just laughed. (When he came to Canada I found out that he drinks hardly anything himself.) Then we sat down and got down to business.

"You know," he began, "this meeting is more political than it is about agriculture." And I said, "It's about whatever you want to make it about." So then he launched into the usual tirade about the wicked United States. But I didn't let him get very far. I said, "Just hold on one minute, Secretary Gorbachev. Before you go any further, I'd like to tell you a little story we tell back home. It's about the three bears. We learn it when we're little kids."

"There's a father bear who's big and gruff, and a mother bear who's always bossing everyone around. And then there's baby bear, who's always getting it from both of them. Well, if the Soviet Union is the mother bear and the United States is the father bear, then Canada is the baby bear. We're caught in the middle." I paused for a bit. "We'd prefer to think we can talk to our parents with respect and that they'll listen with respect to what we have to say." Then I said, "Mr. Secretary, you can continue this discussion any way you want. We can talk politics, or we can talk agriculture. If you want to talk politics, I can say as many bad things about the Soviet Union as you can say about America. It's up to you." That was the last I heard about the bad old United States.

We talked about agriculture and about agricultural research. We touched on world affairs, even Afghanistan. I told him the invasion was not a popular thing in Canada and he replied that they'd had to do it to protect their borders. We had a serious discussion, but friendly – we liked each other from the start. I was particularly impressed with what he had to say about his efforts to improve agriculture in order make life better for his people. Our discussion went on for an hour and half and before I left I invited him to visit Canada – as Yakovlev had suggested – and Gorbachev accepted. So we set a date – the spring of 1983 – and he later received an official invitation from Jeanne Sauvé, then Speaker of the House of Commons. This was designed to make it look non-political.

Sometime after the Moscow meeting, Geoffrey Pearson told me what Gorbachev later said about me: "He not only looks tough, but he is tough too." I felt the same way about him. I could tell even on the basis of our one meeting that he was a good politician. And bright. But hard as nails.

His visit to Canada in May 1983 was his only major trip to a Western country before becoming General Secretary of the Communist party. He'd attended a meeting in Paris one time and that was all. Although it was obvious to many of us in Canada that he was a rising star, the press didn't pay too much attention, so I had him pretty much to myself. He was in Canada ten days and I spent most of this time with him, including five days on the road.

When he arrived I met him at the airport along with Alexander Yakovlev, Jeanne Sauvé, and a number of other Soviet and Canadian officials. I think some of the Soviets were a bit jealous that this old peasant from Canada would be spending more time with him than the official representatives of the U.S.S.R., but he was here to see Canada, not the Soviet embassy staff. Mrs. Gorbachev was also supposed to come, but for some reason the plan was changed at the last minute.

On the tarmac Mikhail greeted me with a great big Russian bear hug. He hadn't forgotten our meeting in Moscow and we were glad to see each other. The first couple of days he spent making the rounds in Ottawa. I escorted him to various meetings and also took him to the Experimental Farm where we put on a steak barbeque for his delegation. We ate under a big tent and served Canadian wine (as agriculture minister I never served anything else). The caterer, Dave Smith, brought along a lobster especially for Gorbachev to try. He said he'd never tasted it, so this was the first time he'd eaten Canadian lobster or drunk Canadian wine – he only drank one glass. We had a wonderful time.

While in Ottawa he appeared before the joint agricultural committee of the Senate and the House of Commons and met with both Ed Broadbent and Erik Nielsen. He also had a meeting with Trudeau. Like most foreign leaders, he was very impressed with the Prime Minister; he already knew a lot about Trudeau's background and admired him a great deal. When I'd returned from the Soviet Union in 1981 I'd brought with me a letter from Brezhnev asking Trudeau to act as a mediator between the United States and the Soviet Union to help bring about peace. I didn't read the letter, but Gorbachev hinted to me what was in it. He brought a similar letter with him in 1983, this time from Andropov.

Gorbachev thought our Parliament Buildings were among the most beautiful he had ever seen and commented that the people who had selected the location must have been very farsighted for a new country. He wasn't nearly so impressed with the Senate – I mean the institution, not the architecture. He would jokingly ask me how the citizens of a democratic country like Canada could put up with legislators who were appointed for life. And when we appeared before the joint Senate/House agricultural committee he asked me, "How can you sit with them? They never have to associate with the people." On that I agreed with him totally. As I've already mentioned, I have long favoured abolishing the Senate.

I hired a plane to fly Gorbachev around – but I even had to fight with the Treasury Board for that. Here he was, our largest grain customer and clearly a man who was going to be very important in the future of the Soviet Union, and they said the jet plane I wanted to hire was too expensive. I wanted to get a DC-9 from Air Canada – for five days it would have cost $100,000. So I shopped around and finally found an old propellor-driven Convair – forty years old – at Air Ontario and paid $39,000 for it. And that was charged to Agriculture Canada; it came out of our budget. This was part of the reason I had such a high bill for travel that year. When I was criticized for it the press and the Opposition always made it sound as if I was flying off on some junket to Florida, rather than providing transportation for the next leader of the Soviet Union.

I rented a plane or used a government aircraft for every important minister who came to Canada – that way they could see as much as possible and visit the far-flung corners of the country in a short time. I've always believed in treating our trading partners as special guests. But the Treasury Board didn't always agree with me.

I took Gorbachev to various places in Ontario and Alberta and, wherever we travelled, he was fascinated with our way of life. We toured farms, agricultural research stations, food-processing plants, wineries, supermarkets, even a distillery. He couldn't get over all the products on the shelves of the supermarkets. He never tried to hide the fact that he was impressed with what Canada had achieved. Remember, he'd never spent any time in North America before and had almost no experience outside the Soviet Bloc.

Before Gorbachev arrived, Yakovlev had told me, "Talk to him just like you talk to me." He meant that he wanted me to be completely frank and talk openly about the virtues of the Canadian system. One time when Gorbachev and I were discussing the merits of the Russian system versus the Canadian system, I could see Yakovlev standing behind Gorbachev cheering me on with a clenched fist. In one of these conversations I told Gorbachev that the problem with the Soviet food system was state control – that as long as he had his system, Russia would never be able to feed itself. Then I turned it into a joke and said, "Of course, if you adopt our system, you'd never have to buy anything from Canada any more. I tell our farmers to pray for your system all the time." He just laughed because he knew it was true. It seems as though he's attempting to introduce more competition and more incentive into the Russian economy. But I doubt it will work as long as the state and its bureaucratic methods remain so strong.

After Ottawa we took him to Windsor – he stayed in the Holiday Inn and we toured my home turf. Then we had him to our home for a country-style roast rib of beef and roast chicken. He was amazed at how informally we did things – he didn't realize that he was with the master of informality. (Unlike other visitors from the so-called socialist countries, Gorbachev and his group didn't comment on our lack of servants. Others from the Soviet Bloc and China invariably expressed great surprise that someone so high up in the government had no staff waiting on him.) It was obvious to everyone that Gorbachev was having a really good time but he usually remained quite reserved. It was often his eyes that told you what he was thinking and feeling. You could tell by their expression when he was annoyed, or when he was bored and wanted to move on to another subject.

For instance, I could tell right away what he thought of Dennis Timbrell, who was then the Ontario Minister of Agriculture and who hosted us at a dinner at Ontario Place. After meeting him Gorbachev asked me, "How did that guy become an agriculture minister? He's never even been a farmer." When Dennis made his speech at the dinner he was trying to be clever and it wasn't working. He tried to make some jokes about me being a Liberal (since he claims he's a Conservative) but they didn't come across. I got the impression that Gorbachev thought Timbrell was sort of a smart aleck.

One particular event in the Ontario part of his trip seemed to stick in Gorbachev's mind, because he referred to it several times afterwards. It happened when we visited Gino Penunzio's greenhouse near Leamington. As Gorbachev was leaving, Mr. Penunzio shook his hand and said, "I'm just a little tomato farmer, and I know you're from a big country, but I don't think my wishes are any different from yours or those of your people. I hope and pray for peace for you and your people." It was one of the nicest speeches I heard from anyone on the trip – politicians included – and I think Gorbachev was quite moved by it.

Gorbachev's personal physician travelled with him everywhere, always with a special kit in a metal box. I have no idea what was in the box or whether Gorbachev required some special medication, but he was certainly very careful about what he ate and he never once drank liquor during the trip, only occasionally a little wine. This doctor seemed to watch everything he did – what he ate, the clothes he wore, his routine.

We also toured the region around St. Catharines (including Niagara Falls) before heading west to Alberta for the last couple of days of the visit. In Calgary we had a special meeting set up with Premier Peter Lougheed and we spent about an hour and a half together. What a sight it was to have this great socialist leader and this well-known Conservative leader in the same room. I'll never forget one of the first things Gorbachev said to Lougheed. He said, "You know, Mr. Premier, you Conservatives and we Communists have a lot in common." When he heard this, Peter pretty near fell off his chair in a state of shock. When he'd recovered he said, "Mr. Secretary, what do you mean?" Gorbachev replied, "We both like to do things in a big way," and then he laughed devilishly and Peter laughed too. I could have said something right then, but I didn't. I could have said that there was more truth to what Gorbachev was saying than even he realized. Conservative Alberta is big on government ownership of the economy – airlines, banks and so on. The Alberta government even owns more than 50 percent of the land in the province – a lot of those so-called independent beef producers are on state-owned land. The first request of almost every visitor from a socialist country was to go to Alberta to see how a successful socialist state is run. The communist system is very conservative: it doesn't change its philosophy very much and it's afraid of change. I would have liked to have told Gorbachev that if he really changed anything, he'd be a Liberal.

This was one of the few times in my career I met with Lougheed, but I never loathed him as many Liberals did. He always treated me very well and I rather liked him, in fact. But I thought his hatred for the East was irrational and unwarranted. A lot of Westerners have a very mistaken view of Eastern Canada; they lump us all in with Toronto and Montreal. But some people in Essex County hate Toronto with just as much passion – and with just as much reason.

There's no question that Gorbachev was most impressed with our country. He marvelled at our technology and our productivity and freely admitted how far behind his own country was in many ways. But the majority of our conversations weren't about agriculture. They were about how we lived and what we did, about our families and our lives and the things that were important to us personally. I told him about my childhood growing up in Anderdon Township, the stories about fighting with the quarrysuckers, and giving the teachers trouble, and getting elected to the school board when I didn't even know I was running, and winning my first election to Parliament, and so on. And he told me about his growing up as a boy during the Second World War – the hardship, the lack of food, the friends and relatives killed and wounded.

He was still very bitter about World War Two – and not just about the Germans. In his area near the Black Sea, every city and town had been destroyed. He said to me, "We fought beside you and we lost twenty million people during the war to destroy a monster." But despite this, the Allies never helped Russia to rebuild. There was no Marshall Plan for the Soviet Union as there was for Germany, no masses of American aid as there was for Japan. When the war ended, instead of helping the Soviet Union rebuild, the U.S. told them to change their ideology. "They never told us that when we fought the war together and died together," Gorbachev said. He was still very bitter. I don't blame him.

I would have liked to work with him to make the world a better place. In 1985, after he became General Secretary of the Communist Party, in effect the most powerful ruler of the second most powerful country on earth, and once I'd become President of the World Food Council, I wrote him a letter. It was the same letter I sent to the Pope and to presidents and prime ministers around the world asking them to help fight the famine in Africa. But I didn't receive a direct answer. I complained about this to the new Soviet ambassador, Alexei Rodionov. I said, "I'm browned off because I've received no response from my friend Mikhail." Rodionov made some excuse about how long it took for letters to get to the top. (I later received a letter from Alexei telling me that Gorbachev had received my letter and shared my concerns.)

One of the last times I met with a world leader of Gorbachev's stature was in March 1984 when I had a private audience with Pope John Paul II at the Vatican. I'd met his two predecessors – Pope Paul and John Paul I – but only as one of many at a large audience. Those first two occasions had both been during the annual meeting of the Food and Agriculture Organization (FAO) whose headquarters are in Rome. I always found those audiences kind of funny – the FAO members included all religions, Hindus, Moslems, Christians, Jews, and here everybody was fighting to get to see the Pope. Even though I'm a Catholic, I never thought of the Pope as being something special. He's simply a man who has been put in a special position. I guess that's always been my approach to important people. I don't treat them any different if they've got three thousand pairs of shoes or just one pair.

When I went to see John Paul II in 1984, I was in Italy for a meeting of world leaders at Bellagio near Milan – a think tank on the food problem. As President of the World Food Council, I'd made a special request to see him and the request was granted. We sat on plain chairs and his desk looked like a plain little bench that had probably been there a few hundred years. Since, like mine, his hearing apparently isn't very good, we both leaned on the corner of the desk – probably not much farther from each other than this book you're holding is from you now. He was very tired the day I met him and had many other people waiting for him, but he paid attention to what I had to say and gave me the time I needed. I appealed to him as a moral leader to help get all the churches involved in the cause of the Third World and to fight the famine in Africa. He promised to do what he could.

I was very gratified when he came to Canada that one of his first speeches was on the importance of assisting the developing world and how the rich countries had to do more. He's a very intelligent and compassionate person, though I don't always agree with him. I don't know if our conversation did any good, but I felt I had to try.

It's funny, but when I think of meeting the Popes I can't help remembering the time my wife and I visited the Pope's country estate outside of Rome, Castel Gandolfo. It's a beautiful estate with quite a sizeable farm and lots of livestock. We talked there to the chief herdsman of the Pope's dairy herd and he appealed to me as a good Catholic to donate some pure-bred Canadian Holsteins to the Pope's herd. I guess he was encouraged by the fact that Stephen Roman, the millionaire chairman of Denison Mines, had already donated a nice big Canadian herd. I told him, "I don't have money to give the Pope no herd of cattle." So he came back, "But you're the Minister of Agriculture." And I said, "That doesn't give me the right to give anybody, including the Pope, a single calf. Besides the Catholic Church is very well off. You don't need any cows from me." He said, "You're not talking like a very good Catholic." And I said, "I never learnt in any book that you can buy your way into the Kingdom of Heaven." Which ended the conversation.

I couldn't get over the way they ran the Pope's farm. They had a modern milk cooler, sure enough, but they milked the Pope's cows by hand. I asked the chief herdsman why and he said "Because there's less chance of getting bacteria in the milk that way." I said, "You must be kidding. An open pail in a barn with bare hands on the udders?" But he was very firm about that. I also couldn't get over the Pope's chickens. They were fine chickens but they were running around and scratching in the dirt just like the old chickens on our farm when I was a kid. I was just amazed to see the Pope's chickens picking in the dirt. I guess you get that old-fashioned flavour so many claim is gone from the chicken they eat today.

11

Feeding the Hungry

My first trip to Africa was in June 1980 when I spent fourteen
days in Tanzania, touring the country and attending a meeting of the World Food Council in Arusha. During the visit I
met with President Julius Nyerere, then took a short trip with
him and his agriculture minister John Malecela to visit the
experimental wheat farm near Arusha that is run by Agriculture Canada on behalf of CIDA, the Canadian International
Development Agency.

Nyerere is a very intelligent man, very concerned about his
people, who call him "Mwalimu," which means "the teacher."
He is often criticized in the West for the failure of his state-
run economy – and certainly Tanzania has had many problems
resulting from its highly centralized planning – but I don't think
people realize how many problems Nyerere has had to face in
dealing with different tribal groups with different languages
and cultural beliefs. And I think it is fair to say that Tanzania
has made great progress under his leadership. But despite his
good intentions Tanzania is still unable to feed its people and
still requires food aid.

Both the amount of progress that has been made and the problems that remain became clear to me when Nyerere, Malecela, and I visited the experimental wheat farm. Malecela had been Tanzanian High Commissioner to Canada and I'd gotten to know him quite well. He was a handsome and intelligent man, well educated and with a sense of humour. He'd gotten his education first in Tanzanian schools and then, as is so often the case in Commonwealth countries, in England. He had a law degree and an engineering degree and he was a very well informed man.

We flew the hundred miles from Arusha on a two-propellor Buffalo transport airplane made in Canada – a good plane. It had one row of little fold-down canvas seats bolted to the floor, and some bolted to the wall, with no padding or anything – just canvas. President Nyerere sat in front of me – no special treatment – and we had a pretty rough landing on a sod runway. I wouldn't mention this except that when I got back to Canada, a press report talked about how Nyerere and I had flown in a fancy jet airplane. It's this sort of thing that makes us politicians lose some of our natural respect for the men and women of the press.

The Canadians who work on our Hananj experimental farm complex, made up of seven farms in all on the Hananj plain, are dedicated people. Usually they are husband-and-wife teams – technicians and farmers – who sign three-year contracts to go work with the Tanzanians. The Canadians live in simple little houses with bare cement floors and where the electricity is shut off at nine every night – except for the refrigerator which has a separate line. What they do there is important. They live and work with the local people and teach them how to farm more productively using modern agricultural technology – tractors, combines, cultivators, seeders, fertilizers. The soil around Arusha is beautiful. You could grow wheat there for fifteen years without needing any fertilizer, it's so rich in nutrients. The only real problem is a species of bird, the *quelea*, that eats the grain, but it can be controlled by airplane spraying.

Some time after this trip – in 1983 or 1984 – the Auditor General recommended that we stop paying the annual several million dollars required to keep the farms going. He said it was a waste of money. And just before the famine became world news the CBC show *fifth estate* made a slashing attack on our program. It seemed like pretty near every year I had to fight like hell at Treasury Board just to save the farm; and they made us back off from building a $5 million agricultural research laboratory in Arusha. Then, when the big famine hit Africa, they found that our farm could produce two tonnes of wheat for what it cost to buy and ship one tonne to Africa. Then the Treasury Board started to say, "Isn't this great how we can now produce two tonnes for what it used to cost us to ship one?" The Tanzanians are now producing 50 percent of the grain they need.

At the time of this visit, I made an agreement with President Nyerere. I said, "When you get up to 100,000 acres of grain, Canada will build a railroad to haul it out. (In 1986 they were expecting to seed 63,000 acres and their yield per acre has been going up.) I don't know if the Tanzanians remember that promise or not. And I don't know if the current government will keep it if they do. The promise was never made in writing but if I was still there, you can be sure it would be kept.

The main reason for my trip to Arusha in 1980 was the annual get-together of the World Food Council, which, as I've mentioned, consists of thirty-six agriculture ministers or their representatives from both the developed and the developing world. It was established by the General Assembly of the United Nations in late 1974 to ride herd on the other twenty-seven UN aid agencies concerned with food so that things like the African famine don't take place. Its job is to oversee and co-ordinate UN policy affecting the world food situation. It was a good idea, but there was one fatal flaw from the start. It didn't have enough power.

The Council has no power to take action, it can only make recommendations – in other words, raise hell. And that's exactly what I'd been doing at every WFC meeting since 1975 and was trying to do again at the 1980 meeting. I wanted to get our member nations off their asses to put big pressure on the UN and the other relief agencies. Many of the multitude of UN agencies involved in food aid were represented at this meeting as observers, among them the Food and Agriculture Organization (FAO), which is by far the largest and most powerful.

This was the first of many public speeches I would make on the topic of the looming famine in Africa. Our Canadian advisers in Africa and many other people were already warning us that the African continent might be on the verge of a huge catastrophe. We knew even then about the developing drought in sub-Saharan Africa and the possibility of widespread famine. I gave the delegates one of my barn-burner speeches. I told them to get their acts together, co-ordinate their efforts, and to work with all the private organizations involved in the food aid business. I demanded proper accounting to the WFC of the activities of all these competing UN agencies and a full report on the situation with recommendations for action at the next annual meeting of the WFC in Novi Sad, Yugoslavia, in June 1981.

But the UN bureaucrats from the FAO who were at the meeting objected and tried to have some of my words struck from the record. This was done behind the scenes but some of my friends told me, and when I found out I got up the next day on a point of order and held up a little portable tape recorder and I looked straight at my old friend Arturo Tanco of the Philippines – who was WFC president that year – and said, "I want you to know that I have a tape, word for word, of what I said, and it better show up word for word on the records of this meeting." But I had to leave before the meeting was finished and some Canadian made a concession and took out part of what I'd said. The FAO people didn't want my words to be there because they showed that they weren't doing their job. And we never did get that report the next year. The UN bureaucrats were all too busy fighting among themselves and studying their computer printouts, instead of doing something. The problem wasn't important enough until it was too late.

I went home from that meeting deeply disturbed and wondering what more Canada could do. I had seen the poverty in Peru in 1968 and since then had seen slums in many countries until they made me sick. I wanted to do whatever I could to prevent a terrible famine in Africa.

What was I doing getting so involved? Well, the fact is that a very high proportion of Canada's foreign aid is in the form of food or of agricultural equipment, methods, research. So Agriculture Canada administered things like that wheat farm in Tanzania on behalf of CIDA, and very often we would send people to help a particular country. For example, we would send our veterinarians and technicians to a country that was having problems eradicating livestock diseases. Sometimes we paid for that sort of thing right out of our own department budget and sometimes we were funded by External Affairs through CIDA. But Agriculture Canada has long had a presence in the developing world and our veterinarians and other agricultural scientists who are helping developing nations are in my view some of Canada's finest diplomats. In fact, Agriculture Canada was involved in aid from the beginning, even before CIDA was established.

As minister, I always kept an eye on what CIDA was doing and if I didn't think a particular aid program was a good one, I'd make that known to the Cabinet. So when I started to get involved more in the problems in Africa, it wasn't so much a departure as an expansion of the role Agriculture Canada had been playing for years and that I'd been playing more actively since the founding of the World Food Council.

Actually, one of the first times I'd ever made news on the subject of foreign aid was in 1979, The International Year of the Child, when I went on my diet. Canadians were raising money for children in other countries and Jean Coolican, wife of Denis Coolican, who was then the chairman of the Ottawa regional government, was looking for people who would participate in the Slim-a-thon sponsored by the Canadian Save the Children Fund. For every ounce or pound you lost, people were supposed to donate money. Mrs. Coolican is a mild-mannered person, but she was good at this job. She called me up and said, "Mr. Whelan, I think you'd be a perfect candidate for our weight-loss program." And I said, "Mrs. Coolican, are you saying that I'm too fat?" And she quietly replied, "I think you could lose some weight, Mr. Whelan, and for a very good cause. Let me explain it to you."

So I had a medical and went on a diet and exercise program.

The doctor I went to at the Department of National Defence was a lady doctor and I'll never forget what she said. She said, "You're stupid, you know, to be carrying the extra weight that you are." (I weighed 245 at the time.) I said, "What do you mean? That's not a very nice thing to say." And she said, "Would you walk around every day with twenty-pound weights on the ends of both arms?" I was starting to say, "No, that would be stupid," until I realized what I was saying. And she said, "That's what you're doing, you're carrying nearly forty pounds more than you should."

In six weeks I lost pretty near forty pounds. I had a big button that I wore when I rode on airplanes that said, "Don't feed me," which I'd put on before I went to sleep – the stewardesses never woke me up. I didn't eat too much when I was awake either. Not many of my sponsors had expected I'd lose so much – I raised the most money of anybody in Canada for this project. One old farmer wrote from Saskatchewan – I've never met him – and said, I'll give you five dollars for every pound you lose. I didn't bill him or any of the others for the full forty. I just billed for twenty-five pounds, and still I raised the most.

When I went to get weighed for the official weighing, they'd set up some scales in a press room downstairs in the House of Commons. Mrs. Coolican was there and some reporters. I had a pair of gym pants on under my regular pants – but Mrs. Coolican didn't know that – and I was wearing a sweatshirt that had International Year of the Child on it. Just before I stepped on the scale I dropped my pants and Mrs. Coolican nearly died. She thought I was going to do a striptease right there in the press room. I got my picture in pretty near every paper in Canada, standing on the scales in my little gym shorts and, I must say, not bad-looking legs, either.

That incident was having some fun for a good cause, but by 1983 I wasn't having much fun. I was getting extremely frustrated about the situation in Africa. Since my trip to Tanzania in 1980, the crisis in the sub-Sahara had been worsening, but in Canada we were distracted by our own economic problems and it was all I could do to persuade the government to maintain aid at its current level. This led to some vicious arguments in the Cabinet, but there wasn't much else I could do in those two years except watch and wring my hands. So, when the opportunity came, I decided to run for President of World Food Council. My old friend Arturo Tanco, who'd been President himself, urged me to run. I was elected in July of 1983 for a two-year term. In August I made a special trip to Ethiopia to look at the worsening problem first hand.

Before I left I had seen a film prepared by the people at World Vision, one of the Christian aid agencies that did so much to publicize the tragedy. Dr. Bill Newell, their executive director, showed it to us and it was as bad as anything you saw on television in 1984. Skeletons of children, masses of starving people waiting for food. But when I stopped in Rome on my way to Addis Ababa, the people at FAO headquarters, and the other UN organizations, who should by then have been co-ordinating a massive worldwide campaign, were too afraid to talk. They were more concerned with protecting their own little empires than doing something about the problem. Each one had his little domain and didn't want anyone else infringing on it. It would be cruel of me to say that they didn't care, but it was obvious to me that they didn't care enough or there would have been so much more done. Not one of them thought it was that serious. They were all contradicting each other and claimed I was overreacting when I told them I thought we should mobilize as if we were fighting a war. I never received any official follow-up from that visit.

When Liz and I arrived in Addis Ababa in August we were met by Tekola Dejene, the Ethiopian Minister of Agriculture. I had met Dejene at our WFC meetings and knew him to be a highly intelligent young man who spoke perfect English. In fact, he had an agriculture degree from the University of Michigan and knew my part of Canada. I found him bright, articulate, concerned and very human. Like most Third World ministers of agriculture, he'd been given very limited resources, but he was quite dedicated to his job. He was trying like hell with little or nothing to work with.

Like many of the Ethiopian ministers I met, I don't think of Dejene as a dedicated Marxist. He believed in the accomplishments of the revolution and wanted to make a better country for his people. The only one of his colleagues I wasn't so sure about was Major Dawit Wolde Giorgis, the head of the Relief and Rehabilitation Commission, the man in charge of dealing with aid. He was the roughest one as far as I was concerned – a military man more than anything else. I really disliked him. He did not want to admit Ethiopia's failure. He almost made it sound as if Ethiopia didn't need the aid so badly, that the problems weren't as bad as we knew they were.

The head of Ethiopia, Major General Mengistu Haile Mariam, whom I met on my two subsequent trips, was different. Both times he thanked me in what I thought was a very sincere way for the tremendous things that we had done in Canada to help the Ethiopians. In 1984, he gave me a personal message of thanks to convey to Prime Minister Trudeau. But as late as 1983, even Dejene, whom I knew best and with whom I got along well, didn't want to admit and indeed tried to stop me from seeing how bad things were. For instance, he kept making excuses why I couldn't go to visit the northern provinces of Eritrea, Tigre and Wollo where conditions were worst. I'm sure a lot of the reason for this was because of the civil war. Eritrea had been a separate Italian colony and had never wanted to be part of Ethiopia.

On that first trip to Addis I also met with all the various UN people stationed there. No two of them agreed on what should be done and it was obvious to me that they were covering themselves. Only Dr. Kenneth King from the United Nations Development Program admitted the real problem. He took me aside and said, "There is no co-operation, no co-ordination here." He was convinced that the worst would happen. And it did.

In 1983 I think the Ethiopians were still hoping that the rains would come and that they would be able to take care of things themselves. They are proud people. But we knew from our satellite pictures and from the reports of non-governmental organizations such as World Vision and Catholic Aid that there was already mass starvation at that time in the northern provinces where Ethiopia was (and still is) at war with the rebels. I believe firmly that some of the Ethiopians were trying to starve the rebels into submission. They were saying, "Either you do what we tell you to or we're going to starve you to death."

In more ways than one Ethiopia could have prevented much of the mass starvation. The government appealed for world aid too late and they hid the full extent of the problem. And they must take full responsibility for using starvation as a weapon in war. They could have spent more of their money on development and less on their military. But knowing these things didn't stop me from trying to help the starving Ethiopian people. I thought that perhaps, once we had helped their people as much as we could, the government would listen to us if we made an effort to negotiate peace between Ethiopia and the rebels. A massive effort to negotiate peace between Ethiopia and the rebels was part of the report that we at Agriculture Canada submitted to Prime Minister Trudeau and the Cabinet in 1983. The time to attach conditions to aid is not when people are starving to death.

Dejene travelled with me wherever I went in Ethiopia. Together we visited small villages outside of Addis, one of which Agriculture Canada sort of adopted. Upon my return we sent them some gifts to commemorate our visit. When I went back there in 1984, I could see our gifts at work – a water pump, a grinder for grain, and a small farm office we built for them out of cement blocks. This may seem like so little as to be practically useless, but I believe small things like water pumps are far more important than big things like hydro-electric dams and airports.

Of course, the area around Addis was relatively well off, yet every time I suggested a trip to the north Dejene would make some excuse – the weather was too bad or he couldn't arrange a flight. So finally I told him, I said, "Look Tekola, I have an airplane of my own and I'm going in the morning. You coming?" So he had no choice but to make the arrangements.

The next morning we flew north in a Canadian Department of Transport Challenger to the city of Asmara, the capital of Eritrea, much of which had been built by Mussolini. (It always surprised me in Ethiopia how much the people seemed to like the Italians in spite of what they'd done. But the Italians had left what little infrastructure the country has – roads, schools, hospitals.) From Asmara we went by four-wheel drive Jeeps into the mountainous area around the city.

Everywhere we travelled we had with us soldiers carrying loaded machine-guns because we were close to the areas of fighting. The north was where the real poverty was – where the famine was at its worst – but we only saw a little of it in terms of people. What I did see was how the desert was taking over as the drought lasted longer and longer. I used to tell Dejene that I wished I'd had my shotgun. I'd have shot all those goats and sheep and camels that were running around eating every damn thing in sight. One of the basic problems in Africa is that not enough land has clear tenure; so land reform is a high priority.

Dejene made sure that even in this blasted part of the country I saw the best – a dam near Adi Keyih, to the southeast of Asmara, that had been built by mountain villagers practically with their bare hands. It had taken six hundred people six months to build and was maybe a thousand feet long and maybe forty feet thick at the base and forty feet high at the centre. There were about six hundred men, women, and children there who had been working on it. And on the surrounding hills they were terracing the slopes to stop erosion and planting trees and grass. We saw this in several areas. But I was told that often even the drought-resistant trees and grasses died on the hillsides.

The Ethiopians hoped this little dam would provide enough water to irrigate about four hundred acres of vegetables; it was basically just a stone-faced embankment of earth across the river. The workers had had no tools of any kind except picks, hammers and shovels – not even a wheelbarrow – yet the building had been completed ahead of schedule. They had even used little plastic pails tied with string or rope on their backs as a method of carrying earth. I learned why the villagers worked so hard when I was told that the more work you did, the more wheat you got.

I'll never forget seeing the local people using material from the bags sent as emergency food relief as suitcases and satchels to carry their meagre belongings. Many of these makeshift carrying cases had the red maple leaf stamped on them, which told me the bag had come from Canada and had held Canadian wheat.

I didn't see the worst starvation in Ethiopia until my third trip, in 1985. During my brief visit for the WFC annual meeting in 1984 they were celebrating the tenth anniversary of the revolution and still didn't want to admit things were that bad. But in 1985 I saw a lot of terrible camps – resettlement camps, hospital camps, refugee camps. It is hard to describe my reaction to these awful things – the refugee camps being the worst, with thousands of people living in tents and many people still starving and many with no protection against the cold nights. At those high altitudes the sun is very strong in the daytime, but nights get very cold. That really breaks down people's resistance when they also don't have enough nourishment. Worst of all was the knowledge that it didn't need to be happening. Over and over again I asked myself, "How can this be going on in 1985, knowing what we knew in 1980 and in 1981, knowing what the world leaders knew?"

In 1985 I went to visit one of the resettlement camps near the Sudanese border. There were sixty thousand people living in little huts and these people were not used to living at such close quarters. Their huts were being eaten up by the termites – the bureaucrats were estimating that the huts would have to be replaced every three years. It's inhuman to put that many people together. It's not natural for them – they used to live in little villages. And they were also making them farm collectively – something they weren't used to. Part of the answer might be to resettle them in much smaller villages, like the ones they've come from.

In the resettlement area I could see the seeds of future drought and future famine. The people had been moved to an area of rolling land, a tall-grass savannah dotted with scrubby-looking trees not much taller than the grass. The way they were settling it I could see it all turning into a desert in five or ten years and then the cycle of drought and famine would begin again. The land was fairly rich but it needed water and it needed vegetation to replace the grasses and trees that were rapidly being cut down to make thatch for the huts of the new settlement. And there was a crazy idea being suggested by some people that the resettlement areas should be given lots of oxen instead of small tractors. Add thousands of oxen and let them go out and forage when they're not needed for planting (a period of six weeks each year). You can imagine what that would have done to the fragile environment.

The Ethiopians are a very intelligent and cultured people with a civilization thousands of years old. Without the civil war I believe they could solve their own problems. It is a country of tremendous resources and Agriculture Canada made a study that showed that with proper management it could support 240 million people instead of the current population which is around 50 or 60 million – and even export food. Great progress has already been made in some areas. For instance, unlike in most of South America and other parts of Africa and Asia, you never see wealthy Ethiopians. Some of the government people live better than others, but I saw no luxury, no lavish mansions. The holdings of the deposed royal family have been turned into government buildings or are used as embassies. And, although most people in Addis Ababa had enough to eat, there was nothing like a big banquet when I had dinner with people like Tekola Dejene.

Even in Addis, however, the tragedy of the famine is just under the surface. There was still a lot of poverty right in the city. On my 1983 trip, Ezio di Emanuele, one of the young assistants I had with me, was in the market shopping and saw two men die right in front of him – they died of malnutrition or the side-effects. The men weren't supposed to be there, but somehow they'd gotten in the wrong area. Ezio was in a state of shock for six months after he came back to Canada.

While I was with Tekola up north Mrs. Pat Agnes, the wife of the Canadian ambassador, took my wife Liz on a tour of orphanages and hospitals in the capital. At one orphanage she saw these little kids sleeping on mounds of dirt. The mound was their mattress and then they put a cloth on top for a blanket. Liz said the stench of urine was so strong she could hardly stand it.

One of the hospitals they visited was being funded by CIDA. It was the place where they did what they could for young Ethiopian women of the Coptic Christian religion who got pregnant and, because of their malnutrition, weren't big enough to have their babies. The problem was that the Coptic religion forbids a Cesarean section, so many of them died in childbirth and those that survived had their bodies badly damaged. That was a real shocker to my wife and she couldn't get over the good work being done in that hospital by an old New Zealander doctor and his wife with funds from Canada. The fact that CIDA was funding this hospital made both of us have much greater respect for the Canadian govenment's aid agency than we had before. After Liz got home, my three daughters commented that for the next several months she was awful quiet. She had no complaints about Canada after seeing the conditions in Ethiopia.

The two Canadian ambassadors who served in Ethiopia when I was there were both fine men, very dedicated. Wilfrid Agnes was one of the voices crying in the wilderness before the world took notice of the famine and I could see the strain was having an effect on him. He looked tired. Marc Lemieux, who took Wilfrid's place when he retired in 1984, was also a tremendous person. By then the famine was beginning to make news and it was easier to travel around the country. In his first six months I think he saw more of Ethiopia than most other ambassadors who'd been there for years. He just hitch-hiked rides on any plane or helicopter he could find.

The potential of Ethiopia is so great it makes you want to cry. They wouldn't need massive Western technology to be able to banish famine forever. But they do need to bring in conservation, reforestation, and regrazing practices that are used in other parts of the world. Ethiopia has a beautiful climate and much beautiful land. With reforestation, the climate would change and what has become cruel desert could be green again. Some people believe that the Garden of Eden was somewhere in this part of Africa. If that's true, Eden could well have been in Ethiopia – and it could be there again.

When I returned to Canada after my first trip to Ethiopia in

1983 I instructed our Agriculture Canada people to get all the facts from every source, both government and private agencies (Agriculture Canada, CIDA, World Vision, The Red Cross, Catholic Aid, and so on), prepare a report on the seriousness of the problem, and recommend a co-ordinated effort to deal with it. Meanwhile I was doing everything I could to persuade the government to increase its aid to Ethiopia, which we knew would be one of the countries hardest hit. Here I had some success. In the fiscal year 1983-84 we were the largest donor in the world to Ethiopia. We went from $12 million to $26 million in one year. And when I visited Ethiopia the same year I was told, "Your forty thousand tonnes of wheat arrived just in time."

I was not so successful in getting our report accepted. I had to battle with the bureaucrats and I had to battle with the Cabinet. Although some of the people at CIDA had helped us to prepare our report during the fall of 1983, others at CIDA and at External Affairs were saying, "Whelan's wrong. It's going to rain and there'll be enough food." Maybe some of them thought that an agriculture minister had no business getting so involved in questions of foreign aid. But someone had to. I had a hell of time with some of those people.

What we recommended was the equivalent of a declaration of war. We wanted to use Canadian NATO troops and NATO equipment – helicopters, airplanes, four-wheel drive vehicles. And we were going to co-ordinate these with other organizations like the Red Cross to send equipment, food and people – doctors, nurses and so on. I'm not saying we could have stopped all the suffering, but there would have been a lot less of it.

In the report, we described the famine in Africa – what was going to happen and what needed to be done. We were so accurate it makes you sad to read it now. By using satellite pictures we could describe the situation in the sub-Sahara – from the Atlantic right over to the Indian Ocean – the part of the continent that was hardest hit. In the pictures you could see how the green belt of Africa was shrinking away. We knew as much or more as the people sitting in Addis Ababa and we were six thousand miles away – we even knew the temperature and the amount of rainfall in every little village.

I knew there would be resistance among the pipsqueaks in the Prime Minister's Office. So I appealed directly to Trudeau. I wrote him a letter in which I described what I wanted to do. I remember saying, "Mr. Prime Minister, you and Canada are held in very high esteem on the international scene. To me it is our moral and Christian responsiblity to 'walk an extra mile' to help those people who are so much worse off than ourselves."

Pierre wrote a nice letter back telling me to go see MacEachen (who was Minister of External Affairs) and Jean-Jacques Blais (the Minister of National Defence), to go before the external affairs committee to request the money I wanted. You see, I was asking for a massive crusade, a peaceful act of war. But Blais and MacEachen wouldn't call the committee into session. I had a hell of time with MacEachen, but he wouldn't budge. Instead of believing our report, they believed a report prepared by a "fact-finding" committee of bureaucrats in their departments. After I read my copy I wrote "bullshit" across the front page in great big letters because it was so inaccurate. When I see some of these people now I remind them of what it felt like to be the mule they hit with a two-by-four. They just say, "You should be thankful; a lot more would have died if you hadn't done what you did."

After my return from Ethiopia, I launched an attack on the UN and called for an immediate emergency meeting of all the twenty-seven UN agencies involved in food aid and for a special debate on the subject at the next session of the General Assembly. But as President of the World Food Council I could only recommend; I couldn't demand. The Secretary General of the UN, Javier Perez de Cuellar, supported us. He told me, "No one has spoken the truth with more heart and feeling than you have." He begged for co-operation from his member agencies, but they are powers in themselves. At a meeting I went to in New York he did what he could. But the head of the FAO, Edouard Saouma of Lebanon, got up and said, "I'm having my own meeting in March 1985 in Rome." That was his way of saying, "No, you can't take away my little kingdom."

That's the root of the problem, all these agencies fighting for control. Saouma is a perfect example. He spends more time on the politics of protecting his job than doing it. He runs the FAO as if it was some sort of personal empire and, in my opinion, he doesn't worry enough about the problems he was hired to look after. In a nutshell that kind of pettiness is the problem with the UN today.

Western world leaders knew what was going on, even though they later pretended that they didn't. They would say things like, "If only we'd had better communications we would have known and could have done something." After the famine became headlines people called for an early warning system, some sort of DEW-line for Africa. Well, we had our early warning system; it's just that nobody listened to the warning. Canada knew and the people who pretend otherwise are just making excuses. As I said more than once, "a blind economist on a galloping horse could have seen the problem, but you claim you didn't."

All I could do was go to meetings and raise hell. I went to the annual meeting of the World Food Council in Addis in May 1984, when the world still hadn't woken up to what was happening. It wasn't until the fall of that year that the BBC publicized the famine and brought it into everyone's living room – which was too late for the millions who died. I went in 1984 even though I was running for the Liberal leadership and had to leave the meeting early to get back to Ottawa for the convention. I was so tired I could hardly drag myself up onto the platform to give my leadership speech. But I did have the energy to say that if I was elected leader and became Prime Minister I would give 1 percent of our GNP to foreign aid. We're at about 0.62 percent.

After I'd left the Cabinet, I made one last trip to Africa while I was serving out my term as President of the WFC. The trip was in May 1985 and during it I travelled to five African countries: Ivory Coast, Burkina Faso, Kenya, Ethiopia, and Somalia. This was the trip when I saw the worst evidence of the famine in Ethiopia. I saw many other terrible things.

Afterwards I wrote a letter to Pope John Paul, whom I'd met earlier the previous year, and to many other world leaders, including François Mitterand and Brian Mulroney. I spoke of the tragedy in human terms, "abandoned children, orphans, displaced and separated families, seriously malnourished and handicapped people, weak farmers who are incapable of cultivating the land." I pointed out that in Ethiopia alone malnutrition "had left one to two million retarded children, both physically and mentally, and over a million of them orphans."

The Pope's representative and most of the others answered my letters seriously, but Mitterand and Mulroney didn't bother – Joe Clark sent me a polite formal response. Everywhere I went in 1985 the problems were similar and the aid was not enough; it showed me more clearly than ever that we must attack the problems at their root, that emergency assistance must be continued but greater emphasis should be given to development assistance on the local and the national level. A huge effort is required, but it is possible. It means shifting the world's resources away from war.

For a short while in Ethiopia the world showed what it can do when everyone works together. On the tarmac at the airport in Addis in 1985 were Polish helicopters and French ones, Russian planes and British planes, East German and West German and American – but no Canadian ones. And I saw the same things on little dirt landing strips all over the country. Soldiers from all these countries in their own uniforms, but hauling food instead of guns. An army mobilized to fight a war but not with weapons, with food. It was something I'd only dreamed about in 1983. So I know now it is possible for us to work together.

If the rich countries spent five times what they are spending now on foreign aid that wouldn't be one-tenth of what they're spending now on weapons and armies. That would mean the developed countries could go from $15 billion a year to more than $75 billion a year in aid. Think what we could do with that money. Think what we could have done.

The press' and public's interest has died down, but the underlying problems are still there – as bad as ever. We must focus our efforts on a massive campaign to help Africans develop their own countries. On the local level we have to help educate these people and make it possible for them to stay and work the land. One of the greatest tragedies of modern Africa is that people have left the land to look for a better life in the cities only to find there poverty as bad or worse. Only twenty years ago there was just one city in Africa that had over a million people. I think over twenty cities now have more than a million inhabitants and the conditions in these places are appalling – terrible pollution and vast slums. In many cases these people are much worse off than they were before.

We must give Africans the technology and the tools they need – not high-tech things that we North Americans or Europeans want to give them. It may sound funny, but even something as simple as the introduction of long-handled hoes to much of Africa would make a big difference. The short hoes they use make the farmers bend over, which is bad for their backs and exposes more of the body to the hot sun. And we need to help them build villages, pump water, plant trees. We can give them things that will help, but they need to learn to do things for themselves.

On the national and international level the need is for an infrastructure – roads, railroads, post-harvest storage and food-processing facilities, marketing boards so that food producers can be guaranteed access to markets and a fair price for what they produce. If they produce a tonne, they must know they'll be paid for it. In many countries there is no incentive. The government simply confiscates what the farmers grow.

And there is a need for massive land reform so that the farmers work land that they own themselves. And there needs to be a massive reforestation of Africa to let the green belt make a comeback and even grow bigger than it ever was before. Where there is now desert, there could be forests and farms. Known underground water reserves in Africa are some of the greatest in the world and we can help the Africans tap these resources. With the coming of green, the climate will change and there will be more rain. Much of the desert will disappear. We in Canada have turned a cold desert – the Canadian prairies – into one of the breadbaskets of the world. And look at what the Israelis have done and the now-productive desert areas of Arizona and California. I know the African desert can bloom.

I don't believe these are impossible dreams. But for them to come about we must have an international will that up to now has only been around to deal with an emergency after it has happened. Once the starving faces disappear from the TV screens, people soon forget and the cycle of drought and famine is allowed to repeat itself.

Of course there is no magic answer to development. There are enough examples of expensive foreign aid going to waste (or into the pockets of rich officials) to make it clear that just increasing development aid is not the answer. The problems of Africa – and other parts of the developing world – are great and complex. The countries themselves are often combinations of tribal groups that don't get along and until they do this makes development even more difficult. We need to help these countries develop economically stable democracies, but I would be very surprised to see this happening in the next fifty years, let alone the next twenty. We have to work with governments that don't always listen to their people or want development that is of greatest benefit to those that need it most.

So many of modern Africa's problems are the after-effects of the colonial period. In many cases if we had left these countries alone in the first place they would have been better off. The colonial powers went in and robbed these countries and taught them enough of our system to destroy their natural abilities to look after themselves. In some instances the colonial powers stripped the resources and wrecked the land with overgrazing. They took subsistence cultures and turned them into cultures of drought and famine. They turned countries that lived off their own resources into exporters of raw resources, but the people didn't benefit. Even today, only about four cents out of every dollar Africans export goes to the primary producers. They say a little knowledge is a dangerous thing. Well, Africa is a good example of how a little development is a dangerous thing.

Most difficult of all is the need for a change of philosophy in the developing countries themselves. They need to shift their priorities to food production and education, reforestation and restoring grazing lands – and away from military might.

The potential of Africa is so great it makes the tragedy seem even greater. We spend a lot of money and yet our aid is so often infantile – spent on big, flashy projects which benefit the international bureaucracies and the elites living in the cities rather than the people who really need it. There are 4.2 billion people in the world today and yet we grow enough food to feed six billion, but we don't have the means to distribute it. Not that long ago Asia couldn't feed itself, and now it can. Zimbabwe, where the British left more of an infrastructure and where the black people are now running the country, has in the last two years produced a surplus of food. The little farmer in Zimbabwe has gone from accounting for 10 percent of food production to over 60 percent. So there's no excuse for letting Africans, or Brazilians, or Indians starve when we can help them learn to feed themselves.

As I said in the letter I wrote to the presidents and prime ministers of the world in 1985, "There will never be peace on earth until this suffering ceases and all people have enough food to eat." And as I've said to many people since in a paraphrase of what I said to Trudeau in 1983, "Come walk this mile with me."

12

Fired Twice

I was the last of the seven candidates to enter the 1984 Liberal leadership race. The convention was set for June 14, but I didn't announce my candidacy until April 12 at which point the others had all been off and running for quite a while and many of the delegate slates had already been elected. When the press asked me why I had waited so long, I told them that my wife Liz had had to have a serious back operation, so I'd waited to declare until I knew she was going to be all right. That was one reason. Then I pointed out that unlike some of the other candidates I was well known right across the country, so I didn't have to go around introducing myself.

I'd thought about the possibility of running back in 1979. But neither then nor in 1984 did I start to run before the starting pistol had been fired. I wasn't working on my campaign before Trudeau resigned. I probably wouldn't have run at all if I'd felt that any of the other candidates were raising the issues I thought were important. But they weren't, not even my friend Jean Chrétien who'd asked me to be the Ontario chairman of his campaign. Not even Jean was talking about the primary pro-ducers and what I call the three renewable resources – fisheries, forestry and agriculture. As much as anything I entered the race to make sure that the people in these vital industries and their concerns were represented. Another thing: none of the candidates were talking enough about young people. So I turned Jean down and ran myself, even though I knew I didn't have a chance of winning.

Chrétien came to me when he was thinking about running – before he'd made up his own mind. We had a long talk and I told him he should go, that the old bogey about alternating French and English leaders was nonsense – that the leader should be the person most qualified to lead the party and the best one to win an election. The principle of alternation is like saying that if you have a black horse one time, the next time you should use a white one, even if the white one can't pull a plough – even if it's balky and incompetent and ready to be sold for glue. To hitch a horse up to a plough just because of its colour is nonsense – political nonsense.

Canada has changed, and Chrétien's support outside Quebec proved this. In fact, if he'd gotten as much support inside the province of Quebec he would have won. Many of the Quebec MPs were urging him not to run but I told him it was mostly jealousy on their part – because he was more popular and had gone so far and was more capable, even though they thought they were better looking and smarter. People forget that Chrétien had been a minister longer than anyone – Pearson appointed him Minister without Portfolio in 1965, the same year Trudeau first went into the Cabinet. Chrétien's problem in Quebec could be summed up in two words – André Ouellet.

Ouellet was jealous of Chrétien and he didn't want to lose his power over the Quebec caucus.

Once Turner had won he should have had the sense to tell André to go jump in the lake and said to Chrétien, "Yes, you're my right-hand man in Quebec."

I also urged Chrétien to run because, other than myself, he was the only candidate who really had the respect of working people and of the ethnic groups that are so important to the

Liberal Party's success. I told him that if I didn't run myself I'd work for him. Perhaps if I'd done better on the first ballot I could have swung enough votes to him to win and been the kingmaker. To have swung the convention over to Chrétien would have been a success as far as I'm concerned. But that wasn't in my mind when I decided to run.

My family urged me not to. They knew I didn't have a snowball's chance in hell and were worried that I'd be hurt and humiliated. When I told Liz I'd made up my mind to go ahead anyway, she was so mad she wouldn't speak to me. But even her surgeon at the hospital was telling her, "You gotta let him run. He means more to the people of Canada than you think." Liz eventually forgave me and supported me – as she's had to do more than once before in our twenty-six years of marriage.

Once I'd decided to run my three daughters really supported me. For the previous few elections they had been old enough to campaign in my riding and were getting some political savvy. In 1984 they worked really hard on my leadership campaign which, like every campaign I'd run, was a lot of hard work by a lot of ordinary people. The most gratifying thing was the support I received from every province right across the country.

In the short time we had we raised $250,000 for my campaign. People just walked in off the street or sent us contributions without even being asked – and these donations aren't tax deductible like regular political donations. One supporter in Windsor, Louis Scodeller, raised $50,000 in about ten days. Louis is a big Italian I've known since he first came to Canada. He put together a little committee of about ten people – farmers, working people – and they canvassed for donations. I think the largest single gift we got was $5,000 and that came from a man who I know votes Conservative, but he told the woman who phoned him, "I always liked Gene and I don't think he's got a chance, but I want to help him." Mostly we got small donations: $50, $100, $200, $300.

Shortly after I declared for the leadership I was in British Columbia at an all candidates' meeting. On the plane back to Ottawa I was wearing my green stetson and I sat down next to this guy who was wearing a green suit. I've always liked the colour green. We got talking and I said, "I'm Gene Whelan." And he said, "I know who you are." Turned out he was an executive with a big trucking firm in B.C. on his way to a convention in Halifax. Before we'd finished talking he said, "I've followed you and I like you even though I'm not a Liberal and I'm going to send you $2,000." A couple of days later the cheque arrived.

If I'd had more time I could have run quite an expensive campaign. As it was, I ran a modest campaign compared to some of them, never had to spend any of my own money, and at the end came out of it with a small surplus; we didn't have to borrow a penny from my friendly banker. I doubt the others could say the same.

One of the funny things during the campaign concerned the picture we used for our literature. We had a nice green brochure with pictures of me at various times during my career, and when you unfolded it, there, almost as large as life, was a poster-size picture of Gene Whelan standing in the middle of a beautiful Prairie wheatfield. The wheatfield was actually within sight of the Brooks Aqueduct, in Alberta and was one of several taken at the big celebration for the new aqueduct opening, by Prairie Farm Rehabilitation Association photographer, Ken Burnett.

In the picture I'm standing in the field wearing my green stetson and a western shirt and with my coat over my shoulder. At the time, I didn't pay too much attention to the wheatfield. But later, when I saw the shot they'd selected for the brochure, the first thing I noticed was the sow thistle and the wild oats right there in amongst the wheat; these are two of the worst weeds in Western Canada and any Western farmer would spot them right away. When I saw the picture I said, "I hope they had the artist take out the weeds before they printed the brochure," but of course they hadn't, and I guess a lot of farmers had a good laugh when they saw it.

Otherwise, it's a beautiful picture. In some ways it reminds me of an old painting you used to see a lot – it was very popular with rural people – a picture of Christ standing in a wheatfield. Some people made the connection when they saw our campaign poster and they'd say to me, "So you think you're like Christ, do you?" And I'd say, "Well, one difference is that in the old picture Christ doesn't have no weeds with him."

In a leadership campaign most of your time is spent going to small meetings of delegates, giving a short speech, answering questions, and shaking hands. By the time I got to many places lots of the delegates had already been sewn up by Turner or Chrétien, but I campaigned hard nonetheless. I entered the campaign too late to have much of a strategy. I figured I'd get support from farmers and from people – MPs and others – whom I'd helped over the years. Quite a few people promised to vote for me, at least on the first ballot, and then didn't when the day came. I guess I felt a bit like old Paul Martin back in 1968. People who'd looked me right in the eye and told me I had their vote on the first ballot switched to Turner or Chrétien. By then the battle was so hot and the two frontrunners had so many delegates that those people must have just got swept up in the tide. But I still couldn't understand it. To me a promise is a promise.

I really enjoyed the all-candidates meetings; although I declared last, I made it to all but one. I'd had lots of practice at this sort of thing and some of the others weren't so comfortable – especially John Turner. I didn't attack him too directly, but I really thought I could do the party a service if I stopped him from winning. I'd say to the delegates things like, "Would you fly in a plane with a pilot who hadn't flown for eight years?" Or, "Would you play on a team with a guy that got mad and took his bat and ball and went home?" (A lot of Liberals hadn't forgotten that Turner had quit in 1975 and gone off to Bay Street to make money. And almost as many had trouble forgiving him for his criticism of the party while he was on the sidelines, particularly that expensive newsletter he sold to his businessmen friends.) But I think my best line of all was one that certainly must have come back to haunt him. I told the delegates, "If the Canadian people have to choose between a real Tory and pretend Tory, they'll choose the real Tory every time." They did, too – although I imagine a lot of people are now wondering whether Brian Mulroney isn't a pretend Tory also.

Before the all-candidates meeting in Toronto – I believe this was the last one before the convention – I was sitting in my hotel room thinking about the speech I was going to give. From the window of my room I could see the Royal Bank building, the one with all that gold leaf embedded right in the glass so it looks like it's pure gold, especially at sunset. (If they ever want to get that gold back, they can't. It's gone for good; there's no known process for taking gold flake out of the plate glass.) That gold leaf got me thinking. And that afternoon when I was in the middle of my speech I said, "If I become Prime Minister, the banks will never be allowed to put gold flake on a glass-plate building, when people don't have corn flake on their plates to eat." I didn't really plan to say it. It just came out that way. Later, as we were walking out of the meeting Turner said to me, "God damn you, Gene, my office is in that building." I hadn't known that, but it wouldn't have stopped me.

In a sense, even though Jean Chrétien and I were running against each other, we were a team. We never attacked each other. In fact, whenever he made his set speech he'd always turn to me and say that if he became Prime Minister, Eugene Whelan would be his Minister of Agriculture. And the audience would just applaud and applaud. Then when it came my turn I'd say, "I haven't decided yet whether or not I'll make Jean Chrétien Minister of Finance when I become Prime Minister. I'll have to consider all the options." We almost had a comedy act going.

The only candidate who gave Turner and Chrétien any run for their money was Don Johnston, the man from MSERD. He got a lot of sympathy when he got all emotional about the atomic bomb, and his vote went up. But I thought to myself, "Where was he when I was trying to talk the Cabinet into doing something more in Africa? He was counting his pennies."

Johnston was considered to be the ideas man of the leadership campaign, but I didn't find his ideas too wonderful then and I don't now. He's one of the lonely Liberals in favour of free trade. And one of the things he comes out for in his book is limiting the term of members of parliament to twelve years. Now there's a dumb idea. That would be like shooting a good plough horse just so you can go spend money on a new one that doesn't necessarily know how to walk, let alone pull a plough.

As the convention got closer I noticed that I was having an effect on the other candidates. Before I'd entered the race you never heard a word about the three renewable resources or the fact that they account for about 70 percent of the Canadian economy. After a while the whole bunch of them changed and they all presented little programs in these areas. But I had to tell the Liberal Party's candidates for Prime Minister that we're the largest exporter of fish in the world. That our forest products industry—wood and paper—is by far the biggest single industry in the country and accounts for a greater return to the federal treasury than any other sector. And that agriculture employs a vast number of people, not just as primary producers but in the processing industries and of course the transportation industry. I also told the delegates that the first thing I'd do once I became Prime Minister was to appoint a woman Deputy Prime Minister with special responsibility for the three renewable resources, the most important portfolio in my new government.

The other candidates also started to talk about young people as I was doing. I stressed that young people were so important for the country and that they were being ignored. I reminded the delegates that during the last war we had schools running twenty-four hours a day to retrain people to fight a war. Then I said, "We are fighting a war: it's a war of unemployment for young people. And the schools that can teach our young people the skills to deal with modern technology in the modern world, I wouldn't run them one-third of the time like they are now— averaging thirty hours a week. I'd run them full time." I said I'd fund huge public works projects rather than pay billions in unemployment. I talked about retraining young people, making sure they had job opportunities.

I've had all kinds of young people come up to me since the convention—even recently—and tell me, "I remember what you said, Mr. Whelan."

My campaign did accomplish its main goal: I got all the candidates talking about the issues that concerned me and so many other Canadians.

You see, I'm not much in favour of the present system of electing a party leader. I prefer the system that was tried by the Parti Québécois when they elected Pierre-Marc Johnson – direct election of the leader by all the members of the party. Then you don't have the various campaigns spending so much energy (and money) attempting to fix the convention their way, tying up delegates ahead of time. There are too many party members for that. The infighting (mainly between the Turner and Chrétien forces) was very vicious in 1984, much worse than anything in 1968.

The people who come to the all-candidates meetings and even the people at the convention outnumber the delegates. If you'd polled the people in the hall at the convention Jean Chrétien would have won, no problem. I even said that to John Turner before he called the election. I said, "John, you know you may have had the majority of the delegates voting for you, but you had a minority of the people in the hall and you've yet to win a majority of the Liberal Party, let alone the country."

The low point of the leadership campaign and maybe the low point of my entire career was when I was accused of being a racist. The whole thing began during a campaign trip to Quebec. I was talking to a group of reporters about the situation in Africa and I was making the connection between climate and lack of food. Many of the worst-off people are living as high as nine thousand feet above sea level where the sun is hot in the day and it gets cold at night. So not only are they suffering from malnutrition, but the elements take their toll. I mentioned that pregnant mothers were carrying babies starving in the womb, babies who would be born brain-damaged or retarded. At this point one of the reporters jokingly said, "Maybe the Africans should wear green hats." And I said, "Well, we always wore a hat in the hot sun at home." One smartass reporter, a guy named Richard Cleroux, took what I'd said, and made it seem as if I'd said that Africans have low IQs because they don't wear hats. That was how I came to be labelled a racist.

The press made a big thing about it – without checking out the story. The *Windsor Star* was especially dirty. They printed a picture of four people protesting my "racist" remarks and cropped it in such a way to give the impression it was a big crowd. If it was today I would sue them.

I think the whole incident teaches a lesson about the power of the press and the responsibility of the press. There were nine press people covering me that day in Quebec and not one of them – including Richard Cleroux – remembered me saying what I said the way Richard reported it. I talked to him afterwards and he said, "I didn't mean to write it in that fashion." He even apologized and said that his editors had changed what he'd written. But by then the damage had been done and everyone in Canada had heard that Gene Whelan was a racist – even the great Charles Lynch put it in his book. All because one press man wrote it wrong.

In the House of Commons the Opposition called for my resignation. The attack in the House came while I was campaigning out West and I wasn't there to defend myself so Trudeau got up and defended me. It was a very strong defence. When I thanked him for standing up for me, his only response was, "Good God, Gene, you a racist? Every damn Cabinet meeting you bring up something about Africa and what we should be doing in Africa and when are we going to expand our aid."

The racism charge is one thing I'll never get over. Once something like that is done, it's hard to undo. Even Liberals I meet sometimes look at me kind of funny. But most of the people in my own riding who know me didn't believe it. Shortly after the whole thing hit the papers, my brother Tom was shopping at the A & P in Amherstburg and Glenna Bell, a black lady my family has known for years and years, yelled over to him across maybe three aisles, "Tom, you tell your brother Gene that all us black people know he's not a racist." No one who knew my background and no one who knew my work in the Third World believed it. Maybe the best summary came from Howard McCurdy's dad. (Howard is currently the MP for Windsor-Walkerville and the only black member of the House.) Howard,

Sr., and I went to school together and he had only one comment: "Why, we beat the racism out of Gene a long time ago."

I found it particularly ironic, in light of all this, that I arrived at the convention on June 14 dog tired and at the last minute because I'd been at the World Food Council meeting in Addis Ababa. When people asked me how come I would abandon my campaign in the final days, I simply replied, "I have a responsibility to the World Food Council as their President. It may hurt me at the convention, but I'm going to keep my commitment to be there."

The convention itself was not my finest hour. I was exhausted and my support was slipping even though I believed it was stronger than it turned out to be. One of the things that made the experience liveable was that my daughters were with me, campaigning their hearts out even though they knew I would lose. Maybe the finest moment for a Whelan at the convention was on the first day when my number three daughter, Cathy, gave a speech at a special session for women delegates.

Each candidate was sending a representative to speak to the group, so I sent Cathy. Of the three she seems the most politically inclined, although my second daughter, Sue, is studying law and used to say she would become the first woman Prime Minister. I keep teasing all three of them that when Mulroney calls the next election each of them can pick a riding and I'll pick one and Liz will pick one, and we'll all run.

Cathy has always been the one who took to politics like a fish to water. She studied political science at Carleton and unlike her dad she's already bilingual. Even when she was little she stood out. The girls would sometimes come to political meetings with me and if I talked for more then twenty minutes, Cathy would just stand up in her chair and look at me. It was her way of saying, "Shut up dad, you've talked too long." That was my cue and I usually stopped pretty soon after.

Anyway, my campaign staff gave Cathy this four-page speech about the issues in the campaign. She took one look at it and said, "I can't use that thing." She just got up there and spoke off the cuff and from her heart. She said, "My dad knows he doesn't have a chance to win, but he's doing it for a reason, he's doing it so he can make sure that the things he believes in get heard. He won't win the vote, but when it's all over my dad will still come out the winner."

She spoke without notes and with lots of feeling – like her dad, you might say – and she had the audience cheeering and crying. You can ask any of the women who were there.

Since I had so few delegates pledged to me, I knew a lot would depend on my speech. If I could raise a little hell and bring out a few tears, maybe I could swing a few more delegates my way. But it wasn't to be. I was just too tired; I could hardly walk up to the platform. So I gave my prepared speech and said what I'd come to say. If I'd been able to give one of my old-fashioned tub-thumping speeches I might have got another twenty votes. The other speeches weren't much. Even Jean Chrétien didn't come across well; he tried to look like a prime minister instead of plain old Jean. I'll bet it cost him votes.

I may not have given the best speech I could have, but the response from the crowd in the Ottawa Civic Centre was very warm – of course, most of them weren't delegates. Many people who'd watched the convention on TV mentioned to me later that I was the only one of all the candidates whom Trudeau applauded, the only one toward whom he showed any emotion. That meant a lot to me.

Leading up to the vote there was a lot of pressure put on me by some of my colleagues who were in the Turner camp to come over and join them as soon as the balloting was over. Some of them thought I should have withdrawn before the vote and gone to Turner the night before. They pressed pretty hard on the people that were sitting with us. They threatened them with being shut out of the party if they didn't come over and join Turner. (The Chrétien people did nothing like this that I know of.) It was a lot more vicious than anything I saw or heard in 1968. But then in 1968 none of the candidates had so many of what I call professional young people – people just graduated from college with law degrees and business degrees – who were doing a lot of the work on the floor. In 1968 there were more plain ordinary people involved. Maybe you need a university degree to learn how to be mean and dirty.

The vote was on Saturday and when the first ballot results were read out I was devastated, destroyed. I'd never expected that I'd have only eighty-four votes. You can't imagine how bad it feels. Even though I hadn't expected to win it was awfully difficult to lose, and to lose so bad. This was the first election I'd lost since 1959. And there were a lot of delegates, including MPs, in the hall who wouldn't have been sitting there if I hadn't worked so hard for them in 1974 and later, so it was even harder to see these people running like lemmings to Turner.

I hadn't made any prior commitment to throw my support to Chrétien after the first ballot. I hadn't really thought about it, but I imagine Jean assumed I would. After the vote his campaign manager, John Rae, called me up and asked me to walk over. And I said, "John, I cannot help Jean, I cannot bring him many votes; he is too far behind." But John said, "We don't care about the votes, we want you." So I said, okay and I just hung up the phone and walked over. When Chrétien greeted me, he just said, "Welcome, Gino." I may have brought him a few votes, but not enough.

I knew in my gut that Turner couldn't win the next election no matter what happened, he was so out of touch with things. And I didn't think of him as a true Liberal any more, if he ever had been. Jean Chrétien was quite different. I think he has the ability to communicate with young people – with all sorts of people – and he has respect right across Canada.

Jean Chrétien would have made a good Prime Minister – as good as any. Of course he still may get there. Contrary to his public image my one fear would be that he might be too tough. I remember how tough he was as President of Treasury Board and as Minister of Finance. But I think he would have made a different kind of Prime Minister, someone who could really talk to people – relate to people and listen to their concerns. He certainly would have given Brian Mulroney a run for his money in 1984. Maybe I made a mistake in not agreeing to work with him from the beginning. If I had, perhaps things would have turned out differently.

At the post-defeat party for our campaign workers, I looked around the room and thought of the old saying we used to have – "Win or lose we drink the booze, but not before." There were tears and laughter and a wonderful warm feeling. And some of them made themselves hoarse singing our campaign song. So the gloom didn't last long. We'd done our best, we'd had lots of support from people right across the country, and we'd got our message through.

After the convention, but before the transfer of power to Turner, I had my last meeting with Pierre Trudeau. He wanted to discuss an appointment for me, but we also just had a general conversation about politics. It was probably one of the longest meetings I had with him from the time I'd first known him as a backbencher. We went over old times, what we'd done and hadn't done, what we should have done. At one point I asked him, "How come you kept me in the Cabinet so long." And he replied, "Sometimes I could have killed you." And I said, "The feeling is mutual." Then he told me, "I kept you because you were my best campaigner, you ran a good department, you were honest, and you were loyal to the government's decisions, even when you didn't agree with them." Then he told me something I hadn't heard about before – that over the years the party had taken polls to test the popularity of the various Cabinet ministers and that I was always either number one or number two.

Then we talked about what I was going to do. We both knew that Turner wouldn't keep me on even though I continued to hope that he would. So the first thing Trudeau said was, "I don't suppose you want to go to the Senate." And I said, "You guessed it right, Mr. Prime Minister." And he just laughed because he'd always known how I felt about the Senate. Some of my colleagues said to me afterwards, "You're stupid, you should have taken the Senate." But after so publicly favouring its abolition for so long I wasn't about to behave like some broken-down work horse that's put out to pasture. So Trudeau asked me what I'd like to do. And I said, "I wouldn't mind being an ambassador." And he said, "Well, we have Ireland and Greece." I said, "I don't want to go to either one of those, but if I could do something with the knowledge that I've gained over the last twenty-two years as a parliamentarian, as Minister of Agriculture, and working with the developing world, I'd be pleased to do that. But I'm not going to move out of Canada just to be an ambassador someplace I don't know much about." And he said he would talk to Chrétien. It was Jean who reminded him that we'd made the decision two years before to appoint a full-time ambassador to the Food and Agriculture Organization (FAO) in Rome and Jean asked me if I'd like that. I said, yes. So Trudeau agreed to recommend my appointment to Turner along with the others he was recommending at the time.

I was Canada's ambassador to FAO from July 11, 1984 (my birthday), to October 11 when Little Joe gave me the bad news. And it was not a pleasant tenure, I can tell you.

After Turner made the appointment, even many fellow Liberals didn't defend me – especially during the election when patronage became such a hot issue. I guess most of them didn't understand the importance of the FAO. After Turner messed up on the patronage subject during the television debate Mulroney grabbed it like a fumbled football and ran with it right to election day, when he scored his touchdown. I'm sure it was a big issue with many of the voters, but I think it was much less the issue than the way Turner handled it. He didn't look much like a leader during that debate, that was the real problem.

I'm certainly not opposd to patronage in principle. The British governmental system which we've inherited was built on patronage. Other countries – including Britain – think nothing of appointing former politicians as foreign ambassadors. And the tradition exists in Canada. Paul Martin made a fine High Commissioner in London, for example, and so did Don Jamieson. If you look around Ottawa, you'll find that many of the ambassadors are former politicians. Political and diplomatic skills are similar. The former Prime Minister of Sweden is currently the Swedish ambassador to Canada and there are several former ministers of agriculture now representing their countries in Ottawa. In fact some countries have a policy that one-third of their top diplomats have to be former politicians. So I don't think it's a question of ending patronage. It's a question of making sure that the people you appoint are qualified to do the job.

What really hurt me was when Mulroney, during the election campaign, questioned my competence. He said, "Whelan, an international figure?" and he made fun of the food issue. No one came to my defence – Liberals or Conservatives who might have – they were purposely lying about it for political reasons. It hurt me most when Liberals damned me by omission. I'll give John Turner credit for one thing; on a couple of occasions he actually did try to defend me. He said I was "eminently qualified" for the position.

The press – especially the editorial writers and the TV editorialists – were particularly nasty. That guy Peter Trueman even said on Global Television: "Let Whelan get an honest job like the rest of us." No comment.

I knew that Mulroney was just using the issue to gain political advantage. I said during the election that when Brian got in he'd make us look like a hummingbird alongside a bald eagle. He lied about patronage. Now he's talking about changing the rules, two years later after he's appointed all Tories except a few token ones like Stephen Lewis and Lloyd Francis to keep the public off his scent. Now that I think of it, even Stephen Lewis criticized my appointment. On the night of the 1984 election he described it – and Bryce Mackasey's appointment as Ambassador to Portugal – as purely political and said it was hypocritical of us to accept. He said, "FAO is part of the UN and the United Nations is an apolitical body." I remembered those words when he accepted Mulroney's appointment to be ambassador to the UN. Here was a man who'd had no experience in foreign diplomacy accepting an appointment that was purely political. That was the greatest piece of hypocrisy I'd seen in a long time.

During my days as a minister, when I was appointing people to boards and so on, I never paid much attention to what party they came from. And I got into quite a few "discussions" with my colleagues from Ontario because I wasn't appointing enough Liberals. Canagrex is a perfect example. After I'd fought for two years to get it past the bureaucrats, we held up that board probably three or four months because we couldn't agree on taking the people being recommended by the farm organizations and the other organizations to go on the board.

Patronage has its place when you reward someone who's qualified. I always used to say about patronage, "Pick good people. Mix them up like a good ketchup into a proper political mix to make it palatable." If you look at Trudeau's record you'll see that he appointed a lot of non-Liberals. The various people I appointed in my area – Conservatives and Liberals and NDP – all did a good job.

As for my own "patronage" appointment, let me quote what Bob Stanfield said in the Ottawa airport after I'd been fired by Mulroney. Bob came up and shook hands with me, then said, "Gene, I never thought they would do it. You have my deepest sympathy." And then he said, "It was just un-Canadian." Whether he'd admit what he said today, would be another thing, but I certainly appreciated it at the time.

Losing so bad didn't actually hurt as much as being fired by John Turner – even though I knew he would. In spite of the things I've said about him, I would have worked with Turner. And I remembered 1968 when Trudeau appointed all his defeated opponents to the Cabinet, no matter what awful things they'd said of him. I knew it was the group around him as much as Turner himself because they'd promised someone else the agriculture portfolio – my old friend Ralph Ferguson, the member from Lambton-Middlesex – and they'd decided I was a political liability. The pipsqueaks around Turner made the pipsqueaks around Trudeau look like angels – Bill Lee and that crowd – they were the ones telling Turner he had to get rid of me, saying I was an embarrassment to the party.

It was certainly an embarrassing situation when Turner fired me – embarrassing for him. The scene took place in his suite at the Château Laurier shortly after he'd taken over as Prime Minister. The whole thing was very badly run. You had to walk down this long hall and there was no way you could avoid the press unless you snuck in and out the back stairs. And of course when the press saw I was going up, they knew it was bad news.

John was alone in his suite when I went in. He was in a gleeful mood, smoking a big cigar and sitting back in his chair looking very pleased with himself. Practically his first words were, "Big Gene, I gotta let you go. I got too many Cabinet ministers and there's too many from Windsor and I have to let you go. I just can't keep you in the Cabinet." And I said to him, "John, you can do what you want, but my whole life has been dedicated to the Liberal Party and I still have three kids in university and I cannot afford to retire." I pretty near begged him to keep me on. When I look back on what I said it seems to me one of the most demeaning things that I ever did in my life.

But I didn't just slink out of the room with my tail between my legs. I told him what I thought of what he was doing. "John," I said, "you're making a mistake if you think you can fire people like me and still win an election. What your advisers are telling you is wrong, because I have a lot of friends out there. They may not all be Liberal, but you're going to need every one of them in order to win." I reminded him that out of the eleven thousand people at the convention he had only eighteen hundred vote for him. And I warned him that the wounds in the defeated camps would take time to heal. I said, "They're wounded and bloody." I knew the party was low on money and that we weren't ready to fight a campaign – especially not in the West. "John, you know that out of the seven ridings I'm responsible for we have only one that we can win – and that one's mine – and it will be a near thing to win that one right now." Of course I didn't know he was going to make all the boo-boos he did during the campaign. (As it turned out the Liberal candidate in my riding ran third.)

Before I left I told him, whatever you do, don't call an election right away, not this summer. We have long, hard winters in Canada and summer is the time Canadians like to be left alone – to be with their children, go to the beach, to the park, or ride to the end of the subway just for the heck of it. They don't want people bothering them with an election. They'll resent it. "Stay the hell out of it until September." And I warned him not to postpone the Queen's visit and to wait to welcome the Pope. But Turner wouldn't listen to anything I said. I don't think he could hear that day at all. The polls were telling him that he had over 50 percent of the decided vote; he was on a power drive and his car was out of control.

Before the Turner regime took over there was one last event of the Trudeau era – the farewell dinner at 24 Sussex Drive. All the members of his last Cabinet and their wives were in attendance. Trudeau just wanted to say thanks and goodbye; it was a very pleasant time, no gnashing of teeth or crying or anything. Pierre was very relaxed, it was a beautiful evening, and there was a feeling of peacefulness – and it was a little bit sad.

I'm not one of those who want to bury the memory of Pierre Trudeau and what he did for Canada. He did things that other Prime Ministers only dreamed of doing. When somebody puts his whole record together, they'll find out he was a pretty amazing guy. I think the Trudeau era will go down as the greatest in Canadian history. Never before did the country grow as much as it did under Trudeau. Never before did we have the respect of the world as we did under Trudeau. And he ran a very honest government. There were no scandals and the few ministers who had to resign over his long period in office – like Francis Fox – had to do so for things that were more personal than political.

Maybe his greatest accomplishment was keeping Canada together when it was threatening to fall apart. He stopped separatism and made the government truly bilingual. People forget what a huge change this was. He will be remembered for bringing home the constitution, but most of all his accomplishment was to keep the country united and to make it grow.

There's a lot of criticism of Trudeau by people who say he was a big spender, that he wasted the public's money. The Tories and some of those smart economists talk about this and about the size of the deficit and the debt that we ran up. But were the provinces innocent? No way. Proportionately they spent much more, and much of the money they spent was transferred to them by the federal government. The provinces and the municipalities spend nearly 70 percent of all tax dollars. I've already mentioned how Trudeau continued Pearson's policy of transferring millions and millions of dollars to the provinces for higher education – and none of the provinces were complaining. And he gave money to the cities. Look at Toronto, Vancouver, Edmonton, Calgary, Halifax, or Montreal. When was their period of greatest growth and expansion? Under Trudeau.

Unlike Reagan, when the economic slowdown came, Trudeau didn't take it out on the poor. During the recession he actually increased some of the social services and I think that will go down in history as a good thing, not an economic error. I've always felt that this obsession with the size of the deficit is wrong. I often used to say to my audiences, "Who holds the debt in Canada? Who are we indebted to? How many Canada Savings Bonds do each of you have? Well, a high percentage of the indebtedness of Canada is in the form of savings bonds held by the Canadian people. Ninety percent of the national debt is owned by Canadians themselves and how can you say that's so bad? How could you foreclose if you held the mortgage yourself on your own house?"

Trudeau wasn't perfect. I certainly could have killed him from time to time, but he made very few mistakes in my opinion. One of his weaknesses was that he hadn't had enough direct experience of life, or ordinary people. But then you could say that about almost all of the Cabinet ministers I worked with. And, hard as he tried, he never could understand agriculture.

Maybe his greatest weakness was that he paid too much attention to advisers like Jim Coutts and Michael Pitfield and not enough attention to some of us. Sometimes he got too isolated from the grassroots of the party and the grassroots of Canada. But he was certainly no dictator. Quite the contrary. I think the press have built up a very false impression. As the effect of Tory policies is felt, I think Canadians will begin to think more fondly of Pierre Trudeau.

It was an odd feeling to watch the 1984 election from the sidelines. When it was called, some press phoned to ask me what I thought. I said, "Turner would be crazy if he didn't go now." But of course I thought just the opposite. I was just being a good party man.

The decision to leave politics, even after I'd been fired from the Cabinet, was a hard one. Marty Goldfarb had taken a poll that showed I would win with about 62 percent of the vote. But I figured my firing would be used against me in the campaign and that it wouldn't be a very enjoyable experience. Paul Martin and a number of others tried to talk me into staying. But I didn't want to go into a summer campaign; after the way Turner had treated me, I didn't have much stomach for another battle on the hustings; and my family was against it, having shared with me the pain of the leadership loss. But it was hard to give up after so long.

Despite everything, my daughter Sue, who was still living at home, worked in the election; she and her friends canvassed door to door. But this was the first campaign they didn't enjoy. People were mean to them. The papers and the people had turned against the Liberals and against John Turner. A lot of times the person just slammed the door in their face – and that had hardly ever happened before. There was a feeling of genuine anger toward the party.

When people ask me how long I think the Mulroney government will last, I tell the following parable. The Mulroney government is like a farmer who buys a well-kept farm that's been run by a conscientious farmer – one who rotated his crops carefully and always kept the soil fertilized. This new farmer comes along and he stops putting on the fertilizer and he stops rotating the crops – he leaves the land to just take care of itself – and he gets maybe four or five good crops from the soil. Then about the fifth year he discovers that the land won't produce anything unless he gives it a big shot of fertilizer. Suddenly he has to spend a lot money to make the farm productive and he goes deep into debt. Mulroney is doing the same thing with the Canadian economy. He's forgotten the importance of fertilizer and he's letting it run unregulated and hog wild. He forgets that if we'd depended on the private sector to build this country, there'd be no country at all.

The decision to fire me as ambassador to the FAO after three months was of course made by old Mr. Clean, the man who fought and won the battle against patronage and so became Prime Minister, but it was Joe Clark who had the job of giving me the news. It happened on October 11, when I was over visiting the new Minister of Agriculture, John Wise. I was waiting in my old office for John to come back from a Cabinet committee meeting when the phone rang. Somehow Joe had found out I was there. So I got the news I was being fired as Canada's ambassador to FAO, talking on my old phone, sitting at my old desk, in my old office. That was a hard thing.

I asked Clark, "Why are you doing this, Joe? Will you give me a reason?" And he said, "Well it is an order-in-council appointment," which means it is made by the Prime Minister and can be cancelled by the Prime Minister. I said, "There's lots of order-in-council appointments. Don't you think the FAO is a worthy organization and one that deserves a full-time ambassador who knows as much about food and the Third World as I do?" He didn't have an answer to that. So I said, "Then give me a letter explaining your reasons." But he never bothered. They didn't appoint anyone in my place so Canada has no full-time ambassador to FAO.

In the space of three months I'd been fired by two Prime Ministers. I have the dubious distinction of being the only person I know of ever to have received such an honour. The only good thing I can say about it is that when I give speeches these days, the line always gets a good laugh.

Not long after I'd been fired the second time, I wrote a letter of consolation to Judge Francis Carter, whom I'd named to head a commission studying the potato industry. The Tories had just terminated the potato enquiry and Carter had lost the job. In the letter I included two quotes that had been of help to me. One of them is an old saying: "Man's disappointments are God's appointments." The other was from Alexander Graham Bell: "When one door closes, another opens; but we often look so long and so regretfully upon the closed door, that we do not see the ones which open for us."

Mr. Mulroney was kind enough to let me serve out my term as President of the World Food Council with my staff of one. I imagine it had something to do with the fact that I held the highest position of any Canadian in the whole United Nations system and they didn't want the bad publicity of losing that. I doubt if any concern for the World Food Council or the developing world went into the decision. Brian handled that very smoothly. He simply left me in my post and pretended I didn't exist.

It's difficult to predict what the future holds for the Liberal Party or what the future of Liberalism is in this country. Right now, I'd say that the best thing Brian Mulroney has going for him is John Turner, although John has been doing better lately and Mulroney has been working hard to help him. The Conservative Party under Mulroney isn't listening to the people and it hasn't kept its promises. I've never seen a party in my life that has ignored the platform it asked people to vote for as much as the current Tories.

The main problem is that the Liberal Party right now isn't very representative of the views of the ordinary Liberal – or the majority of Canadians. The ordinary Liberal wants things done in an open and fair way and resents the cliques that run the different parts of the party apparatus. For instance, the recent Halifax meeting that was trumped up as a great time for the reform and renewal of the Liberal Party was nothing of the sort. It was a stage show designed solely to make Turner look good. The last thing the Turner Liberals want is reform.

And if you look at the so-called reform group that helped him win the leadership, they're just a group that wants power in the Liberal Party. It's worth noting that this is the same group that openly criticized Trudeau before he resigned while calling for a more open party. Now they argue that the party comes first and don't want any criticism of the leader or his policies. They fought to have the review provision put in the party constitution and now they don't want a genuine review.

What's happening to all the parties in Canada is that they are increasingly run by an elite group at the top who are interested only in keeping power for themselves. I believe the party base has to be expanded. Perhaps every constituency association should be required to have a minimum number of active members before it can participate in things such as a leadership review or leadership convention – this number could be related to the population of the riding. And the membership should be a cross-section of the total society in that riding, not just some narrow slice – a kind of affirmative action for ordinary people. Maybe we should have a minimum number of farmers in certain ridings, a minimum number of accountants, or bricklayers.

I think the rules that permit instant Liberals should be abolished. And perhaps even better than choosing a leader by direct election of the whole membership would be some kind of primary system similar in principle to what they have in the States. It would certainly be more democratic.

I believe the Liberal Party should always be free and open to debate from the rank and file. What the party needs right now is for the leader to open the windows and let in some fresh air, but I think the people around him are afraid he might catch cold. That's the only way to ensure that the Liberal Party remains as liberal as possible. Right now it doesn't know what it is. But there's still time. The current system we have is old-fashioned, it's out-dated, and it's turning people off. This is something the current crowd better understand: you don't fool the people with a phoney form of democracy.

As for leadership reviews, if I had anything to do with it, every Liberal delegate would go armed with a copy of the page in the dictionary that has the definition of "liberal" on it.

As for me, it's a strange feeling not to hold elected office. Until 1984 I'd continuously held some public position since I was first elected to the local separate school board at the age of twenty-one. Not bad for a farm boy who didn't even wear shoes to elementary school. Just after my mother died in 1986 at the age of ninety-three a man who'd been reeve in one of the neighbouring townships wrote me a card of condolence in which he said, "Your mother must have been very proud that she had a son who went as far as you did, did as much as you did, met as many people in as many parts of the world as you did." It's true, and I take with me from my political career a richness that you can't deposit in the bank, a richness no banker or anyone can take away from me, a richness of knowing I helped a lot of people in a lot of different ways. I've done so many things and met so many people, I would never have imagined it possible.

The ordinary Canadians I've come to know over the years have been my greatest source of satisfaction, in spite of all the great and important people I've been privileged to meet. I sometimes like to hold out my hand and say to an audience, "This right hand of mine has shaken hands with many leaders around the world, from the smallest nations to the most powerful, including the United States and the Soviet Union, the heads of the Anglican and Catholic Churches, and the Queen of England." I never would have dreamt when I was starting out, that little Gene Whelan from Anderdon Township who lived just across the railroad track from Hell's Corners would have ended up as Minister of Agriculture or would have run to be Prime Minister of Canada. As a boy my only ambition was to drive one of those big black steam locomotives. I just loved the sound of those old trains as they went hissing and roaring by our farm. I loved it when the engineer tooted his whistle and blew steam before the train disappeared off into the distance.

Those steam engines are gone now. But I'm still around. And unlike those old-fashioned engines, you haven't necessarily heard the last from Gene Whelan. Not yet.

Acknowledgements

I'd like to thank the following people without whose help this book would not have happened: Liz, Terry, Sue and Cathy for collecting pictures and memorabilia and providing a family perspective and critique; Dr. Tom Anstey for providing fascinating additional background to my collection of facts on the history of agricultural research in Canada; Linda Clifford, for her careful attention to the details of every phase of the work, including proofreading the manuscript and galleys at various stages, spending many hours going through my papers and photograph archives in search of buried treasure, and reminding me of stories or people I'd forgotten to mention; Roger and Cathy Crowe-Hollander for emergency office space; Rick Feldman for word-processing technical support; Sharon Gignac, who transcribed the miles of taped interviews; David Haines for his knowledge of TV trivia; Susan Macdonald for expert fact-checking; Nancy Sheppard of Canapress Photo Service for helping find photos; John Smiley of Agriculture Canada for confirming details on foreign trips; Morris Wolfe for information about Tonto and the Lone Ranger.

And I'd like to thank the people at Madison Press and Irwin Publishing who ushered this book into being: Hugh Brewster and Al Cummings for seeing the possibilities and making the deal; John Pearce for expert editorial advice; John Parsons for reading and commenting on the manuscript; Elizabeth Wilson for careful proofreading; Lynn Shannon, the patient production manager; and Jennifer Leonard, promotion person extraordinaire.

I would also like to thank here the many hundreds of people who have helped me throughout my long political career–during election campaigns and in between. In particular I want to acknowledge the members of my political staff as a member of parliament and later as Minister of Agriculture. My personal secretaries: Loretta O'Regan; Joan Kufner; Joan Berube; Janis Harry; Ilona Redmond; Linda Lomax; and private secretary Norma Lamont ("Them"), who later was also my special assistant and saw that our office on the Hill ran smoothly.

My executive assistants: Henri Vandermeullen; Keith Matthie; Dr. Ken Wells; Gilles Choquette; Jim Fay; and Linda Clifford ("Sgt. Major").

My policy advisors: Peter Christensen and Henri Vandermuellen.

My speech writers: Jim and Bill Romahn; Sarah Gunning (Trant); Henry Heald; Mike Sage; Sharon McKay; and Janet Hunter.

My press assistants: Jane Logan; Joanne Duguay; Nicholas Mesley; and Lilly Haddad.

My special assistants: André Pigeon; Jean-Paul Marchand; Alan Minz; Ezio di Emanuele; Ted Mieszkalski; Vincent Bloem; and Vince Meechan.

My research assistant: Mary Ann Allen.

My Ottawa/Windsor assistants: Brian Ducharme; John Commisso; Milan Meleg; and Louis Durnbeck.

My constituency staff: Larry Wigle; Fern Clark; Elsie Cusinato; Kirk Walstedt ("Little Gene"); Shirley Oleynik; and Juel White.

My Parliament Hill office staff: Gert White; Francine Boucher; Suzie Sauvé-Cardinal; Isabelle Seguin; Danielle Vinette.

My legislative assistants: Doug Lousley; Mike Ellis; Terry Hayward; Ron Davidson; Terry Hall; Lise Beauparlant; and Frances Lemon.

My Regina office staff: George Leith and Irene Lamothe (the pioneers); Linda Clifford; Sonny Anderson; Jake Vanderschaaf; and Genny Gross.

The employees of Agriculture Canada, with special thanks to Bernadette Richard, Carol Paquette, and Colleen Griffin, who were there with me during all of my time as Minister; departmental drivers Moe, Ollie, Pierre, Bob, Red, and Eddie; and the great team in the file room.

I'd also like to acknowledge the student interns who worked for me during the 1980s. I believe strongly in getting young people involved in government and the ones who worked with me made a great contribution: Jon Sims; Ted Mieszkalski; Alex Cameron; Kerry Hamilton; Richard Pollack; Paul Bosc, Jr.; Becky MacEachern; Vincent Bloem; Shannon Jones; David Lamont; Andrew Harvey; Robert Couture; and Jack Bryson.

INDEX